The Soddit

NOT!
The first few minutes of prologue in
A MAJOR NINE-HOUR MOTION PICTURE EPIC!!!

When he's not being A. R. R. R. Roberts,
A. R. R. R. Roberts writes proper books under the
pseudonym Adam Roberts. Ones we publish are:

Salt

On

Stone

Polystom

The Snow

The Soddit

or,
LET'S CASH IN AGAIN
or,

There, and Back Again, dammit, where did I put it, where is it, I don't believe it, I must have left it There, over Again to There, oh for heaven's sake, it's not here either, Back Yet Again, fuming, oh there it is, it was by the front door all along.

A. R. R. Roberts

Copyright © Adam Roberts 2003
All rights reserved

The right of Adam Roberts to be identified as the author of this work has
been asserted by him in accordance with the
Copyright, Designs and Patents Act 1988.

First published in Great Britain in 2003 by

Gollancz
An imprint of the Orion Publishing Group
Orion House, 5 Upper St Martin's Lane, London WC2H 9EA

This paperback edition first published in Great Britain in 2004

A CIP catalogue record for this book is available
from the British Library

ISBN 0 575 07591 0

Typeset at The Spartan Press Ltd,
Lymington, Hants

Printed in Great Britain by
Clays Ltd, St Ives plc

www.orionbooks.co.uk

Bingo

Chapter One

THE UNEXPECTED PART

⌘

In a hole, in a highly desirable and sought-after portion of the ground (the hole two doors along went for three hundred thou last month, near enough, although admittedly it was double-fronted and had a newly turfed roof) lived a soddit, the hero of our story. His name was Bingo 'Sac' Grabbings. Not a name he chose for himself, of course, but one decided on by his mother. Easy for her to say, of course; she didn't have to live with it all through school and adult life. Parents, eh?

Where was I? Oh, yes.

In a hole, then, lived Bingo. It was a fair-to-middling soddit hole, with a circular blue-painted door, fine blue tiles in the bathroom with a cheesy blue mould growing on them, blue beetles, silverfish, silvery worms, all manner of moistness and a kitchen area from which it was next to impossible to clear out cooking smells. Nevertheless in soddit terms it was a reasonably desirable residence. Bingo's aunt, the severe Vita 'Sac' Vile-Vest, had designs upon this very sod-hole, although

Bingo was in no mood to give way to pressure from that branch of the family. He was a soddit of forty, which in soddit years was next to nothing, a mere bagatelle, less than a bagatelle in fact; well, technically about four fifths of a bagatelle, but still young, that's my point.

Soddits are a race of little people who live *in the earth*, which is where their name comes from (you'll learn a lot about names and where they come from if you pay attention as you read, believe me). Scholars and philologists have established the derivation of the name, evidenced by an ancient rhyme:

> *Cleave the sod with your trusty spade*
> *Dig out a house that's quite like a grave*
> *And should your neighbour not return your wave*
> *Cleave the sod with your trusty spade*

Now it is an interesting thing that soddits don't tend to call themselves 'soddits', for reasons I'll come to in a minute. But 'soddit' is the generally accepted term. Once upon a time a traveller from the country of the bigger people roamed far and wide through the country of the littler folk, through the County of the Hunchkins, Shrimpville, Littleputia, the Land of the Lepercorns[1],

[1] A brave little folk afflicted with the most repulsive and contagious foot diseases. Foot diseases are, it must be said, something of a common theme for the Counties of the Little.

Jockeyton, and into Hobbld-Ahoy!, the home town of Bingo, the hero of our tale. On his return to the human town of Brie this big 'un traveller found his way to a tavern, and sat meditating on his adventures, and his fellow big 'uns gathered around him curious as to what he had seen. 'What did you discover?' they pressed him. 'Who did you encounter?' 'I met a—' he started to reply, and drew a great shuddering sigh into his body, before concluding in a lowered tone, 'soddit,' and reaching for his tankard of ale. The name of the particular soddit he encountered has not been recorded, but it was clearly a meeting that had a profound impact upon the big man, for he stayed inside the Dragon-Queen Inn at Brie for two days and two nights drinking all the time and speaking to nobody, and soon afterwards left the area never to return.

Soddits build the accommodation portion of their houses under the ground, and they build their coal-cellars, wine rooms and sometimes large rooms with ping-pong tables in them above the ground. They insist that this is the most logical manner of arranging living space, and indeed Hobbld-Ahoy! planning regulations have made any other form of domestic building illegal, although this does tend to result in living quarters prone to damp, to worms, to mould, to associated asthma and bronchitis for the inhabitants, whilst coal, wine and ping-pong bats are the most burgled items in this burglary-prone town. But a tradition, after all, is a tradition.

Soddits, as I say, don't call themselves soddits. In their own tongue, which is queer and old and full of syntactical-grammatical inconsistencies, they call themselves *hobblds*. Now, there's a reason why they refer to themselves in this manner, and not by the name of soddit like everybody else in the world, and the reason is found in their feet. Shocking feet, they have. Just shocking. Whatever the reason – and soddits down the ages have blamed the gods, or an ancient wizard's curse, or inadequate orthopaedic practice, or congenital disease, or a dozen other factors – whatever the reason, soddits are almost all of them afflicted with appalling arthritis of the feet. Their feet are swollen and gnarled, many three or four times their normal size, with toes like coconuts and ankles like condoms stuffed with pebbles. This arthritis is extremely painful, and is indeed no laughing matter, although queerly it is a condition that does not spread to any other part of their body. But it gives their feet a strangely deadened, different colour from the rest of their bodies. Moreover, it makes it impossible for the adult soddit to wear shoes, for the pressure of leather against the inflated flesh of the feet is too, too ghastly. This means that the diminutive folk walk only with difficulty and excessive slowness; and accordingly adult soddits spend much of their time searching for the cushion of perfect softness, making little grunts as they collapse into their sofas and using their hands physically to lift their feet on to their footstools.

And now you know everything that you need to know about soddits, or hobblds, excepting only one or two minor details, such as the fact that they are food-loving and drink-loving and enjoy conviviality. And that they like to wear waistcoats and corduroy. Oh, yes, and that they smoke pipeweed a great deal and that accordingly they die younger than they otherwise would of cancers of the mouth, tongue and throat as well as of heart disease. What else? That they are conservative, rural, bourgeois, middle class. That they speak with a slight Birmingham accent, oddly. And, also, that despite their manifest disadvantages – their diminutive stature, their crippled elephantiasitic feet, their small-mindedness, their disinclination to listen to strangers or change old ways, their addiction to tobacco and alcohol, their stagnant class-ridden 'respectability' – despite all this, they have developed the most modern semi-industrial culture in the whole world, with water-mills, steam-foundries, comfortable housing, pipes, pop-guns, spectacles, velvet clothes, charming little flintstone churches, books and fireworks, whilst the rest of Upper Middle Earth is languishing in the dark ages of swords, horses, and burying their dead under enormous mounds of earth. Funny that. But, you see, the ways of the world are strange and sometimes inexplicable.

Bingo was sitting on his most comfortable sofa one morning, with his poor swollen arthritic feet resting on a green velvet cushion on the footstool in front of him. He was staring at the knuckled toe joints of these feet, the place where the individual toes meet the body of the foot, and these joints were staring back at him, like ten radishes. He was feeling the full weight of the misery of existence, poor old Bingo.

There was a series of bangs on the door, loud and startling, the sort of noise that might be made by a naughty soddit child stuffing a firecracker in the key-hole, lighting it, running away, hearing the dis-appointingly soggy pop, coming back vexed and kicking the door off its hinges with his as-yet unspoiled, bovver-booted feet. Young people today, eh? What can you do? Tch.

Bingo sighed. 'Go away,' he called. After a pause he added, 'Go away.'

The banging continued on the front door.

There was nothing for it. Bingo got slowly to his feet, and made his way to the door, flinching with each step and uttering all his usual expressions of pain, including 'ah!', 'ouch' and, half under his breath, 'ow-ow-ow'.[2]

Bingo did not like having a round front door. Who would? Geometry dictates that such a door be held in place by only one hinge, and that this hinge cannot be placed in the most effective load-bearing position, so that the doorway is draughty and the door unwieldy to open, and able easily to be kicked completely in by any soddit still young enough to be wearing boots. But tradition is tradition is tradition, and this was a tradition which Hobbld-Ahoy! planning regulators enforced with particular zeal. Bingo pulled open his door.

Outside, standing in the sunshine, was a wizard. Bingo had never seen a wizard before, but the 'W' on the front of his poncho could only mean he was one of that magic brotherhood. Either that, or he was a Munchkin of unusually developed stature and had put his poncho on upside down.

The knocking noise was continuing, louder than before.

---

[2] Which is to say, the noises somebody makes not when they are in actual pain, but when they wish to communicate to the world at large that they are experiencing a sensation of slight discomfort. Nobody suffering *actual* pain – let us say, a broken leg, or having their shoulder pierced all the way through with a Wharg-rider's arrow – would ever say 'ouch'. If somebody in such a situation *were* to say 'ouch' we would think not that they were in pain, but that they were taking the piss.

Bingo looked up at the wizard.

'Yes, well,' said the wizard in a booming voice. 'I'm sorry about that.'

'Sorry?' Bingo repeated, uncomprehending. He looked at his still-knocking door.

'The knocking spell I put on your door. It's a common enough wizardly spell, you know,' he bellowed, as if talking into a gale. 'I'm too fragile at my time of life to go banging at doors. Banging at doors! I'm too old and fragile for that. So I've put the knocking spell on, do you see?'

Bingo looked at the door. 'Can you turn it off, please?'

The wizard seemed not to hear. 'Thank you!' he said, in his stentorian voice. 'But, really, you're *too* kind. It's a small spell, but potent. Potent!'

'How long does it last?'

'Yes, yes,' boomed the wizard indulgently. 'But can I turn it *off*? That's the question. And the answer? The answer is "can I buggery". Hard to do, do you see? Easy to turn it on, that spell, but fiercely difficult to turn it off.'

'How long does the spell last?' said Bingo, leaving a space between each word and moving his facial muscles in a more marked manner as he spoke.

'Grabbings?' shrieked the wizard, his shaggy eyebrows rising and his eyes staring intensely. 'Grabbings?' He stepped forward, filling the doorway, bent down and stepped into the hallway of Grab End.

Bingo spun around as the huge figure of the wizard, bent nearly double, moved rapidly along the hall and into the main sitting room, shouting Bingo's surname at the top of his voice. All the while the front door carried on making its deafening racket, like a heavy item of wooden furniture clattering down an endless flight of stairs. Bingo stumbled after the wizard, calling out 'hey!' and 'ow-my-feet!', and came through to the sitting room to find the old wizard parked there in Bingo's own sofa (which though large for a soddit was chair-sized for the man), beaming toothlessly at him. 'So you are *Grabbings*, are you?' he shouted.

'Yes, yes I am,' replied Bingo. 'But, look, I'm sorry but I'm afraid I'm going to have to ask you – I'm sorry – to leave. You can't come in. You can't sit there.'

'It said "Grabbings" over the door, you see,' said the wizard.

'I'm going to have to ask you to *leave*,' said Bingo, in a louder voice.

'Grabbings,' said the wizard, putting his finger to his cheek to mime contemplation. 'A burglar's name, is that?'

'I'm a gentlehobbld of independent means,' said Bingo, wincing as a sudden pain arrowed up his leg from his left foot, 'and I'm asking *you* to *go, now*.'

'I thought so,' said the wizard, smiling knowingly. 'I thought so.'

'*Leave! Please!*' screeched Bingo.

'Too kind,' said the wizard, taking off his hat and placing it on his lap. 'Two sugars, for me. My name is Gandef and I am a wizard, yes indeed. The famous Gandef. Don't be scared. I promise,' he said, chuckling to himself, 'I do – I promise – although I *am* a wizard, I promise not to turn you,' he went on, his chuckling bubbling up until his shoulders and his whole head were shaking with the hilarity of what he was saying, 'not to turn you into a *toad* – arch-CHHTTGH QOOF-QOOF-QOOF,' he added, coughing so abruptly, so prodigiously and body-spasmingly that it looked, for a moment, as if he were going to shake himself out of his seat and on to the floor. 'AWARGH – SCHW-SCHWO'AH KOH-KOH,' he coughed. 'K'OAH K'OAH K'OAH K'OAH K'OAH K'OAH K'OAH.'

Bingo, alarmed, sat down in the second-best chair.

'K'OAH, K'OAH K'OAH K'OAH K'OAH,' the wizard continued.

'Are you all—' Bingo started to say.

'K'OAH K'OAH K'OAH K'OAH K'OAH,' the wizard concluded, and let his head flop backwards. His colour had drained away, and little dregs of spittle were visible on the grey of his beard just below his mouth. 'Blimey,' he said in a strangulated voice. 'Oh dear, oh dear.' His right hand fumbled in the pocket of his gown and brought out a pipe, his left hand brought out a wallet of pokeweed, and with trembling fingers he filled the bowl. 'I'll be better in a moment,' he croaked, muttering a small spell to bring a yellow flame from his right thumbnail so that he could light the pipe. For long minutes the wizard simply sucked noisily at the stem of his pipe, making orgasmic little moans between breaths, and swiftly filling Bingo's front room with a smoke so acrid and dark it made the little soddit's eyes smart. 'Oh that's better,' Gandef murmured, sucking in another lungful of heated tobacco particles and air, 'so much better.'

'Are you all right?' Bingo asked, a little nervously.

'Eh?' Gandef shouted. 'What? You'll have to speak up. My hearing's not what it used to be.'

Away in the hall, behind him, Bingo could hear the door still knocking away to itself. 'I —' he started to say, but realised that he didn't know how to finish the sentence.

'Oh, *once* upon a time,' said Gandef, 'my hearing was better than an eagle, and my eyesight better than a – well, a goodly eyed animal. I don't know. Something with a very good and acute sense of sight. An eagle. Yes. But age takes its toll, you know.' The wizard hawked, and so enormous a noise of wrenching phlegm emanated from his chest that Bingo shrank back. 'I tried a most potent Noise Amplification Spell once upon a time,' Gandef was saying, his voice meditative, though still loud. 'Marvellous spell. I could hear the birds speaking to one another in trees over the horizon, I could hear the rustlings as the clouds rubbed against one another in the sky. I could hear the sound a rainbow makes as it arches its back over the world. Then a dog barked behind me and I burst my left eardrum. Won't try *that* again in a hurry. I actually wet myself – imagine it! A wizard! Wetting himself in terror! Wouldn't do for that piece of news to get around, the forces of evil and all that, important to keep up appearances of, you know, magic and potency. I'm not actually a man, you see – I'm a sort of angel.'[3]

[3] This is true, actually. The best theological thinking today suggests that when you die and go up to heaven you'll find God surrounded not by people in white with wings, but instead by a large crowd of crotchety, beardy men in big hats with nicotine-stained fingers and swords. As the Philosopher once said: The world is not only stranger than we imagine, but stranger than we *can* imagine, and more imaginative than we can imagine too, which is something of a contradiction, don't you think, where was I? Hold on, bear with me for a minute, angels, old men, ah yes, ahm, ahem, stranger than we imagine, stranger than we *can* imagine, stranger than we *will* imagine, stranger than we *shall* imagine, stranger than we *can't* imagine, stranger than we *shouldn't* imagine, stranger than we *wouldn't* imagine *if we could*, stranger than you can imagine *but not me*, and so on. Anyway, I think we can both agree I've made my point.

He chuckled to himself. 'Covers a multitude of sins, that. Sharp's the word!'

'I don't quite follow,' said Bingo.

'They'll be here in a moment, Our Friends from the Dwarf. From, uh, the dwarfland. They're the salt of the earth. Which is to say, they've dug up and sold the salt of the earth. And also that they've ploughed salt *into* the earth of people they didn't like. But we'll stay on their good side. Oh yes. We'll draw up a contract, I'll get the map out, and we can head off tomorrow. Be on our way.' He cleared his throat, or to put it more precisely, he moved half a stone of snot from one internal location to another, and then drew a deep breath through his pipe.

'Come again?' said Bingo.

But Gandef had fallen asleep, his head lolling, his still lit pipe rolling from his fingers and tipping smouldering tobacco over the matting that served for a carpet in Bingo's soddit hole.

The first four dwarfs[4] arrived half an hour later, hammering on the door so violently that it jolted off its latch and collapsed inwards. 'My door!' squealed Bingo, scurrying as fast as his deformed feet could take him out into the hallway.

---

[4] This, by the way, *is* the correct plural form of 'dwarf'. Look it up if you don't believe me – really.

~ 15 ~

'Apologies,' said the first dwarf, treading on the wreck of the door as he stepped inside. 'We were knocking for a while, look you, but seeing how the door was knocking anyway by itself I don't think we were being heard. I got a mate who does doors.'

'Does doors lovely,' said the second dwarf.

'Oh, he'll do you a *lovely* door,' said the first dwarf, with a flush of agreement. 'Lovely big *hefty* door. Soon as he pops along, he'll quote you, lovely boy, la, bach.'

'There's been a misunderstanding,' Bingo gabbled at them. 'I'm sorry that you've been inconvenienced, but you've got the wrong hole. Nobody here called Grabbings. No wizard, there's no wizard here. You'll have to go away.'

From behind him, in the sitting room, came a series of axe-like chopping noises such as can only be produced by a man who has scoured the walls of his lungs red and smooth over many years of dedicated smoke inhalation.

'That's the boyo,' said the first dwarf, stepping past Bingo. 'Failin,' he said. 'I'm a dwarf, la, boy, see, yow, bach, dew,' he added. 'This is my cousin Qwalin.' The second dwarf bowed. 'And behind him are Sili and Frili, also cousins, see?'

'I haven't the victuals—' Bingo began, in desperation. But the four dwarfs were already in the sitting room, singing tunelessly but loudly, one of them bouncing lustily on the wizard's chest to wake the fellow up. Bingo turned about, cursed the gnawing pain in his left toes, and turned again as four more dwarves[5] stepped boldly into his house.

'Mori,' said the first dwarf, who was holding a clipboard. He was a strong-nosed dwarf in green, with a waterfall of beard and eyebrows thick as caterpillars. Or as actual pillars. 'Allow me to introduce my cousins, Tori, Orni and On. Oh *my*,' he added, stepping towards Bingo. 'Haven't *you* the smoothest of chins!'

The four dwarfs kicked their beards out from under their feet and clustered around Bingo, treading on his toes as they did so. 'Oo,' they said, running callused fingers over his chin. 'Oo.'

'Get off,' Bingo said, flapping his hands before his face like little wings.

'You'll have to excuse us, see,' said Mori, leaning his clipboard against the wall and taking off his dwarf hat. 'It's a rare sight for us, a bare chin – a sight of rare beauty. Wouldn't I love a bare chin!'

'Wouldn't *I*!' said Orni.

'You'll say, shave,' said Mori, clapping Bingo in a manly clasp, his arm around the back, his powerful hand crushing Bingo's shoulder. 'You *will*, you'll tell me, shave.'

[5] Sorry, that one must have slipped through the proofs.

'I won't,' said Bingo.

'Can't,' said Mori, as if in correction. 'Psoriasis. Terrible. Allergy to bauxite. Couldn't shave if my life depended on it. Stuck with this ap-*surd* hippy beard.[6] I hate it.'

'We *all* hate it,' said Orni. 'All hate our beards.'

'All of us in the same boat. Smells, la,' said Mori confidentially. 'Food gets stuck in it. I found a chicken bone in mine yesterday. Anyway, anyhow, anyhew.' He released Bingo. 'Is the King boy here yet?'

'King boy?' said Bingo.

'Thorri, our King, heavens bless him. No? There you go. I can hear merry being made, though, look you, begorrah, la, bach, boyo, see, dew, bach, look you, so we'll go on through.'

Bingo stumbled to the larder, and brought out a selection of the food he possessed. The dwarfs devoured it all in quarter of an hour. In dismay he tried telling the group that he had no more, but they wouldn't take no for an answer, explored his hobbld hole thoroughly and completely ransacked it. They rolled out his one and only barrel of Soddit ale, and tapped and drank it. They sang all the while, whilst

[6] Which is to say, a beard that reaches down to one's hips. Why? What else did you think this might mean?

Gandef sat in the corner tapping his foot not in time to the music and smoking. They sang:

> *When you walk with a dwarf keep your head down low*
> *So as not to draw attention to his height,*
> *For a dwarf's hold on his temper is only so-so*
> *And a dwarf has no fear of a fight.*
> *Walk on, walk on, crouching all the time*
> *Though your hips are racked with pain —*
> *Walk on, walk on, with a bend in your spine*
> *Or you'll ne-ver walk again,*
> *You'll NE-ver walk again.*

After which they sang, or rather they howled:

> AND! WE! WERE! *SI-I-INGING!*
> SONGS AND ARIAS –
> DWARFS IN THE LARDER –
> OH ME, OH MY.

After which they insisted that Bingo join in with the quaffing, despite his protestations that he was normally a very moderate drinker. They drank toasts to his smooth chin, and his smooth upper lip, and they sang more songs: raucous songs, caucus songs, ribald songs, dribbled songs, hymns, whims, theramins, chim-chim-cherees, songs that were hard, songs by bards, songs that left you scarred (emotionally speaking), drinking anthems, looting anthems, puking anthems, footy anthems, beauty-pageant anthems, and 'Bess You Is My Woman Now'. They sang a-capella, a-patella[7] and *any umber-ella-any-umber-ella*. At some point in the proceedings the remaining dwarfs came in, Ston, Pilfur, Gofur, and Wombl; and finally there entered a diminutive little creature, small even for a dwarf and barely an inch taller than Bingo, who introduced himself as 'Thorri, King you know', but who seemed to be accorded remarkably little respect from the other dwarfs. But by this stage Bingo was well drunk, tanked-up, reeling and rocking, and soon enough he was falling over and getting up with a silly expression on his face. He was as unsteady on his feet as a newborn colt that had been force fed half a bottle of whisky. Then Gandef began singing a song, and got halfway through the first stanza before he started coughing with shocking vehemence, making a series of noises like a roof-load of snow collapsing twenty feet to the ground. Forty-five seconds of this and the wizard was too weak to stand, and collapsed back on to the sofa gasping and fumbling with his tobacco pouch.

'My new friends,' said Bingo, with tears in his eye

---

[7] The sort of song you sing when somebody has just kicked you in the kneecap.

and alcohol compounds in his bloodstream. 'My new friends! How sweet it is to have friends – to make new friends!'

'Strictly a business arrangement, Mr Grabbings,' said Mori. 'We have a quest to undertake, and we need your help, that's all.'

'You need my help!' repeated Bingo joyously, his cheeks wet. 'My friends!'

'Yes, yes,' said Mori, pushing the over-affectionate soddit away. 'Let's not lose proportion, look you, bach, la. There's a dragon, see, and he's got, eh, well shall we say . . . treasure. Let's call it *treasure*.'

'Gold?' asked Bingo, his eyes circular.

'What's that?' said Qwalin, 'Yeah – yeah, that's it. Gold. That's a good one.'

'Gold,' said Mori, looking significantly at his fellow dwarfs. 'All right? We all clear? Mr Grabbings here is to help us nick us some *gold*. Yes, that's it, we're on our way to steal the dragon's gold. See?'

The dwarfs made various noises of dawning comprehension.

'So,' said Mori, turning to Bingo, 'we figured – and this is only a rough plan, see – that we'd go over there and distract the dragon boyo with some close-harmony baritone singing whilst you steal the, eh, *gold*, you being a thieving little tinker, or so we've been led to believe – no offence.'

Bingo's heart was flush with new comradeship and love. He sobbed like a child, trying to hug Mori and unburden his heart, to say how he'd always felt, somehow, distanced from the other soddits, as if there was something that held him back from them, and held them back from *him* – it wasn't easy to say what exactly, but on occasion he'd stand at his door with a glass of dry hobbld martini in his hand and watch the evening traffic making its way up Hobbld-Ahoy! high-street and over the bridge into the thickening gloom and feel, somehow, a great emptiness inside himself, a sense of purposelessness of it all – the way the narrow respectability of his world felt sometimes like a suffocating velvet cloak – and all along the thing he'd been missing was right here, this sense of purpose, belonging to this band of brothers, united in a common aim. Sadly the ale, which provoked this chain of thought in Bingo's mind, also prevented the articulate expression of it, and the best he could manage was a 'such-a-lovely-buncho-blokes-lovely-feller-love-you' and a further series of throaty syllables like the noise a dog makes just before it throws up.

'Now,' Mori continued in a louder voice, backing against the wall, 'are you OK with our plan, boyo, look you? Remember, the only problem to this quest thing is that the – eh – the *treasure* is in the possession *of a dragon*. Right?'

'Dragons!' said Bingo. 'They don't frighten me. Insectivores, aren't they?'

'No,' said Mori. 'I wouldn't describe them as insecti-vores.'

'Well,' said Bingo, waving his hand dismissively and wobbling on his feet. 'Does it matter?' He'd long since reached the level of alcoholic uncoordination where it becomes difficult to place the right thumb upon the end of the left little finger, and indeed had gone somewhat beyond it, to the state where it is difficult to get one's upper and lower lips to connect.

'Smug the Dragon,' said Gandef, erupting apparently from sleep. 'A fearsome, terrible sight, he is, the mighty wyrm in his desolation.'

'Terrible, terrible,' said the dwarfs in unison.

The ale swirled in Bingo heart. 'I'm not afeared!' he squealed, trying to clamber on the table.

'Smug the Dragon!' Gandef bellowed, rather carried away with himself. 'Terrible Smug! Marvellous great dragon! Bah!' He coughed once, twice, and then thrummed a long, enduring note on the taut surface of the mass of phlegm held in his chest.

The dwarfs brought out their own pipes, and soon the smoke was so thick in Bingo's sod hole that you couldn't see the smokers for the smoke.[8] Moreover, the

---

[8] I've got a PhD you know, from Cambridge University. I just thought you might be interested in that fact. I'm not some bloke making this up from thin air, I'm a proper scholar, I studied Anglo Saxon and everything.

smoke that came out of the dwarfish pipes had a strange savour to it, a slightly herbal, fruity, pleasant, drowsy, hey-man edge to it, a whiff of 'Rings, eh? They're, like, all hard round the outside and all, like, nothing at all in the middle, isn't that weird? The way they can be both really *really* hard on the edge and *really* soft in the middle, d'you ever think of that?' and a slight odour of 'Hey I'm really really hungry, you got any, like, scones or something?' The excitement and passion drained out of Bingo wholly, and he lay on the floor with his feet in the grate, humming along as the dwarfs sang another song.

> *Smug the Magic Dragon*
> *Are we afraid of he?*
> *In his Magic Dragon-grotto-place,*
> *No-o-ot like-a-lee —*
> *We'll travel over earth,*
> *And we travel over sea,*
> *To beard that dragon in his den, look you now*
> *Most assuredly.*
>
> *Oh yes we will, I tell you now,*
> *You better believe we'll do it*
> *We will, oh yes we will, oh*
> *Yes we will, we're going to it,*
> *I'm telling you we will*

It's practically good as done,
We're going that way right now,
That dragon's, well, let's just say, I wouldn't want to be in his
*   shoes.*

Gandef was shouting something at this point and had to be calmed. Then, under the illusion that he was whispering discreetly into Mori's ear, he boomed, 'I was thinking, why don't we tell the young soddit that we're off after some *gold*? Eh? Wouldn't that be sly?' Mori's voice, much lower, came murmuring indistinctly through the fug. 'You see,' Gandef bellowed, louder still, 'if the soddit *thinks* we're after some *gold* then he won't ask after the *real* reason for our quest – do you see?' Again, Mori's voice, now more urgent but still indistinct, muttered in the dark. Bingo, from where he was lying, could just about see the pyramidical shape of the wizard's hat, and the hunched silhouette of Mori trying to communicate with the old man. 'I can't hear you if you *mutter* like that,' bellowed Gandef petulantly. 'All I'm saying is that this would be a *good cover story* as far as the soddit is concerned. That way we don't have to tell him what we're *really* going for yrkh, yrkh, mmbbmmmdd.'

It seemed to Bingo's eyes, in the smoke-obscured candlelight, as if Gandef's hat had been dragged sharply down to cover his whole face. But the young soddit's eyelids were slipping down in irresistible sleep, and he couldn't focus any more.

Trollps

Chapter Two

ROAST MUTT

෴

Bingo was woken by the smell of Gandef's pipe, the smoke of which caused a stinging sensation in the mucus membranes of his sinus and gave him a mixed impression of singed hair, burning bark and smoking rubber. The young soddit, coughing, pulled himself into a sitting position to find Gandef reclining lazily on the sofa.

'Good morning, young master Grabbings,' the wizard said genially, and sucked at the stem of his pipe so hard that his eyeballs shrank back in his skull.

'What time is it?' Bingo squeaked. But as he asked the question his eye lighted on the half-hunter squatting on the mantelpiece. The hour lacked some minutes of nine. He rubbed his eyes, and *some minutes* came into more precise focus as *fifty minutes*. 'Ten past eight?' he gasped. 'Ten past eight *in the morning*?' (Soddits, as I'm sure you know, like to sleep until noon – a habit so entrenched in their culture that the idea of a clockface having the dual function of 'a.m.'

and 'p.m.' is for most of them only a notional and theoretical hypothesis.)

Gandef nodded intelligently. 'Bright and early,' he said. 'Ah! The first pipe of the day. The first is always the sweetest.' He took another drag.

'Dwarfs!' said Bingo, getting unsteadily to his feet. 'Drink! Potweed! Hallucinations!' His head felt like it had been turned inside out, had tent pegs hammered into it, and then folded back in on itself again.

'Yes, yes,' said Gandef indulgently. 'It is late, I know. But Thorri didn't have it in his heart to wake you. You looked so peaceful. But you'd better get a move on. Did you read the letter?'

'What letter?'

'Good. I'm glad that at least you read the letter.'

Bingo found the letter after a ten-minute search through the desolation and chaos that had once been his front room. Written upon the finest dwarfish parchment, a form of scraped and treated stone, it read as follows:

Honourable sir,

On the offchance that you have forgotten our arrangement, we beg to remind you that should you fail to present yourself at the Putting Dragon Inn at Byjingo by nine a.m. we would be obliged to consider you an enemy of all dwarfkind and would thereafter hunt you down and

slay you like the vermin you are. At nine sharp, mind
for we depart on our great quest eastward to confront
the evil and condescending dragon Smug in his lair.

Yours dwarfully,
Thorri (King) and Company.

P.S. Mori begs to remind you that the purpose of our
quest is *gold*, honestly, *gold*, lots of gold, and nothing
else, certainly not anything non-gold.

'Hunt me down and slay me like the vermin I am?'
said Bingo, a catch in his voice.

'Lovely illumination on the "H" don't you think?' said
Gandef, looking over the soddit's shoulder. 'That's a little
rugby ball flying through the top portion, and Barijon
standing to the left of it. A great dwarfish hero, he.'

'Will they really kill me if I don't turn up?'

'Oh no, of course not,' said Gandef, shaking his head
forcefully and chuckling a little. 'No, no, nothing like that.
On the other hand,' he added, tamping some more
tobacco into his pipe bowl, 'they certainly will kill you if
you don't turn up. It's a sort of dwarfish tradition, you see.
Punctuality. That,' he added, mysteriously, 'and sheep.'

In a blind panic Bingo fled from his front room,
stepping over the wreckage of his still-knocking door,
and scurried along the main street of Hobbld-Ahoy! as
fast as his sore feet would permit in the general direction

of Byjingo.[1] He arrived at the Putting Dragon Inn with one minute to spare, panting and clutching at his agonised feet. The dwarfs were waiting for him, standing underneath the painted inn sign (which represented a trouser-clad dragon attempting to hole a tricky twenty-foot putt whilst a salamander stood in the background).[2]

'Just in time, lad, la, boyo,' said Mori, as the Byjingo town clock chimed the hour, or rather thudded once, which is what it did every hour of the day, ever since a bored soddit youth had stolen the bell to wear as a hat. And with that the dwarfs shouldered their packs and started away on their great quest, Bingo limping complainingly along behind them.

[1] The Jingo, upon which Byjingo is located, is a clear, fast-flowing stream that joins the Great River Flem a score of miles south-east of Hobbld-Ahoy!. Legend has it that the stream is named for its resemblance to an alcoholic drink of clear purity and great strength popular amongst the soddits. Flowing from the ice-capped northern mountains, through the fruit orchards of the County of the Hunchkins (to the north of Soddlesex), the Jingo often carries chunks of pure mountain ice, and bobbing whole lemons in its stream.

[2] Golf is a popular Soddlesex game. Its origins are to be found in ancient Soddit religion, a faith which involved worship of a deified potato, and to which attached a ritualised contest to plant next year's crop by striking the potatoes one by one with a magic staff so that they flew into predug holes. This, it hardly needs adding, was a highly inefficient way of planting potatoes, and the potato crop was always very poor, something the soddits blamed on the anger of their god Spahd rather than their own incompetence.

They stopped in Cremone to buy a beast of burden, a
pack-animal called Bony – which name was (the salesman, 'Honest Anthony', insisted) a wittily ironic refer-
ence to his fat girth and good health, 'like calling a
really large feller called John Little John, you see,' he
said. Neither Bingo nor the dwarfs saw, but didn't want
to reveal their ignorance. None of them had much
experience with ponies, and believed the salesman's
explanation that the protruding rib-like spars running
round this creature's torso were a form of protection
against predation, somewhat after the manner of an
armadillo. 'Ain't Mother Nature a wonderful thing?' he
added, as he pocketed their money.

Having loaded their supplies on to this one sorrowful
beast the party made its way east, through gently rolling
hills, gently downing downs, gently platting plateaus
(platting in the sense that river, road and crops appeared
to weave and unweave, drawing together and pulling
apart as they crossed the land). By noon on the third day
they had entered the Tiger Woods, where dangerous wild
animals lurked in every sand trap, and where the potato
game was originally invented. After many adventures,
which I don't have time to go into, they got out the other
side of this dangerous and exclusive place. They travelled
over the river Tim's, named for one of the most famous
legendary heroes of the Little Counties (Tim the Tiny,

River-Namer), and into Ply Wood. Here the going got slower. Bingo had to sit down every thirty or forty yards to rest his feet, and the dwarfs became crotchety with the delay. Pilfur and Gofur finally picked him up between them and carried him, but he complained at the bumpiness of the ride and they dropped him.

By sunset of the following day[3] the party had reached the Wood of Wooden Trees, and all were exhausted. The dwarfs had taken it in turns to carry the soddit, and had reached the end of their tether. In fact, they had tied a second tether to this end, and had reached the end of that too, which gives some indication of just how far they had gone. Really quite far, tether-wise, as I'm sure you will agree. Sadly their packhorse, Bony the tiny Pony, the only pony for sale in all of Cremone (sold them by phoney Tony the only pony-owner in Cremone) had

---

[3] I'd just like to say that the publishers have cut out *pages* and *pages* of my best stuff from here . . . I originally had the group enjoying all sorts of adventures in the Counties of the Little, fending off an attack of the Not Nice Mice, hurrying through the infestation of Piccadilly Flea Circus and the like. My favourite episode, which I begged and begged to keep in, but they didn't listen to me, was all about the land of the Tellurite Tubbles – those hard, metallic tub-shaped creatures, cyborg beings of terrifying inhumanity with computer screens inlaid in their torsos and weird shaped antenna coming out of their Upper Processing Units. Their ear-piercing cries of 'Annihilate! Annihilate!', 'You! Will Be! Annihilated!' and 'Tubble-tora-tora-tora-die-die-aaaiiee!' have charmed and delighted young children for many years.

fallen into the River Flem and drowned, carrying away nearly all their supplies. They were left only with a cauldron (that Tori was wearing as a helmet).

Dark fell as they made camp. It was a fell dark. Everybody in the company was hungry.

'You,' said Mori, prodding Bingo with the blunt end of his axe pole. 'Go and find us something to eat.'

'You're joking?' asked Bingo, rubbing a dock leaf on the soles of his aching feet. 'That's, you know, exactly like a joke, right?'

'There's firelight through the wooden trees,' said Gofur, pointing at a glowing splodge of orange light in the distance. 'Go and see who it is, and pinch some of their food, grabber, that's what you're here for, look you, a, yes, oo, bach, la, very.'

The other dwarfs made various noises of agreement. Amongst these noises were grunts, growls, two 'I agrees', one 'yes, off you go boyo', one 'I should say *so*' and one 'Mavis!', but this last was from a dwarf already asleep and was probably unrelated to the matter in hand.

Bingo was too tired to argue the case. He crept, biting his lower lip to stifle his grunts of pain, through the wooden trees of the wood of trees, moving always towards the gleam of the firelight. Soon, with a minimum of snapping twig sounds, rustlings, hootings of disturbed ground-nesting birds, sotto voce 'ouches' and 'ows' and the like, he got to the edge of a small clearing, and had a clear view of who was warming themselves by the fire within it.

Trollps! Four, great, whopping, stony trollps. Enough to give even the bravest soddit the collywobbles. They were sitting in a circle, roasting three dogs over the open fire. 'Ah,' said the nearest of them, licking his lips with his massive, stony tongue, 'roast mutt again.'

'Yer likes yer roast mutt, don't you Burt?' said a second trollp.

'That I do, Gerd,' agreed Burt, pulling one of the carcasses from the fire, dripping and sizzling on a stick, and taking a great squelching bite from its flank.[4]

Trollps, as you know, are fearsome creatures. It is

[4] The publishers have asked me to make it clear that they in no way endorse the cooking and eating of dogs, particularly not bassets, ladies, tramps, dogs that can say 'sausages' if you stick a thumb against their soft palate, the dog from the Famous Five or any other household-pet-style animal. Dogs are for Christmas, and for leaving on the side of the A308 in the new year, *not* for eating. *Cows* are the ones for eating, not dogs. They're big enough to look out for themselves, after all, whereas a brown-eyed whimpering Jack Russell is not. Remember the slogan of the 'Dogs Are People Too' organisation: 'Dogs Are People Too!' (The 'Cows Are People Too' organisation slogan is far more equivocal: 'Cows Are People Too, Though Not Very Bright People, And We Got To Admit It People With Extremely Tasty Flesh When Roasted Or, Better, Grilled, And Served With A Mustard And Dill Sauce, Some Chips, String Beans, A Nice Glass Of Red Wine, Oooh, Go On Then It Won't Matter If We Have Just The One, There Are Millions Of Them In Big Sheds Up North').

now many years since they left their traditional sub-pontoon habitat, and their traditional diet of goats, to roam far and wide in search of a fuller sense of self-expression and some quick cash. They are of course gigantic in stature, five foot eleven is not uncommon and some are as tall as six foot one and a half, and their proportions are similarly huge, bellies like boulders, arms like the roots of great oak trees, a head that looks from a distance as if it's wearing a steel helmet until you get closer and realise that that's just the shape of the head. Trollps, being creatures of nature, grow a straggly moss on their chests, arms and legs; they grow a stubble of little thorns from their chins, but the tops of their heads are smooth as water-polished stone. Their eyes are red as garnets, and their brows are beetling – not in the sense of having independent legs and a tendency to scurry away, but rather in the sense of jutting or overhanging in a threatening manner.

These four hefty trollps had come down from the mountains hoping for some business from the north-western cart salesman and middle-farm-management population. They were dressed in the traditional costume of their race: lacy underwear, garter belts, stockings (made of the same wire mesh used by some to construct fences), little fluttery red silk skirts which tended to ride suggestively upwards in the slightest breeze – and which, if the breeze were anything more than slight, tended to become cummerbunds – and a saucy little French Trollection low-halter button-up top, also in red. Burt had personalised his outfit with a natty little silk-ribbon neck bow, very continental, and Bill – the tallest of the four – wore flats rather than the brick-heeled Ralph Lauren trolletto shoes of the others. Gerd wore elbow-length gloves that had been a bridal white once upon a time, although they had now gone a rather muddy pink colour in the wash on account of being put in the laundry with man-blood still on them one too many times. Old Gil, the fourth member of the group, was the master make-upper of the four. His slab-like lips were carefully outlined in fifteen pounds of lipstick, very fetching. His tiny glowing eyes were surrounded by four thick, tangled rows of eyelashes, giving him the appearance of having large and grotesquely overfed Venus fly traps fitted to the front of his face. Which, indeed, may have been how he achieved the effect.

Bingo had not enjoyed a hot meal since the day before, and his mouth started watering at the smell of the roasting dog. He peered from behind a tree trunk, and slipped soundlessly to another tree trunk to get a better view, pressing himself close against this for cover and taking another cautious look. Sadly for him this last tree trunk was not a tree trunk at all, but Gerd's leg. He was suspended in midair, squealing and kicking his legs, before he knew what was happening.

'Hey! Crikey, blimey, love a duck and apples'n'-pears,' said Gerd, displaying his catch to the rest of them. 'Look what I've found!' He pronounced this last word 'fanned', but Bingo assumed that he meant 'discovered by chance', 'obtained' rather than 'cooled by agitating the air with a fan'.

The trollps clustered round, and gave a few exploratory pokes of Bingo in the ribs with their massive fingers.

'A snack!' said Gil. 'Bags he's mine!'

'There's bare enough in 'im for a mouf-ful,' said Bill.

'Lumme, cor, 'Ackney and Bermondsey,' said Gerd, 'a mouf-ful is all I want.'

'But ooze?' challenged Burt. 'Ooze to get the mouf-ful?'

'I caught 'im,' said Gerd.

'I bags'd him fust,' said Gil.

'I say we draws lots,' said Bill.

'Lots of wot?' said Burt.

'Are there any *more* of you mouf-fuls round about?' asked Gil, bringing his great stone face close up to Bingo's. The stench of Amour de Troll washed up the soddit's nose.

'No!' Bingo squeaked.

'Gah,' said Bill, grimacing. 'Bound to be,' said Gil, nodding.

With nary another word Bill, Gil and Burt lumbered

off into the woods. Bingo, gasping, dangling in midair, consoled himself by thinking that the three trollps were making such a loud noise that the dwarfs would surely be warned of their approach. Then he thought that the dwarfs were fierce and hardy warriors and would quickly defeat the trollps, and his captors would soon be nothing but rubble. Sadly, he was wrong in both these thoughts. No more than ten minutes later the three trollps returned, each with a brace of dwarfs. All the members of Thorri's band had been tied with their own beards, a humiliating circumstance that did not so much add insult to injury as multiply insult plus injury by shame to the power of agony. When they were all deposited, like giant hairy pupae, in a pile by the fire Bingo was trussed with an old trollp garter belt, and placed on top of the heap.

'That's more like it,' said Gil, sitting down on the broad boulder he'd been using as a stool and rubbing his great stony hands together at the fire, sending stone chips skittering into the air. 'That's a feast, that is.'

'Dwarfs,' said Burt, smacking his lips, or to be more precise, clacking them together. 'Tasty! Pukka!'

'I got nettles in my garter,' complained Bill, fumbling under his fine silks. 'Bloody forest.'

'Hark at 'er,' said Gerd. He affected an effeminate voice, or as close to one as his enormous stone vocal cords permitted him, to add: *'Got ne'els in my gar'er'*.

Then he sniggered, a sound like a row of gravestones falling over domino fashion. 'Ponce,' he concluded.

'Nance,' snapped Bill.

'Dunce,' said Gerd.

'Berk,' said Bill.

'Jerk,' said Gerd.

'Merck,' said Bill.

'Oi!' said Burt. 'Cut it out.' Actually he said 'Cu ih ah', but the other two trollps understood what he meant well enough. They glowered at one another. Bill smoothed out the creases of his red silk skirt against his enormous thighs. Gerd looked haughtily away into the forest.

'All we got to do now,' said Old Gil, 'is work out the best way to cook 'em.'

'The best fing with dwarfs,' said Bill, 'is to soffen 'em up, with a meat tenderiser, or a shovel maybe, and then chop 'em up.'

'Nah, nah, nah!' said Burt with scorn in his voice. 'You dahn't *cut* dwarfs, you *rip* 'em. And then you put 'em in a pot wiv onions, peppers, dozen cloves o' garlic, some cardamom, *green* chillies not red ones, and a lemon. Forty-five minutes, take the pot off the 'eat, *then* add the basil, bay leaf, touch of mint, frow in four dozen carrots, put them on the 'eat again, only *don't scorch* 'em, two hours, layer over with cream and brandy, Demerara, stir some more, 'nother lemon, fish out their 'ats and boots (keeping 'em for stock) and serve the whole fing up with six hunnert-weight of spuds. Cushtie, that. Lovely. Pukka.'

'Or we could just sit on 'em,' said Bill.

'All right,' said Burt.

The trollps regarded the pile. 'Tell you what, Gerd,' said Bill. '*You* sit on 'em.'

'Me?' said Gerd, outraged. 'Why me?'

'You got the biggest bum.'

'Bugger *off* have I!' said Gerd, standing up in his fury. 'Gil's is twice my size.'

'Yer lie!' roared Old Gil, standing up also.

'Remember that leather skirt you bought in that Dongor boo-teak?' taunted Gerd. 'Oh we laughed at that, all right. Made your bum look like two cows fighting in a leather tent, that did.'

'Laugh at me behind my back!' Gil yelled, and put his fist into Gerd's face. The ground shook with the terrible force of the blow, but Gerd did not so much as flinch, nor did his expression change. He pushed out with his right arm, aiming a devastating hook and catching Gil, smack in *his* face. The blow made a noise like a thunderclap. Cups containing water that happened to be standing on the ground nearby jiggled little bullseye patterns of ripples in their surfaces. But Gil didn't flinch either. The huge trollp made no sound. To be honest with you, there's little point in trollps fighting, since it's almost impossible for them to injure one another and they don't really feel pain. But they sometimes go through the motions, just for the form of it. After a few more punches on either side Gerd and Gil sat down.

'Please kind sirs,' squealed Bingo, who had been summoning his courage and trying to think of what to say. 'Don't eat us! We'll give you gold!'

'Gold,' mused Burt. 'I ate some of that once. A corn factor in Bardbury gave me a gold bracelet, had it engraved 'n all – "to my darlin' in memory of the happiest weekend of my life, your snugly-puggly J. Harrow Whettlestone Jr, Corn Factor and Mercer, Seasonal Rates".' Burt sniffed as if moved by the memory. 'I ate it, o' course, but it did somefink shocking down below . . . you know what I mean.'

The other three trollps grumbled their agreement.

'It ain't specially digestible,' said Bill. 'Gold.'

'Wait a minute,' said Gil. 'Corn factor in Bardbury? You got a arrangement wiv a corn factor in Bardbury? What we doing skulking in these woods if you got a comfy berf in Bardbury?'

'Well,' said Burt shiftily. 'Trufe is, he's a special little feller of mine.'

'Share and share alike,' insisted Gil.

'And I would,' said Burt. 'Only I et him last spring. He used to take me on special trips, it was lovely, the best hostels, fine clothes, as much dog as I could eat, but then one morning I woke up and looked at him and thought, "You're a pretty tasty gent," so I et him, and there it was.'

'Enough natter,' said Bill. '*I'm* going to squash me a dwarf. Better do somefing or we'll be ere all night.'

He stood up and picked a wriggling dwarf from the pile. But whilst he was up, Gerd pulled another dwarf from the bottom of the pile, and quickly slipped it on to Bill's boulder. As the unwitting trollp sat down there was a sound of revolting flatulent squelchiness. He looked startled, and his three friends began their rolling, ponderous, stony laughs. 'Oho,' said Bill, with a stern face. 'Oh that's very funny, that is,' he said sarcastically. 'Oh, I'll split me sides laughing at that.'

'Should have seen your face, Bill,' said Burt.

' 'Ere,' said Bill. 'You 'av this one.' He tossed his dwarf to Gil, and got gingerly to his feet trying to unstick the object that was now adhering limply to his hindquarters. Meanwhile, the three other trollps took their own dwarfs, placed them carefully on whichever slab or boulder they were sitting on, and sat back down. The whoopee-cushion noises sounded wetly round the ring. For several minutes there were no further sounds in the clearing save the gnash and gulp of four trollps eating.

Things were looking grim for the company.

'This one,' said Gil shortly, 'tastes a bit of chicking.'

'Everyfing tastes of chicking to me,' said Bill. ' 'Cept gold,' he added.

'Are you supposed to take the shell off of 'em before you eat 'em?' asked Burt, picking a mangled chunk of chain mail out of his great teeth with a fingernail like a paving slab.

'You smell,' came a rather quavery but fairly deep voice, the sort of voice an adolescent boy might inadvertently employ when he is on the cusp of slipping into manhood. 'You smell and, ah, nobody likes you.'

'Oo said that?' snapped Gerd.

'It was Bill,' said the quavery voice.

'No it wasn't,' said Bill.

'It came from over there,' said Gill, standing up and pointing towards the trees.

'No it didn't,' said the quavery voice. 'It was Bill. He said you all smell really unpleasantly and, uh, that you, oh I don't know, that you're a disgrace to the name of trollp.'

'Oo *is* that?' said Gerd.

The voice cleared its throat in a moist fashion, and seemed to slip down a semitone: 'Don't you speak to me like that, young Bill, you're the one who's a disgrace. I happen to know that the other two agree with me when I say that you've let down the honour of trollps everywhere.' There was a momentary pause. 'That was Gerd.'

Gerd was standing. 'I don't sound anyfink *like* that,' he declared, reasonably enough.

'No, no,' said the voice, 'that was definitely Gerd. I'd say that he's trying to pick a fight. Are you going to stand for that, Bill? Are you aHurgh Hurgh! Hurgh! Hurgh! Hurgh! Hurgh!' The voice was suddenly coughing so hard it was making the leaves nearby shudder. 'Hurgh! Hurgh! Hurgh! Hurgh! Hurgh!' it said.

Gil reached into the trees with his enormous hand, and brought out a wriggling figure dressed in a grey poncho and sporting a conical hat.

'Hurgh! Hurgh! Hurgh! Hurgh!' said the figure.

'A wizard!' said Gerd. 'Now don't that just cap everyfink?'

'I've never et a wizard before,' said Bill with glee in his voice.

'He's a bit scrawny, like,' said Gil, examining him. 'But 'e'll do.'

'Hurgh!' said the figure, the coughing subsiding. 'Hurgh!'

'Gandef!' squealed Bingo. 'Save us.'

Gandef, suspended in midair by the stone grip of a trollp's fist around his neck, managed to twist his head enough to look down upon Bingo. The look on his strained face seemed to say, *What do you think I'm trying to do, you twit?* It seemed to add, *And now look at the situation I'm in. What are we going to do now? It's all very well for you, but I'm a man of advanced years, I can hardly tackle four fully grown adult trollps by myself, bearing in mind my chronic lumbar pain and everything, not that I'm one to complain, I'm only saying.* A twist of a wizardly eyebrow seemed to ask, *Can't you reach one of the dwarf's swords, cut your bonds, free the rest of Thorri's company, dig a large pit, lure the trollps into it and quickly cover it with several hundred tons of earth?* As the despair on Bingo's face implied a negative answer, the look concluded, *You're a waste of space, useless, the lot of you.*

All in all, it was an exceptionally eloquent look.

'Now,' Gandef rasped, addressing the trollps. 'Gentlemen. I advise you not to be hasty. I should warn you that I'm a wizard.'

'So?' said Old Gil.

'Well, I could be trouble for you. In fact,' he wheezed, trying to loosen Gil's fingers with both his hands, and kicking his legs pitifully, 'in fact – isn't that the first ray of sunshine, dawn creeping up on you unawares, ha-ha?'

Burt looked over his shoulder. 'So it is.'

There was a pause.

'Well,' said Gandef, his face growing increasingly purple and his voice increasingly gasping, 'shouldn't you make a dash for your trollp cave?'

'Why would we want to do that?'

'Well – you know. The dawn, the sunshine will, you know. Kill you.'

'No it won't,' said Gerd. 'Wot a odd notion.'

'Oh,' gasped Gandef. He seemed to be casting around for something else to say. 'You sure?'

'Quite sure,' said Gerd.

'I went on holiday to the Souflands last year,' said Bill. 'Lovely sunshine there. Got a nice tan. I say tan, it was more a sort of process of oxidisation.'

'If you could just—' Gandef hissed, the purple of his face deepening almost to black. 'Be so kind as to – just put me down—'

'Wot's he saying?' said Burt. 'Put him down for a mo. Gil.'

The wizard dropped to the ground. For a while he lay panting, whilst the trollps discussed amongst themselves the best way of adding him to the meal.

'That's it,' said Gandef, pulling himself shakily to his feet. 'You've made me really quite tetchy now.'

The four trollps stopped talking, and looked down at the wizard.

'As a gentleman,' Gandef went on, 'I'm prepared to give you fair warning. Untie my companions here, apologise to them properly, and I'll let you be on your way. But I warn you, if you persist in this boorish behaviour, I won't be answerable for the consequences.'

'Wot consequences?' said Bill.

'Terrible consequences,' said Gandef, shaking his fist, or, possibly, simply holding his fist out such that it manifested his tremulous old-man wobble.

'Don't believe yer,' said Burt. 'Terrible conscience-quenches for *oo*? That's what I wants to know.'

'Terrible for *'im*, I'd say,' agreed Gerd.

'Shall I stamp on 'im right away?' offered Gil.

'I *am* a wizard,' Gandef observed, with a tone in his voice that might have been hurt pride. 'After all.'

'And?'

'I'll put a spell on you. I've got some pretty uncomfortable spells, you know.'

'Har har har,' said Burt, speaking the laughter rather than laughing it in order to convey a sense of condescending and sarcastic dismissal.[5]

'I do so know some spells!' said Gandef. 'Terrible spells, some of them.'

'Bad, are they?' said Bill.

'Oo, yes,' said Gandef.

'What's your *worst* spell?' asked Bill.

'I could,' said Gandef, with dignity, 'turn you all to stone. Easily.'

---

[5] Why does this only work with laughter? If somebody tells you a bad joke and you say 'ha ha' you express a withering contempt for the feebleness of their sense of humour. But if they throw poor quality pepper in your face and you say 'sneeze sneeze' instead of actually sneezing, it doesn't have the same effect at all.

'But we're already stone,' Gerd pointed out. 'Why should that frighten us?'

It seemed to Bingo that Gerd had a point. 'Hmm,' said Gandef, as if considering this.

'Turn us to stone!' said Burt. 'That's a good 'un!'

'Go on,' said Gil, 'do your worst.'

It wasn't easy to see in the dimness, for the shadows of the trees threw an obscurity over everything in spite of the growing light of dawn, but to Bingo's terrified eyes it seemed that the towering figure of the trollp froze for a moment, and then drained away to nothing. The other three turned to their comrade with puzzlement on their faces, and a moment later each of them also shrank away to nothing, losing the substantiality of stone and dribbling away downwards. They vanished completely. For a while the soddit could not believe his eyes.

Gandef settled himself on a bounder not stained with dwarf blood and lit his pipe, puffing meditatively for a while. Then, as if remembering something trivial that had slipped his mind, he got up, shuffled over to Bingo and undid his bindings. The two of them freed the remaining dwarfs, and in five minutes everybody was huddled round the fire, rubbing their stiff limbs and eyeing the still-singeing dog carcasses with hungry, if disgusted, eyes.

'Gandef?' Bingo asked in a small voice. 'You can hear me properly now?'

'Oh yes,' the wizard said, sucking on his pipe. 'You all seemed to be in a sticky situation, so I ratcheted my hearing spell up a notch or two. I don't like to leave it on all the time,' he added. 'It runs my magic strength down.'

'What did you do,' Bingo pressed, 'to the trollps?'

'Turned them to stone, just as I threatened.'

'You turned them,' said Mori, who was kicking his feet through the remnants of the creatures, 'to sand.'

'I didn't say what *kind* of stone I was going to turn them into,' said Gandef. 'It only goes to show, never cheek a wizard. I'd suggest you scatter that sand through the forest in all directions. It's still alive, you see, and it'd be better for us if we stop it from, well, *accumulating* again. Then we ought to be off.'

Coward(ly) Elf & Wild(e) Elf

Chapter Three

A 'SH'

ᏻᎾᏗᎧ

'Sh', said Gandef.

They had been travelling for three days, sorrowfully at first in memory of the four fallen comrades, then wearily, and finally in a crotchety fashion. They did not tell tales, or sing songs. Neither did they sing tales or tell songs. The mountains grew on the horizon, but grew very slowly.

'Is that *the* mountain?' asked Bingo. 'The one to which our quest is directed?'

'I wish,' said Mori dismissively.

'Phumf,' said Tori, a sort of nasal equivalent of the same sentiment. 'Look you,' he added, with his mouth rather than his nostrils.

They walked on for a while.

'I'm terribly sorry,' Bingo hazarded, 'for the loss of your – um, comrades. Comrades? Brothers?'

Tori looked grumpy. Bingo felt dopey for having asked.

'We dwarfs,' said Mori, 'do not like to parade our

grief, look you. We're a secretive folk, a tough, stout, thrawn people.'

'Right,' said Bingo. 'I understand. What's "thrawn" mean?'

'Thrawn,' repeated Mori. 'Well it's sort of . . . it's a word that refers to the dwarfish, to the dwarfish, um. Well. Hmm. Wombl,' he called. 'Boyo, what's "thrawn" mean?'

Wombl was trudging along on the far side of the group. 'Thrawn,' he grumbled. 'Is that, you see, a word for slave?'

'No,' interjected Frili. 'You're thinking of "thrall".'

'Oh, so I am, so I am.'

'Is it that, kind of, sea creature?' piped Gofur. 'Looks a little like an insect. Lives on the ocean floor.'

'No, no,' said Mori. 'It's a *dwarf* word, isn't it? It's got something to do with dwarfs, see.'

It was at this point that Gandef said, 'Sh!'

Everybody stopped.

'Elves!' said the wizard. 'See them, in the trees?'

The party stopped at the edge of a great forest, glorious in silver birch, golden-green leaves like sequins, fragrant and expansive. Gandef pointed, and Bingo could just make out thin, sharp, clever-looking faces looking back at them from boughs in the wood.

'Elves!' he gasped.

'Elves,' grumbled the dwarfs.[1]

'Do we have to go through this damn elf-infested forest?' demanded Mori. 'Wizard? Can't we go round?'

'Well,' said the wizard, apparently in reply to some completely different question. 'There are two different races of elf, you see. I'll tell you. There are the Star Elves – or the "In The Gutter Looking At The Star Elves" as they are more properly known – and there are the Tree Elves, the *Herbertbeerbohmtree* Elves. I won't attempt to translate the elvish epithet. Of these two great people, the former likes the plants of the world, particularly the carnations, and especially the purple carnations, which they like to pluck from the places of greatest danger and to set in the front of their clothing to display to all the world. This delight in the dangers of carnation-plucking has led to them being called the Wild Elves – but do not call them so to their face, for

---

[1] As is well known, there is no love lost between elves and dwarfs. By *no love lost* I mean that they do not love one another. Now that I come to think of it, I suppose the phrase *no love lost* might be taken to mean that the two peoples loved one another so completely and with such zealous stewardship of their love that all of it was directed at the loved party, and none of it went astray, none of it was wasted on ants or milkmaids or fine clothes or things like that. But that wasn't the sense I intended to convey. I meant the other sense. Perhaps I should have said something like *dwarfs and elves hated one another*. That would have been less ambiguous. But it's too late now. Oh dear. Too late! Too late!

the phrase was not meant kindly. The Tree Elves, however, avoid all such danger. Elves are immortal provided no external force kills them, and the Tree Elves take the understandable view that they should do all they can to avoid being killed by some external circumstance. The Wild Elves despise them for this reason, and call them the Coward Elves – but do not use the name yourself, or call them so to their face, for the phrase was not meant kindly. And it is true to this day that the Wild Elves are often truly Wild. I have known a Wild Elf wear bright purple breeches with a lime-green and orange-checked tunic. No Coward Elf would have the courage for such attire. Tweed is about as courageous as they can be.'

Mori smiled warmly at the old wizard. 'The fact that you can't comprehend a single word I'm saying,' he said, clasping the wizard's old hand in his, 'encourages me to call you, to your face, the most tedious old codger in all of Upper Middle Earth.'

'Thank you, my dear dwarf friend,' said Gandef, his eyes moist with emotion. 'Thank you indeed.'

'So,' said Bingo, who had actually been quite interested by Gandef's little exposition. 'So – these elves in the Last Homo House; are they Wild Elves or are they Coward Elves?'

'I've no cladding idea,' said Mori, utilising a mild dwarfish stone-based expletive.

'The answer to your question,' said Gandef boomingly, 'is no. On the other hand, you're probably wondering whether these elves of Bluewaterdel are *Wild* Elves or *Coward* Elves. It's a complex matter, but I think I can explain it.'

Mori sighed.

'Elsqare himself is a Wild Elf. But he took as his partner a Coward Elf, the beautiful Olthfunov, and accordingly groups of both races cohabit here. But their time is not our time. The days pass differently for them, as a fleeting flicker; they do not rise until noon, and they often nap. Alas!' he cried suddenly, 'For the tragedy of this forest is that the two races do not cohabit contentedly.'

They were walking between the trees of the beautiful forest now, and an elf sauntered from the shade to stand in the path before them. He was tall and elegant and his garb was of green velvet and silk, and he stood leaning his torso at a slight angle to the vertical, supporting it by placing a hand upon his own hip. His eyes glittered; or one of them did, for in front of it he wore a circle of purest glass.

'Gandef the wizard,' he said languidly. 'And companions. I *do* declare.'

'Ah!' said Gandef. 'Sunblest, the Elf of the Morning, is it?'

'*I* am Elstree the Tree Elf,' said the elf in a hurt voice.

'Surprised I am, O wizard, that you did not recognise me. Did we not once share a small lakeside cottage for a fortnight of relaxation and occasional swimming? Nevertheless, I greet you, and shall take you and your companions to Lord Elsqare himself.'

'Oh, well, I suppose that's a fair question,' said Gandef, beaming. 'I'd say the answer was bread, except in the winter months when it's probably a meal of chaff.'

Elstree's eye shield of glass twinkled in the sunlight. His head leaned five degrees to the left. The wind moved in the trees behind him.

There was silence for the space of several minutes.

Eventually, Elstree beckoned to them all to follow him through the woodland.

Lord Elsqare himself was seated in a throne made of boughs and carved branches, high in a tree. He was an elf of indeterminate age, dressed in purple and blue, and he wore the carnation and the polished crystal eyepiece of the Wild Elves. Mori whispered to Bingo that all the elves lived in trees, odd though that seemed to the rest of the world. And, truly, Elsqare was surrounded by elves in amongst the leaves, all of them peering haughtily down at the travellers.

'Gandef the wizard,' said Elsqare. 'How good it is to see you again. Fares your quest well?'

'About half past four, I'd say,' returned Gandef. 'Hard to tell precisely,' he added, 'without a watch.'

'And *you* are Thorri, King of the Dwarfs, or I am mistaken,' continued Elsqare, unfazed.

Thorri bowed so low his beard inched along the ground before him like a caterpillar. 'I am honoured to be in thith thelebrated palath of elvithneth,' he said.

'I'm sorry?' asked Elsqare. 'Didn't quite catch . . .'

'Our noble King,' struck in Mori, 'declares himself at your service, Lord Elsqare.'

'Thorri,' said Thorri, in a miniature voice, casting his face to the ground.

'We have suffered on our travels,' Mori continued. 'We have lost some of our company – brothers, comrades, glorious in death.'

'Really?' said Elsqare, perking up. 'How so?'

'Trollps,' said Mori severely. 'They took four of our comrades before we were able to destroy them. Qwalin, Orni, Ston and Pilfur, may their names be writ in glory.'

'Dear me,' said Elsqare. 'To lose one dwarf might be regarded a misfortune. To lose four looks like carelessness.'

The elves twittered their twittery laughter.

'What did you say, look you?' said Mori, his face reddening.

'To lose one dwarf,' Elsqare repeated, 'might be regarded a misfortune. To lose four looks like carelessness. It's a witticism.'

'A joke?'

'A witticism.'

'You mean,' said Mori, 'that you regard the death of four individuals as the occasion for humour? In what way is it *careless* to have you friends killed? Where's the carelessness in that? Surely that's tragic, not funny.'

Elsqare looked marginally perturbed. 'The good end happily,' he said, 'the bad unhappily, that is what dwarfishness means.'

'Wait a minute,' said Mori. 'Have you ever had four friends die on you all at once? How would you like it if somebody accused you of carelessness, when—'

'I think,' said Elstree the Tree Elf stepping forward, 'that there has been a misunderstanding. Let us not, elf and dwarf, become enemies.'

'Indeed not,' said Elsqare languidly. 'After all a man cannot be too careful in the choice of his enemies.'

A few elves in the tree behind him tittered and chattered at this.

'The choice of your enemies?' said Bingo. 'How do you mean? People don't *choose* their enemies. That's not how it goes. Your statement doesn't really mean anything.'

Nobody spoke.

Gandef broke the silence with a single percussive cough. But then he too fell silent.

Bingo became conscious of the fact that everybody was looking at him. He cast around for a topic of non-contentious conversation. 'Must be hard living in a tree,' he said eventually. 'Couldn't you dig a nice, modern little ditch and live under the soil as God intended? If it's good enough for dead people, surely its good enough for you? There's quite a lot of soil over there, for instance.'

'We're with the soddit on this one,' said Mori. 'Living in trees? I ask you.' He looked around. 'I don't *actually* ask you, bach, you see, look you, it's only a figure of speech, isn't it?'

'Tis true, life is hard,' stated Elsqare. 'There is only one thing worse than being an elf, and that is *not* being an elf.'

A dozen elves laughed, twittering like swallows. The laughter died away.

'I don't get it,' said Bingo. He became uncomfortably aware of dozens of elvish eyes, each pair focusing a cut-glass look down upon him.

'You don't *get it*?' said Elsqare, sounding, for the first time, peeved. 'What d'ye mean?' He fitted his cunningly worked elvish monocle back into his eye.

'Well, I only mean to say,' said Bingo cautiously, 'that I don't quite . . . I mean, when you say that. Don't you *like* being an elf?'

''Course I do,' snapped Elsqare. 'Absurd question!'

'Well,' said Bingo. 'It's just that if you say "there's only one thing worse than being an elf", you're implying that being an elf is a miserable thing, and that only "being anything else" is *more* miserable. In effect,' he went on, warming to his theme, 'you're saying that *any* existence is appalling, and that the only salient characteristic of an elvish existence is that it is marginally *less* appalling than any other existence. I suppose I can understand somebody expressing a position of such nihilistic absolutism, but it's difficult to construe it as a . . . as a joke, do you see? I don't see why that's funny. I mean, if existing is *so* terrible, wouldn't tears and lamentations be more appropriate?'

There was silence amongst the trees for the portion of several minutes. Finally Elsqare spoke. 'Anyway, you'd better come up and have some tea.'

They clambered into the trees up elegantly carved wooden ladders, and after much bouncing of boughs and unsteady steps, they were all arranged in a semi-circle about Elsqare's throne. Tea was brought. Everybody sipped, and nibbled at the scone-like Elvish weybread. Gandef smoked. Elsqare's face assumed a pinched, rather pained expression as if he expected more from his guests. At one point he announced, 'I have always felt that work is the curse of the tea-drinking classes,' and smirked. But although a few of his followers hiccoughed briefly with laughter, the line was greeted with non-comprehension by the dwarfs and he fell silent again.

The tea was finished. The last crumbs of Elvish weybread consumed.

The silence grew longer, taller, and more oppressive.

'At last,' Elsqare said. 'Here comes my partner, Olthfunov the Fair. He'll liven proceedings up. Olthfunov! Coo-ee! Up here.'

A stouter elf in green, with a high forehead and a somewhat lumpish nose, was coming up the ladder. 'Guests?' he said. 'How delightful. How wonderful. Is that Gandef I see, snoozing against the trunk back there? And dwarfs, how marvellous. We must have a party.'

Introductions were made.

'So you're a soddit, are you?' Olthfunov enquired of Bingo. 'Where are you from, little man?'

'Soddlesex,' said Bingo. 'Do you know it?'

'Indeed,' the elf replied. 'Very flat, Soddlesex.'

'Oh,' said Bingo. 'Well, quite flat, I suppose. There are several hills, though, and —'

'You're off to the Minty Mountains?'

'In that direction, yes.'

'Very,' said Olthfunov, with a catch of suppressed glee in his voice, '*uppy-downy*, the mountains. Don't you think?'

Bingo could hear tittering behind him. 'I suppose so,' he said.

'Ol,' said Elsqare. 'I'm sorry to say that our friends have lost four of their companions.'

'Dear me,' said Olthfunov, sipping his tea. 'How so?'

'Eaten by trollps, it seems.'

'Ghastly creatures, trollps,' murmured Olthfunov.

'Indeed. And,' Elsqare added, in an aside, 'they're somewhat touchy on the topic, so have a care.'

'A care,' said the Coward Elf. 'Naturally. Sensitive area, I'm sure. But,' he added, bursting into song, or – to be strictly accurate – if not quite bursting, then certainly sidling into a sort of half-song, half-recital:

> *Oh, don't let's be beastly to the trollps*
> *When our Victory is finally won,*
> *And when peace inevitably followps*
> *We can give them a sugar-topped bun.*

He concluded with a rapidly murmured, 'Thank you, thank you, too kind,' and sat back.

The wind shuffled through the higher leaves of the trees. Away below them a fox barked.

'Lovely,' said Elsqare acidly.

'Followps?' queried Bingo.

'Obviously,' announced Mori, 'we'd love to stay, love to stay, look you, but we've a long journey ahead of us.'

The dwarfs stirred, as if rousing themselves to leave.

'Of course,' said Elsqare. 'Off you go. Bon voyage. Please allow us to help you on your way with some supplies – salted goods and such. Where is it you're off to?'

'Over the mountains,' said Mori. 'Through the great forest.'

'I say,' Elsqare burbled. 'How exciting.'

'To the Only Mountain.'

'Really? Isn't that the estate of Smug the Dragon?'

The dwarfs nodded, looking grim.[2]

'Well, best of luck, best of luck. Do call in again on your way home, if you're passing.'

'Oh!' said Gandef, who was helping himself to a fifth scone as he noticed that everybody else was on their feet and climbing down from the trees. 'Are we off then?'

---

[2] Mind you, it's easy to look grim with a great big beard. The tricky thing, with a great big beard, is *not* to look grim.

Sollum

Chapter Four

RIDDLES IN THE DA-DOO-DOO-DOO, DA-DAH-DAH-DAH IDIOM

☙

The following morning was a midsummer's morning as bright and beautiful as could be imagined. The sun danced on the water.[1] Gandef, Bingo and the dwarfs walked towards the Minty Mountains. They reared from the horizon.

'Is that our destination?' asked Bingo as he limped alongside Mori. He asked the question more in hope than in expectation of a positive answer.

'No,' said Mori. He added, in a singsong, 'No no no no no no no no', running down the notes of the musical scale. 'No, boy, no, boyo, no. We've somehow to get *past* those Minty Mountains, and then cross the mighty

[1] Not literally, obviously. This sentence is meant metaphorically – which is to say that sunlight waltzed and pogoed from wavelet to wavelet like little parcels of photons on amphetamines. Dear me, imagine if the sun were *literally* dancing on the waters! My! That would mean the agonising and fiery death not only of our heroes, but of the whole world, a global apocalypse and ultimate disaster! Dear me!

River Misissiisiisisiissississippisipisipisipsofactoisisipi-sipi,[2] then find our way through the scary and inhospit-able Mykyurwood. Only then, my laddo, only then will we approach the Only Mountain.'

'Only Mountain?'

'Well – not the only mountain, of course. *Strictly* speaking, look you, there are plenty of other mountains. But it's the Only Mountain Worth Mentioning if you're a dwarf, see, la. It's many days' march from here. And thrice as many days' stumble.'

Bingo limped on in silence for a while. Then he spoke.

'Mori,' he said. 'I can't quite shake the sense that the purpose of our quest—'

'Gold,' said Mori at once, without looking at him.

'Sure, yes. Right. Gold. Yes. But I can't quite shake the sense that our quest – although ostensibly under-taken for gold—'

'—gold—' agreed Mori.

'—gold, yes, it not *actually* being undertaken for gold at all.'

The two marched on for several minutes.

'So?' Bingo prompted.

'Eh?' replied Mori.

---

[2] For convenience sake this river in future will be referred to as the River M.

'Am I right?'

'Right?'

'About our quest?'

'Gold,' said Mori in a loud voice. 'That's what it's about. Now if you'll excuse me I have to go talk to— to one of the others, you know.'

He scurried away.

The whole party slept under a large gooseberry bush that evening, and by noon the following day they had reached the feet of the Minty Mountains. This great chain of mighty snow-skullcapped peaks stretching from the frozen eminence of Mount Gungadin in the north all the long leagues down to the Gap of Next in the south. The steep sides of the myriad denticular mountains that made up this chain were, all of them, sparkling with clean, bright ice: gleaming and white with snow. To stand at the foot of this gigantic and impenetrable wall of towering rock is to be awed by the sublimity of the natural world; the mountain's slumberous voice echoes through your very being. In the mountains you feel free; there you can read all through the night, if you fancy it, and go south in the winter. The air of the mountains is clean, fresh, sharp, inspiring.

'Buggeration,' said Bingo, as he collapsed on a boulder and started rubbing his sore toes. 'We got to go over those, now, have we?'

'Mountains,' said Mori, with a tear in his eye and a finger twisted into his beard. 'Beautiful beautiful mountains, look you. Beautiful beautiful beautiful beautiful beautiful beautiful beautiful beautiful beautiful beautiful beautiful beautiful beautiful beautiful beautiful mountains.'

'Dwarfs like mountains, then, do they?' asked Bingo.

'Well, not really, look you,' said Mori. 'We prefer the underneath of mountains. But just look at those lovely things! Look how smooth the sides are – how hairless and smooth and perfect! That mountain there, for instance, lovely, lovely, smooth as a baby mountain.'

'And we need to get to the other side of them.'

'Ah yes,' said the dwarfs in unison.

Bingo looked at his swollen, ruddy, throbbing feet. 'Do we have mountaineering equipment? Ropes, thick socks, that sort of thing?'

'Ah no,' said the dwarfs in unison.

'Well I really don't think we should go over those mountains. I don't think my feet would stand it. They're not good in snow. Gandef?' Bingo appealed to the elderly wizard, although he had to raise his voice. 'Gandef? Do you intend that we climb over those mountains?'

The question was repeated only eight or nine times before Gandef finally understood. He had been silently counting the mountain tops, pointing to each of them in turn and munching his lips as if fixing the number in his mind: a curious exercise, but something – Bingo assumed – wizardly. Perhaps the number of peaks visible had a mystic aspect. Perhaps Gandef couldn't count anything without silently moving his lips and pointing.

When Bingo's question was finally beaten into his skull, he snorted with derision. 'Climb them?' he snarled. 'Do I *look* to you like a counting mimer?'

'You what?'

Miro placed his right hand behind his right ear in dumb-show of *say again*.

'Are you deaf?' snapped Gandef. 'I *said*, do I *look* like a mountain climber? No, no, no. We'll not attempt to climb – we'd never make it. Luckily we can go *under* the mountains.'

'Through the Coal Gate?' asked Tori, in awe and terror.

'Through the cavernous and echoey spaces under the mountain?' added Fili.

'And out via the Cavity through which plunges the icy River Floss?' said Sili.

'No, don't be ridiculous,' said Gandef in annoyance. 'I mean go *through* the Coal Gate – and *out again* through the cavemouth Cavity on the other side. It's the only sensible way.'

'But the Coal Gate is enchanted, Gandef,' Sili pointed out.

'Ah,' said Gandef, settling himself down on a tree stump and getting out his pipe. 'I'm glad you asked me that, young dwarf. Yes, that's a good point. But I've carefully counted the mountain peaks, and there really don't seem to be any more here than there were the last time I came.'

Dwarf looked to dwarf looked to soddit, but none had any idea what the wizard was talking about.

'So I don't think we need to worry about *that*,' said Gandef with satisfaction. 'On the other hand, the door of the Coal Gate is enchanted – I don't know if any of you were aware of that. I'll have to rack my brains to try and come up with the magic word. I'll use some of my most powerful opening spells.'

After the wizard had finished smoking his pipe, and after the ten-minute phlegm-hawking episode that followed, the party made their way through the stumpy valleys and past an evil-looking pool to the Western Coal Gate. It was mid-afternoon. Shadows were lengthening. A roseate light lay like a red film over the land to the west: the fields, copses and forests, haystacks, the occasional cottage. Bingo stood looking at the land he was leaving behind, a tear in his eye. Behind lay everything he knew. Before him lay only darkness and mystery.

Gandef was having a spot of trouble with the Coal Gate. Carved from one gigantic piece of anthracite, forty foot tall and forty foot wide, this mighty entrance was sealed by a Great and Terrible Spell cast by Yale of Yore. Gandef sat smoking for a while, muttering. 'There are two portions to the spell,' he explained. 'First we need to see where the door is exactly. No good me firing Opening Spells at a blank piece of coal!'

'And how can we see where the door is?' asked Bingo quaveringly, looking in awe at the perfectly sheer, black face that faced him. As faces, I suppose, are wont to do.

'Oh no,' said Gandef. 'Whatever gave you that idea? First we need to find out where the door actually *is*. But the edges of it are only visible by moonlight. And tonight is a new moon, so no moonlight. And tomorrow I doubt if there'll be enough moonlight to show it up. And it looks like cloud. All in all,' he said, sucking his pipe between the sentences, 'we could be here a fortnight at least. Perhaps we should give up?'

Bingo expected the dwarfs to complain noisily at this wizardly suggestion, but in fact they were lying on the floor in a state of some dejection. Perhaps, he thought to himself, the loss of their comrades had affected their morale.

'Moonlight,' said Bingo, 'is only the light of the sun reflected *off* the moon, after all. Can't we shine reflected sunlight on the door? How would the door know the difference?

Gandef acted as though he hadn't heard the little soddit, as perhaps – indeed, as probably – he had not. But Mori was heartened by the idea. He roused himself from his despondency, and with Bingo's help they unwrapped one of Thorri's shields, leaning it against the rocks in such a way that sunlight bounced off the silvery inner surface and fell on the black cliff before them. At once the outline of a great door became visible, together with several lines of elegantly carved elvish.

'What do the silvery letters say, Gandef?' an awed Bingo whispered to the wizard.

'Wassit?' Gandef replied.

'The elvish writing on the door,' he said more loudly, pointing. 'What does it say?'

'What?'

'What does the *ELVISH* mean in *COMMON SPEECH*?' yelled Bingo, directly into the wizard's ear. 'There! There!'

'What?' said the wizard, following the line of Bingo's arm. 'Ah! Look at that! Some elvish characters! Will you look at that!'

'What,' three dwarfs hollered in unison, 'do they mean?'

'What's that? What do they mean?' said the wizard.

He examined the writing for long minutes. 'Squiggle, squiggle, squiggle,' he concluded. 'I don't know. That one there looks a little like a *p*,' he offered. '*Poqqop*? That mean anything to anybody?'

The dwarfs, standing in a line, did not look impressed. 'You mean you don't know?' asked Mori in disgust. Gandef could read the dwarfish expressions even if he didn't hear Mori's rebuke.

'And how should *I* know?' he asked, sulky. 'I'm not an elf, I'm a wizard. You should watch out. Have more respect for wizards. Miserable dwarfs.'

'Never mind interpreting the writing,' said Mori, his beard twitching with annoyance. 'Can you just open the door?'

'I just told you,' said the querulous wizard. 'I *can't* interpret the writing. But I'll tell you what: why don't I just open the door with a spell?'

The dwarfs nodded, an action – given the shortness of their necks, and indeed of their whole bodies – more evident in the waggling of their beards than in any other respect.

Gandef settled himself before the door and lit his pipe. 'You watch this,' he told nobody in particular. 'It's the most powerful opening spell I know.' He breathed out, breathed in deeply, and intoned in a booming voice: '*Quandog quandoggli*.'

Nothing happened.

'*Quandog quandoggli,*' Gandef repeated.

Nothing happened.

Gandef sucked his pipe for a while. 'Try a different opening spell,' Bingo offered. The wizard looked at him, nodded his sage head sagely, and cleared his throat.

'*Quandog quandoggli,*' he said.

'I'm not sure that spell is working terribly well,' Bingo suggested.

'*Quandog quandoggli, quandog quandoggli, quandog quandoggli,*' Gandef said, with tremendous rapidity.

'I don't think—'

'*QuanDOG,*' Gandef tried. '*QUANDoggli.*'

'I'm almost certain that neither of those words is the magic word,' Bingo said, in as loud a voice as he could manage. The sunlight was starting to fade. Once it had gone, and with a moonless night in the offing, they would have to camp there until the morning: and Bingo didn't like the look of the evil-looking pool. It looked evil. 'Perhaps—'

'*Qua-aa-andoggli,*' said Gandef, putting the word through a strange musical contortion, starting warbling and high and dropping to a baritone for the final syllable.

'Perhaps if you tried some other magic words—'

'QUANDOG!' shouted Gandef. 'QUANDOG-GLI! QUAN-AGH! ACH! A-KOOFKAH-KOOFKAH!'

It was the worst coughing fit to seize the wizard that Bingo had yet seen.

Gandef went, 'UH-KHOO! UH-KHOO! UH-KHOO! UH-KHOO!' He went, 'KLAK! KLAK! KLAK!' He drew enormous amounts of breath into his lungs prior to going 'HOOOGH! HU-HOOOGH!' and shaking his hat off as he swung his head back and forth. He went, 'WHO-WHO! WHO-WHO!' as if he were asking a question. He went, 'K'OAH K'OAH K'OAH K'OAH K'OAH K'OAH K'OAH.' He went, 'oooohh god' in a low and miserable voice and then immediately added, 'Hurgh! Hurgh! Hurgh! Hurgh! Hurgh!' with great emphasis.

When he had finally finished, he slumped slowly to the ground moaning, gasping 'I'll be all right in a minute,' and scrabbling ineffectually in one of the pockets of his poncho for his tobacco.

'Look!' said Bingo.

It was impossible to say which of the many noises inadvertently produced by the wizard had been the one to open the door, but there it stood, open as wide as you like. It seemed he had chanced upon the magic word in extremis without even realising it. The dwarfs cheered weakly. It seemed that at last their luck was changing.

They picked up the whimpering, ash-faced wizard and carried him inside. As they stepped over the threshold, the door started to groan, heaving shut behind them.

They lit torches, and explored the space within. It was a towering lobby, carved, it seemed, from the very living rock, with numerous stairways going up and down away from the space. 'Let us camp here,' said Mori. 'After a rest we can choose a path and make our way under the mountain.'

All were in agreement.

They lit a fire under the portable cauldron and stewed up some salt beef, with some salt potatoes and salt garlic for taste, and salt-preserved beer to wash the meal down. It was belly-filling, thirst-creating stuff. After about forty minutes, Gandef seemed to have recovered sufficiently from his coughing spasms, and helped himself to a hunk of beef ('I'll just have a hunk of this,' as he put it), a chunk of potato ('. . . just a chunk . . .'), and got a little drunk on the beer. For a while he amused himself by repeating 'hunk-chunk-drunk' sixteen or seventeen times. Then he grew sombre. 'Dark in here,' he observed, several times.

He lit his pipe, and smoked in silence for a while.

'It's an amazing place,' said Bingo to Mori, who was sitting next to him polishing his cleaver.

'Ay,' said the dwarf laconically.

'And this enormous hallway was carved from the massy living rock by dwarfs?'

'This,' said Mori, 'and caverns a hundred times as huge! A thousand yards tall, leagues and leagues long, supported on carefully fashioned pillars of intricate design and towering height, enormous staircases carved from pure marble, great groined spaces the length and breadth of the whole Minty Mountains! You are seeing with your own unworthy eyes the Great Dwarf Halls of Dwarfhall, the Mines of Black Maria, the great achievement of our race!'

'Blimey,' said Bingo.

They sat in silence for a while.

'And all this,' Bingo said, the question occurring to him as he asked it, 'carved out with – what? Hand axes?'

'Trowels,' said the dwarf. He seemed to be looking, studiedly, in another direction.

'Trowels? All of it? Gracious. And are there – if you'll excuse the question – many dwarfs in the world?'

'We don't,' said Mori, 'like to talk of our personal affairs.'

'But, let's say,' said Bingo, becoming interested, 'that there are – I don't know – ten thousand dwarfs in the world. How much stone can one dwarf clear in a year with a trowel?'

'These be the great mysteries of the dwarf miners,' mumbled Mori, still looking away.

'Let's say half a ton. That's five thousand tons a year,

~ 83 ~

five hundred thousand tons over a century assuming every dwarf in the world worked at the project without break. That would barely empty even this lobby.'

Mori mumbled something else, of which only 'maybe' and 'difficult to judge' were audible.

'To carve out halls running the whole length of the mountain range,' Bingo carried on. 'That must have been the work of hundreds of thousands – no, of *millions* of years. How long have dwarfs existed? To say nothing of the enormous number of trowels you must have gone through . . .'

'All right,' said Mori hotly, putting his face close to Bingo's. 'All right, don't go bleating and blurting, look you. Have you *tried* chopping into solid rock with a little bronze trowel? It's no easy matter. But don't give the game away, boyo. Some of the others still believe the legends.'

'Legends?'

'Yes, yes, yes. That dwarfs are great miners, so speaks the legend. There *were* mines once, or so we believe, yes, certainly, look you. But it's been a long time since any dwarf worked in one. They were all closed down long ago.'

'Oh,' said Bingo. 'What do dwarfs work at now?'

'In shops, mostly. Markets. Sometimes in the entertainment industry. Singing dwarfs have a certain appeal to certain bookers. Perhaps you've heard of Qyli the Singing Dwarf? No? Lovely singer. Big teeth. But our legends are important to us, do you see. Don't take them away.'

'Does this,' said Bingo, with renewed interest, 'have something to do with our quest? Does the real reason for—'

'Gold,' said Mori firmly and finally.

Bingo didn't think it worth pursuing that line.

'But I don't understand,' he said. 'If you didn't build these great under-mountain halls, who did?'

It was hard to say in the ruddy half-light of the dying fire, but it seemed to Bingo and Mori shrugged. 'Nature,' he said.

'Nature?'

'They're hollow. All the mountains. In fact, although you may not realise it, everything's hollow here, even the trees. The hills have got chambers and rooms inside them – nothing's solid all the way through.'

'What a bizarre notion,' said Bingo.

'I know, bach, but the world's stranger than most people realise.'[3]

'But how can it be? The mountains hollow?'

'According to one myth of creation,' said Mori, 'the world was blown up like a big soap bubble by the Great God at the beginning of things. The smoky breath of

---

[3] See? I told you so. Oh, but nobody listens to *me*, I know.

life puffed up the thin crust of the Primordial Flatness into the bumps and peaks and curves of the world we see today. 'Course, that's only a myth.'

Their conversation was interrupted by a distant thudding noise. Suddenly the party were gathered in the centre of the lobby clutching each other in fear and apprehension, all except Gandef who hadn't heard the thudding and was caught up in the scrum.

They prevailed upon the wizard with much shouting and repetition, to place upon himself a hearing spell. Grumbling and complaining Gandef did so. 'Ah,' he said, when the spell was successfully achieved. 'What's that noise?'

He stood with his head cocked, listening.

'Drums,' he said finally.

'But whose?'

'Gobblins, of course,' said the wizard. 'Who else?'

'Gobblins?' said the dwarfs, shrinking back.

'They're bad, then, are they?' asked Bingo. 'Gobblins?'

'Terrible,' said Gandef. 'Servants of the Dark Lord who must not be named . . .'

'You mean the Great and Evil Sharon,' said Tori.

'The Dark Lord must not be named!' snapped Gandef. 'Yes, Gobblins. Terrible, bad. Dear me, they must have taken up residence down here, the evil creatures. Perhaps I should have thought of that before

I brought us here. It slipped my mind. But actually, now you come to mention it, there's no doubt that these mountains are absolutely swarming with Gobblins. Dear me, yes.'

'What are they?' asked Bingo, who didn't like the sound of this at all.

'What? Gobblins?' said Gandef. 'Long ago the Evil Lord took races of harmless, virtuous turkeys and chickens from the fields and yards of Upper Middle Earth, tortured them hideously and transmuted them into a warped, monstrous and easily suggestible species to fill the ranks of the mighty armies of Darkness and to do the Evil One's bidding. You'll know one when you see one, my young soddit: you'll recognise the turkey provenance of their ghastly and monstrous appearance: the wattles of flesh at their neck, the small heads, the alarmed expression in the eyes, the tendency to scurry around in circles shrieking and so on.'

Gandef puffed at his pipe.

'Perhaps,' he concluded, 'it might be better if we retreated out through the door and climbed *over* the mountains, after all.'

No sooner had the dwarfs expressed their complete agreement with this proposition, than there was a mighty crack, a bang, and Gobblins swarmed into the hallway.

Enormous Gobblins! There were four to each dwarf,

and two even for Bingo.[4] They were over the group before anybody knew what was happening, and legs were shackled, arms pinioned, beards yanked and the great swarm was carrying the prisoners away, clucking and ducking their heads in triumph, in an instant.

Things looked black for the company; both in the sense of 'their prospects looked unpromising' and in the more literal sense that 'they couldn't see anything because of the dark' – since they were carried down unlit corridors, through unlit hallways, and on on. 'Take 'em to the Gobblin King!' the Gobblins sang. 'Take 'em to the hall of the Gobblin King!' Then they sang their terrible song.

> *I feel like ∂wa-arf tonight!*
> *Like ∂wa-arf tonight!*
>
> *I feel like ∂wa-arf tonight!*
> *Like ∂wa-arf tonight!*

---

[4] Obviously, when I say 'enormous' here I don't mean it in an absolute sense. Given that we've already established that Bingo the soddit is a fellow of diminutive size, it would be pretty stupid to suggest that a creature half his size is 'enormous' in any objective sense of the word. 'Minuscule' would be the better word, if I were framing this in objective terms. But I meant 'enormous' in comparison with other Gobblins. That, and the fact that 'tiny, miniature, hardly-there-at-all Gobblins swarmed into the hall . . .' lacked the necessary smack of the alarming. Or so it seemed to me.

Then they flapped their hideous arms up and down, and sang another of their songs in their own brutish language which went like this:

> *Ga-ARG ga-ARG*
> *Guggle-guggle-guggle*
> *Gugg-ARG guggle-guggle*
> *Guggle-guggle-guggle*
> *Guggle-guggle-guggle*

It went on and on.

'Gandef,' hissed Mori. 'Do something!'

'My head hurts,' called the wizard. 'The noise of that explosion in the lobby was amplified by the hearing spell. It's most annoying. My ears are full of this infernal ringing noise. Hang on – hang on.'

There was a dazzling, silent flash of blue-white light. For an instant Bingo could see everything in the broad corridor down which they were being carried: the curving upward arches of the tunnel walls; the hideous seething mass of Gobblins carrying their helpless cargo. Then his face smacked against the rock floor, and he rolled to the wall. Gandef's spell seemed to have snapped the iron chain that held his hands, and he tried dizzily to pick himself up. More than a little dazed by his fall, he saw Gandef standing tall in the middle of the Gobblins, wielding a great shining sword, slicing it back and forth. His face was grimmer and more determined than Bingo had ever seen it before. 'Take that, you Gobblins!' he was yelling, and his sword went snicker-snack and snacker-snick. 'Cleaver and Carver!' the Gobblins cried in terror, running hither and thither in their confusion. 'Chopper and Decapitator!' And, truly, Gandef's sword was making short work of the long Gobblin necks, cutting off head after head. The newly beheaded Gobblins ran hither and thither with, if anything, more eagerness than the ones with heads. Sili the dwarf, freed from his bonds by Gandef's spell, rose to his feet amongst a crowd of swarming, panicking Gobblins. The glowing sword, scything backwards and forwards, swept towards the hapless dwarf and in a moment his head, still in its tight-fitting helmet, was bouncing and rolling down the corridor. 'Sorry!' Gandef sang, as he continued chopping.

Then, from behind, came a terrible war cry, and by the light of Gandef's shining sword Bingo could see an enormous mass of Gobblins filling the corridor, all with hatchets and beak-shaped axe heads, and all charging towards them.

He got to his feet and ran as fast as his soddit legs could carry him. For long minutes he ran, his chest pumping, until a stray rock tripped him, and he fell down a side-staircase towards a smack on the head and oblivion.

When he came round it was dark. Very dark. Very dark indeed. Imagine the darkest you can image. No, really, go on. Have you got a good mental picture of darkness in your head now? Right – this was *darker* than that. That's how dark it was. Bingo crawled around in the dark, and knocked his head against the wall. He tried to stand up but he found it hard, in the dark, to distinguish up from down and he ended up falling over. After this he crawled on.

Then something happened. Something of the utmost significance, something that was to change his life for ever – and the lives of everybody in Upper Middle Earth, everything. Nothing was ever the same again afterwards. The most significant thing to happen in Bingo's life, although *he* didn't realise it at the time. But just because he didn't recognise the significance of the moment, and just because it isn't, actually, now I come to think of it, actually *alluded* to at any place in this book – just because of that, I wouldn't want you to miss this moment. It's terribly *terribly* important. Do you see? I can't tell you why, exactly, not at this stage. Indeed, it may not become apparent even by the end of the book. But take my word for it.

What happened, terribly important as it was, was

this: Bingo stumbled upon a Thing.[5] It was a small Thing®, and was lying in the corridor out of the way. It did not seem to Bingo to be a terribly important Thing® either (although, as I have said, he was wrong in this, and it was indeed terribly important). But he put it in his pocket, and continued crawling.[6]

Almost immediately he heard a voice. The voice said: 'Hello.'

Bingo had crawled, he saw, into a cave. He stood up. The cave was very, very dimly lit – by a sort of phosphorescent lichen that grew on the roof of the cave, although Bingo didn't know that. In the cave was a pond, and in the middle of the pond was an island, and on the island lived a creature called Sollum. Now, Sollum was a mournful and solitary soul. He lacked the gregarious playfulness that endears people to their fellow creatures. He lacked the ability to pretend interest in stupid or repetitive things. His interests were philosophy, metaphysics, ontology and psychology (especially the schizophrenic condition). Month by month he had been alienated from his original community, until, ultimately, he was driven down deep into the mountain's depths, to live in a solitary hut by a

---

[5] The Thing® Bingo found is a Registered Trade Mark and may not be used, invoked or quoted without permission of the Estate.
[6] That's it. There's nothing else to say about it at the moment. But it is, believe me, a really really imortant development.

chilly pond eating raw fish and occasionally killing passers-by – an existence too common to our academics and university lecturers. Hearing somebody coming down his corridor, Sollum had splashed through the water to meet the newcomer.

'Hello,' said Bingo.

Sollum sighed. The sigh started as a hiss, and ended with a reflex closure of the soft palate that closed the noise off with a labially approximately sound. From this noise, if you can believe it, had he derived his name: for his sighs were the most notable thing about him.[7]

Bingo looked around. He could just make out the smooth surface of the pool and the nearer walls of rock that surrounded it. He peered at Sollum, and noted the knobulous bald head, the large thoughtful eyes, the doleful cast of the mouth.

'How do you do,' Bingo said, remembering his manners. 'I seem to have lost my way.'

---

[7] His original name was Seagul, although it was a name he had not heard for many years. Now, if he ever thought of it, it only brought to his mournful mind the memory of mockery and jibes, of his neighbours and relations pouring scorn upon his dedication to philosophy with cries of 'Jonathin Leadenstone Seagul! We shall chase you from our community with mockery and jibes, for we are happy to be blind to your wisdom and relish our own idiocy, oh yes.' Such speeches had left Sollum no choice but to flee far, far underground.

'Indeed,' said Sollum, imbuing the word with tragic overtones.

'I'm Bingo Grabbings,' said the soddit. 'I'm a soddit, you know.'

'Ah,' said Sollum, on a dying fall. He thought to himself that his own origins were not far removed from soddit life, and that he had cousins who had married soddits, and it all brought miserable and depressing memories into his head. It was an unfortunate turn-up. He had been pursuing a train of solipsistic philosophy for seven years, and had been uninterrupted save for the occasional gormless Gobblin getting lost and ending up roasted on Sollum's Sunday lunch table. Nothing is better suited to the prosecution of a truly solipsistic philosophical line of thought than absolute solitude. And now he had been interrupted.

'What's your name?' Bingo pressed.

'Sollum,' said Sollum.

'Splendid name. I say – can you help me?'

Sollum sighed. 'Help you?' he said eventually.

'Yes. I seem to have lost my way. Banged my head, too.'

'Your head,' repeated Sollum slowly. Then, as if he were reciting the lines with a certain distaste, he added, 'Tasty head, a choice feast, a tasty morsel it'd make me.' Then he sighed again.

Bingo, not really following this but feeling more than a little uneasy, said, 'Right,' in a nervous voice. 'Can you help me?'

'Well,' said Sollum unwillingly. 'Perhaps the question is, whether there is such in the cosmos as an action willed unconditionally, which is to say, freely, or whether all creatures are determined by the doctrine of Necessary Causes.'

'Quite,' said Bingo, after a pause.

'On the other hand,' said Sollum, 'if you were to claim rights of victory – if you were to defeat me in some contest or other, such that my compliance was compelled . . .' He trailed off.

Bingo stood and waited.

'Riddles?' offered Sollum.

'Yes,' said Bingo.

'Very well. I'll riddle me you, and you can riddle you me,' said Sollum, his immovable face looking simultaneously haughty and sorrowful, as if he were examining Bingo's pathetic little life from on high and was under-impressed by what he saw.

'Riddles,' said Bingo. 'All right. You ask first.'

'Very well,' said Sollum. He swallowed noisily, making a sound like a rubber ball bouncing on a springy mattress. 'I shall go first. This, we have agreed. Then you will go. The first to be unable to answer a riddle loses the contest.'

'All right,' said Bingo, sitting on the floor and crossing his legs.

So Sollum asked:

Given that the ontological necessity of existence must be defined as essential to Being itself, how can such grounding of the epistemological function be articulated without assuming an a priori and unwarranted existential premise?

It was silent in the cave for a long time. Somewhere, far out in the pool, a fish brushed against the underside of the water's surface, disturbing it for a moment before sinking back into the depths. It made a noise like this: *plop*.[8] Bingo took a deep breath into his lungs and then exhaled slowly.

'So you want an answer?' he said.

'Yes,' said Sollum.

'An answer to your riddle?'

---

[8] Indeed, the fish in quesiton was called Plop by his friends for this reason. His proper name was Smeagoldfish, but the other fish tended to call him Plop as it was easier to pronounce. On formal occasions he might be addressed as Smeagoldfish-Plop, but for most occasions it was just Plop. But I'm getting off the point. The fish isn't important to the onward movement of the story. Not at all, in fact. You won't encounter the fish again. Stop reading this note right now, and go back to the main body of the text. Do as I say! No argument – or you can go straight to bed, and I won't finish writing the book for you.

'Yes.'

'The riddle that you just asked me?'

'Yes.'

'Right. Well, I'd say that the answer to that one is,' said the young soddit, pulling at his left ear lobe with his right hand. 'Is,' he repeated, drawing the syllable out, 'I-i-i-i-i-is'. He sniffed, rubbed his eyes. Then he said, 'The answer to that one,' very slowly, lingering over each word. Then he said, 'I-i-i-i-i-is' again. Then he sat in silence for two minutes.

Eventually Sollum prompted him. 'Yes?'

'Yes what?'

'Your answer?'

'I thought I'd finished,' said Bingo.

'Oh,' said Sollum lugubriously. He pondered for a while. Then he said: 'I don't understand.'

Bingo, with only a momentary hesitation, lighted on the opportunity. 'Oh you don't *understand*?' he said, with a sarcastic inflection to his words. 'My answer too complex for you? I *am* sorry. I *do* apologise. It's a shame I didn't put it in simpler terms. Would you like me to try and phrase my answer in simpler terms for you?'

'No, no,' said Sollum hurriedly. 'I wasn't saying that. Your answer is, um, *is*. Is that right?'

'You're the one who says so,' retorted Bingo.

'No, no,' said Sollum again. 'I think I see. The present participle of the verb to be, is that what you mean?'

'Ah,' said Bingo knowingly. '*Is* it, though?'

'You're right, I suppose,' said Sollum in a small voice. 'Any act of questioning can only take place within a semantic framework that assumes one or other tense, one or other relationship to the contextual temporal configuration. Perhaps by foregrounding the is-ness of is, the continual process of existing that is necessarily embodied in the process of time itself, you do answer my riddle.'

'Well,' said Bingo, trying to colour his voice with suggestions of mysteriousness and veiled wisdom. 'If you say so, *I* shan't contradict. *I* shan't,' he added, as if he couldn't rule out the possibility that somebody else in the vicinity might.

A fish twanged at the surface of the still pond from beneath, and sank again. This was a different fish from the one before mentioned.

Bingo, who was inwardly congratulating himself for getting out of that tricky position, was startled by Sollum's moist and mournful hand on his knee.

'Your turn,' said the creature.

'You what who's-it, what?' returned Bingo.

'You can ask your riddle now,' Sollum explained with quiet and doleful patience, 'and if I can't answer it then you win.'

'I win,' Bingo repeated. 'Very well. My riddle.'

So Bingo asked his riddle:

When is a door not a door when it's ajar?

Sollum contemplated for a while, and then sighed softly. 'I wonder,' he said gravely, 'whether you have inadvertently included the solution to your riddle in the question?'

'Aha!' said Bingo. 'But do you *know* the answer?'

'I was only suggesting,' Sollum repeated, 'that perhaps you meant to ask only the first part of your question, and perhaps intended to retain the second portion *as* the answer?'

'Don't try and weasel out of it.'

'You could ask another one if you liked . . .'

'Answer!'

'But you've already —'

'Answer!' chanted Bingo. 'Answer! Answer! Answer!'

'When,' said Sollum, through tight teeth. 'It's. A. Jar.'

Bingo rubbed his chin. 'So you knew that one, did you?'

'It's my turn,' said Sollum. 'It's my riddle. And if you can't answer this one, then I win.'

'Sure,' said Bingo jauntily. He felt he had done rather well with the previous riddle, and his confidence was building.

Sollum asked:

What happens when an irresistible force meets an immovable object?

'Goes around it I'd say,' replied Bingo quickly. 'Like the wind and a fencepost. My turn! Now then, let me see, let me see. Riddle-riddle-riddle.'

'Wait a moment,' said Sollum. 'I'm not sure your answer addresses the point of the riddle . . .'

' 'Course it does.'

'I don't think so.'

'Does.'

'No,' said Sollum. 'It doesn't.'

'Does.' Contradiction was a game much more in the soddit's taste than this abstruse riddling business. Bingo was getting his contradiction to Sollum's denial more and more rapidly.

'Does not.'

'—Does!'

'No, Mr Soddit, it really—'

'—Does!'

'But if the force alters in some way, then it is surely a resistible force, and that's denied by the terms of the riddle—'

'Isn't,' said Bingo.

'It is,' said Sollum.

'Isn't,' said Bingo.

'It *is*,' said Sollum.

'Isn't,' said Bingo.

'*It is,*' said Sollum.

'My turn! My riddle now! Don't be sour-grapes. You have to answer my riddle or I'll win.'

Red lorry, yellow lorry, red lorry, yellow lorry, rellery yellery, red yellory?

'Now,' said Sollum, his serious manner starting to fray at the edges a little, 'that's not *actually* a riddle at all, is it? Be honest with me, little soddit. That's a *tongue-twister*, isn't it, and not, in fact, a riddle at all? I mean – isn't it?'

'Definitely not,' said Bingo, looking to one side. 'Where I come from that's quite a famous riddle. Down my way. That's definitely a riddle. You could ask any of my people and they'd all say, oh yes, riddle, that's a riddle. So, yes, now the question is, can you answer it?'

'Answer it? You haven't *phrased it* in the form of a question,' said Sollum, his voice starting to warp with hints of frustration and annoyance. 'Be honest, play fair, and admit that it's a tongue-twister.'

'It sounded like a question to me,' said Bingo piously.

'Naturally, since you inflected the line with a rising tone at the end to mimic a questioning delivery. But that's not actually phrasing a riddle in the form of a question. That's just putting a question mark at the end of it. You could put a question mark at the end of any sentence whatsoever, but that wouldn't necessarily make the sentence a question.'

Bingo whistled a tune he had just invented, which consisted of four randomly chosen musical notes. Then he said, 'Is that the answer you're giving me? Because I have to say you're *not even close* with that answer. Not even close.'

'No of *course*,' snapped Sollum, 'that's not my answer. That was me pointing out that the *so-called riddle* you *pretended* to ask me was no such thing.'

'So is *that* your answer?'

'No, no, no,' said Sollum, becoming quite agitated. By the faint blue light of the phosphorescent lichen, Bingo could just about see Sollum's dark froggish hands flapping in front of him. 'Why aren't you listening to me?'

'I'm going to have to press you for an answer,' said Bingo.

'But you haven't asked me a proper riddle!'

'Time's running out – you need to give me an answer now.'

'Don't be ridiculous!'

'Red lorry?' said Bingo, leaning forward. 'Yellow lorry? Your choice!'

'I insist—'

'Ga-ah,' said Bingo in a warning tone. 'Answer!'

'But—'

'An*s*wer! Come on, come on!'

'I just—'

'Time's running out, seconds ticking away.'

'Red lorry!' shrieked Sollum.

'Ha-hah!' crowed Bingo. 'Wrong! Wrong! The answer was *yellow lorry*. It's obvious when it's pointed out to you, isn't it? I win! Hurrah for me!'

'That doesn't make any kind of sense at all,' steam-whistled Sollum. His earlier serious and grave manner seemed to have been evaporated by his annoyance. 'You picked one at random.'

'Now don't be a bad loser. Nobody likes a bad loser.'

'If I'd have said "yellow lorry" you'd simply have told me that the answer was red lorry.'

'Oh really?' said Bingo in a reasonable tone. 'That wouldn't work at all, now, would it? Red lorry – that wouldn't fit.'

'*You*,' said Sollum, his voice dropping almost an octave and acquiring a gravelly undertone. But he didn't finish the sentence.[9]

'So,' said Bingo, hopping to his feet and hugging himself in the near darkness in glee at his victory. 'I win. Incidentally, what do I win?'

---

[9] My guess, for what it's worth, is that Sollum was either going to say, '*You* are right, you're the winner fair and square,' or else '*You* want to share a fish and gluten fondue?' But I could be wrong.

Sollum sulked for a minute. 'You get to eat me,' he said shortly.

'To eat you?' repeated Bingo.

'That's what we were playing for. If I'd have won, I'd have certainly eaten you. Since you won you have to eat me. To tell you the truth,' the creature added, his tone becoming self-pitying, 'I'm almost glad. I'm more than sick of living down here in the dark. Go on, eat me. Start with my legs.'

'I don't want to eat you,' said Bingo, alarmed at the thought.

'Oh,' said Sollum. 'You must. It is a function of inevitability, the doctrine of necessity. And besides, you won.'

'Can't I just get you to show me the way out of here?'

'Ooh,' said the creature. 'No, that wouldn't be right.'

'We could have another riddling contest,' suggested Bingo. 'If I win, then you have to show me the way out of here. And if *you* win, than *I* have to show you the way out of here.'

'But I don't want to be shown the way out of here,' said Sollum.

'And I don't want to have to eat you,' snapped Bingo. 'Come along now. Be fair. I did win the riddling contest, after all.'

'Are you,' asked Sollum morosely, 'surrendering your

rights to me qua meal, and freely giving up the opportunity to eat me?'

'Yep,' said Bingo.

Sollum sighed. It was a deeply sorrowful noise. Had Sollum's pool been a pool of tears he had himself cried at the inherent sorrow of things, his sigh could not have been more sorrowful.

'You wound my honour, sir,' he said. 'And my honour is the only value I have remaining in my life. My life must end, sir, or I must dedicate myself – carefully, cunningly, inexorably – to wreaking my revenge upon *you*. In fact, apart from my honour, I have only one Thing® in the world of any value. It is a Thing® of great antiquity, a Thing® of great value and many uses. With it I find the only consolation my miserable life affords me.'

'Now there's a turn up for the books,' said Bingo. 'Wouldn't you know it, but I found a Thing® in the tunnel as I was coming down here. It's in my pocket now.'

There was silence. In the dim blue light Sollum opened his mouth, a downward-crescent scowl. His teeth, Bingo noticed, were sharpened to points, like golf tees.

'Really?' he said, his voice a little strained.

'I daresay it's the one you were just talking about,' Bingo continued. 'Finders keepers of course, but isn't that a wonderful coincidence? First I win the riddling business fair and square, then it turns out I've got your Thing®! Funny old world.'

'Perhaps you'd care to return it to me?' asked Sollum. His whole manner bespoke a pessimistic anticipation of an answer in the negative. Bingo, accordingly, provided one.

'No,' he said. 'I say, could you show me the way to—'

His soddit instincts saved him. Sollum, incapable of simply abandoning himself to his rage, was advancing upon Bingo with a steady, determined, serious gait, fully intending to tear out his throat and feed on his quivering corpse in a steadily determined and serious manner. He made a clawing sweep at Bingo's head, and only a sort of half-duck, half trip saved the soddit's life. After that Bingo was running, as fast as his little soddit feet could bear him, upwards this time, away from the silent pool and the enraged philosopher.

'Give me back my Thing®!' howled Sollum, a little way behind.

'Not likely,' Bingo whispered under his breath. His hand went to his pocket and there his fingers apprehended the Thing®. Its myriad magical properties, amongst which were included a form of compass-orientation device, a means of seeing in the darkness, and a means of adding speed to running heels, propelled Bingo at tremendous speed along the corridors underneath the mountain. He ran up, along ledges, mounted spiral stone stairways, ran through cavernous hallways, and at last – panting severely – emerged blinking at a precipice high in the sunshine.

He had reached the easternmost extent of the mountains. To his right a mighty and ice-cold river – the Great Floss – tumbled and gushed out of this cavemouth in the eastern flank of the Minty Mountains. The sunlight glassed his eyes momentarily, but, blinking, he could see that he was almost free. Only a forty-foot drop into the bubbling icy whirlpool that the Floss made as it tumbled out of the mountain was between himself and escape.

'Good grief,' somebody below yelled. The voice was only barely audible above the grinding chomping clatter of the waterfall.

Bingo squinted. Below him, a long way below, a group of eight dwarfs and a stooping old wizard stood next to the water's edge. One of the dwarfs, Bingo couldn't see which from this distance, was pointing up at him.

'It's Bingo,' he heard. 'He's not dead after all!'

Behind him, Bingo heard a hiss. He glanced back, and saw Sollum slinking up the ledge towards him, keeping his left hand on the rockwall at his side, and making menacing shaking and swiping gestures with the right. 'First,' the philosopher said in a bitter tone, 'you refused to eat me. Then you stole my Thing®. A painful death is too good for you. On the other hand, since it is the most I can inflict, it'll have to do.'

Several of the dwarfs below were now waving and shouting. Bingo looked at the rapidly approaching figure of Sollum. He looked at the mighty flowing torrent to his right, as solid-looking as stone though it foamed and flexed in its fall. He looked at the drop beneath him. There was nothing for it. He clasped the Thing® in his pocket, hoping devoutly that one of its magical properties was to enable a person to fly, or at least float, and he jumped.

For a moment it seemed as if his prayers had been answered. The world seemed to freeze, and he had a wonderfully clear view of foothills leading down to open pasture and the fertile fields surrounding the Great River M. But then, with a stabbing sense of panic, he realised in the pit of his stomach that he was falling. The view slid upwards, and with a sensation of sharp pain tangible on every single inch of the outside of his body he was immersed in the churning outflow of the Floss.

His world was now white, bubbling, rotating, and utterly disorienting. There was no breath in his lungs. Had a firm dwarfish hand not grabbed his ankle as it snorkelled its way momentarily above the surface and hauled Bingo out he would certainly have drowned.

But there he was, gasping and shivering on the grass under the clear blue sky of morning. Away in the sky, seemingly very far, he heard a wavery voice cry out in its frustration and malice: 'Grabbings! You have incurred the wrath of a philosopher! And a philosopher, once he hates somebody, hates for ever! *For ever!*'

Biorn the Bare Man

Chapter Five
QUEER LODGE

ᏳᏙᏙᎧ

'I know this land well,' declared Gandef. 'Two days' march down the side of the Floss and we come to the famous Mill. There we may replenish our supplies – needful, since *some* of us,' – he glowered round at the dwarfs – 'left our baggage behind when Gobblins attacked.'

'And *some* of us,' Mori retorted, 'were too prissy to be carrying any baggage in the first place, you idle great wizard.'

'Well said, Master Dwarf!' Gandef replied, laughing and clapping him on his back. 'Well said! I like a fellow who's big enough to admit his own failings! And I like a chap with the sense not to cheek a wizard – *very* important that, sharp's the word. But we needn't worry. When we come to the famous Mill we'll replenish.' He clearly like the sound of this word (Bingo wondered how he could hear his own speech when he was so deaf to other people's), and repeated it over and again as they walked. 'Replenish. Replenish. Replenish. Replenish.'

'I may have left the bags behind,' Mori muttered, 'but 'twas not I who chopped off Sili's head by mistake.' He scowled.

'Replenish. Replenish. Replenish. Replenish,' said Gandef, in time to his strides.

And in this fashion the company marched for the rest of the day, the dwarfs complaining of their grumbling bellies and sore feet, the soddit going 'ouch' and 'ow-ow-*wah*' intermittently.

They spent a chilly night camped under a riverside tree; but it was not their fate to get an uninterrupted night of sleep. They had just settled down to rest, the dwarfs wrapping their beards duvet-like about their bodies and Bingo shivering in his corduroy, when wolves sprang upon them. It was as if the darkness took shaggy shape: the night sky transformed into muscle and pelt, the stars jagging into the form of white teeth, the low red moon being swallowed by a lolloping tongue.

'Wolves!' shrieked one of the dwarfs.

Bingo smelt the hot, sharp stink of wolf, and heard a growl by his ear. He leapt awake.

In two minutes everybody had scrambled up the tree, Bingo levering himself up in the midst of a knot of beards and stocky limbs. By the dim starlight Bingo clutched his branch as tightly as a gonk clutches the end of his pencil.[1] 'Gandef!' he called down. 'Gandef!'

But the wizard was still asleep on the ground, as the wolves milled around him. 'Gandef!' called Mori. 'Oh savannah! This is terrible. Somebody wake him up!'

The wolves did not pounce on the snoring wizard immediately, suspicious perhaps of his lack of move-ment. 'Gandef!' the dwarfs called. 'Wake up!'

It was useless.

The lead wolf, grey and lean, moved his muzzle slowly towards the wizard's face. His jaws clicked apart. His white fangs glinted in the starlight. 'Gandef! Gandef!' shrieked the crowd of dwarfs in the tree above. 'Wolf!' they cried.

The wolf angled his head through ninety degrees, all the better to be able to vice the wizard's neck between the two rows of his terrible teeth. Bingo leaned as far

---

[1] A gonk, as of course you know, is a small marsupial from the land of Gonkor, far to the south. They are intelligent creatures though small – the smallest of all the peoples of Upper Middle Earth, which is saying something – and they admire learning above all things. But their own books, written with their own tiny pencils on *teeny-tiny* pieces of paper (ahhh!) are too small for other scholars to read. More adventurous gonks have tried writing with man-sized pencils, a process that resembles, for them, nothing so much as tossing the caber, and although they have written little more than fragmented wavy lines by this method they persevere. Plucky little fellers. Ahhh-hhh! Swee-eeet.

down from his branch as he dared. 'Wizard! Beware! Be wakeful! Be watching out for your throat!'

And then the soddit saw something startling. A wisp of smoke crept up from Gandef's mouth, though his pipe was cold and in the pocket of his poncho. Further puffs followed. Tentacles of smoke drifted upwards. The wizard yawned in his sleep. And then, quick as a lightning flash, fire jabbed out of his open mouth and caught on the dry fur of the wolf.

The beast reared back, yelping, but the flames were already wriggling on the top of its head and spreading down across its neck. As the wolf writhed, butting into its fellows, it spread the fire. In an instant the whole pack was whinnying like horses and dancing a macabre dance as their fur caught aflame. Gandef was on his feet, shouting, 'What? What? What?' at the top of his voice, waving his arms and staring wild-eyed about him – the better, Bingo assumed, to nurture the panic in the wolf pack. And if this was indeed the wizard's plan, it was working. The wolves howled, scattering over the hilltops. Some raced as flaming torches. Some, unlit, skeetered away from their fellows' whimpering, and stretched their long legs in flight. In moments the landscape was empty of wolves.

The stars twinkled, as if in silent silvery applause.

'Gandef!' the soddit called down in glee. 'A brilliant spell! That put paid to them!'

With remarkable rapidity, Gandef scaled the trunk and positioned himself on a branch next to Bingo.

'What?' he asked. 'What?' Bingo had never seen the wizard's eyes quite so wide.

'You lured the beast on!' Bingo enthused. 'You enticed it to come close, and then you put out a fire spell and burnt it up!'

'Where the *bloody hell*,' asked Gandef, 'did those *wolves* come from?'

'You put them to flight, Gandef!' said Bingo.

'They're dangerous, are wolves,' said the wizard, blinking and looking about him. 'Who was on watch duty? Why weren't we warned?'[2]

The dwarfs were reaching down from branches higher up to clap him on the shoulder, laughing at the plight of the wolves. 'They eat people, do wolves,' Gandef said.

It was at this juncture that somebody noticed Wombl was missing. They called his name a few times, in a desultory fashion, and then explored the ground under the tree, but it was clear enough what had happened to him.

---

[2] Advertently or inadvertently, Gandef is here quoting from a famous Upper Middle English poem, the *Hex of Fish*:

Wild weather woke us worryingly   Why weren't we warned?
Hurricane hurled from the heavens   Old oaks uprooted sevenfold
Whose fault but the weathermen?   Typical TV types.

They spent the rest of the night in the tree.

The following day Gandef led the company along the banks of the river. 'Don't be downhearted,' he announced. 'Soon we'll arrive at the famous Mill, and then we'll feast and replenish.'

They reached the Mill by noon, but it was nought but a fire-blackened ruin, timbers poking from the ground like shards of coal, the land all about laid waste. The trees had burnt to the ground, leaving only charcoaled twigs and tar-black stumps. Gandef stood, puffing on his pipe, and surveyed the desolation. 'Gobblins,' he said at length.

'I'm hungry,' said Bingo.

'This is a sorry pass,' said Gandef.

'I'm hungry,' said Bingo.

'Wizard?' said Mori. 'What shall we do? Is there none other who can give us shelter in this dangerous, open land? What if the wolves should return? What if a huge army of Gobblins, in their rage, should flock out of the Minty Mountains to track us? What if we should die of exhaustion and hunger and our bones be picked clean by eagles?'

'Your optimism does you credit, Master Dwarf,' said Gandef. 'But no matter what you say, I'm afraid this *is* a sorry pass we find ourselves in. There is no help for it, we must go visit Biorn.'

'Biorn?' the dwarfs echoed.

'I'm hungry,' said Bingo.

'Biorn,' said Gandef, shaking his head.

'Do you mean Biorn the Bear-man, who is a man by day and a bear by night?' asked Failin, a quaver in his voice.

'No,' replied Gandef crisply. 'I didn't catch a word of that.'

'What's it?' said Bingo. 'Bear-man?'

'Biorn,' said Mori, picking a burnt twiglet from the ground and examining it. 'The legends that surround him are dire. Bestial, is he.'

'There's nothing for it,' said Gandef. 'He's a moody man, so we'll have to be on best behaviour. But his house is very neat and tidy. Don't do anything to enrage him, though, or he'll like as not rip your arms and legs from your torso and then jam the red soggy ends of the arms into the sockets where the legs should go, and vice versa with the legs in the arm sockets, afterwards making you dance upside down on your leggy-arms for his amusement.'

Nobody knew what to say to this. Gloom settled on the company.

They carried on alongside the river, Gandef regaling the company with several anecdotes of Biorn's reputation as bear-man, all of which involved the words 'wrenching', 'ripping' and 'agonising', and two of which ended with the same phrase: 'to join the heap of still-quivering flesh'. He seemed to find these stories rather heartening, and laughed several times, or to put it more precisely produced on several occasions a sort of hybrid laugh-cough. But the dwarfs became more and more sombre as he went on.

Soon enough they cut away from the river and made their way through fields of honey-smelling clover tall as a dwarf's chest. 'Come!' called Gandef, marching through the meadows up a gently sloping hill and leaving behind him a wake in the grass like a boat in the water. The sun was hot above them. 'I'll need to cast a hearing spell on myself in Biorn's house,' Gandef announced to the party. 'So, please, no sudden noises.' He summoned his magic spell, and it appeared in his hand in the general area of his right ear.

Finally, as they crossed the brow of a broad hill, they came across a great log-built hall standing in the midst of the open land. As they came closer, through a perfectly planed wooden gateway into a neatly tended market garden, Bingo could see how precisely and elegantly the timbers of the house had been put together.

There, in a yard before the house, stood a towering, broad-muscled blond man. He was holding a chicken by its legs and eyeing it. 'Teasing me!' he chided the bird. 'There's that look in your eye. But I can't take a chance on a chick like you.' He shook his head and put the bird back in the pen. 'It's something I couldn't do,' he added, to nobody in particular. His voice though carefully enunciated, had a strange flattened and pursed accent to it, a manner of speech the like of which Bingo had not before heard.

'See those hands!' whispered Gandef, with the booming-echoey whisper in which the wizard specialised. 'How huge and muscled! He could tear a fat book of spells in half with those hands! He'd make short work of you lot, that's for sure.'

The owner of the hands looked up at his visitors.

'Biorn,' called Gandef, with a forced heartiness. 'Hello!'

The big man stared impassively at the approaching company. 'Wizard!' he boomed. 'And Gobblins? No – no – dwarfs. Dwarfs are better than Gobblins. You are all welcome.'

'Thank you kindly, Master Biorn,' said Mori, bowing low. 'And may I compliment you on the extraordinary and beautiful smoothness of your chin?'

'My chin,' said Biorn. The expression on his chiselled features did not change at all as he spoke, but he seemed to Bingo more courteous than Gandef's description had suggested. 'Yes, yes, I have a smooth chin. My brother has a blond beard, and a great musical talent on the fjord-horn and the stringed linchirping. But my chin is smooth.'

'Biorn!' said Gandef. 'It is many moons since last we met. You may indeed have forgotten, it is so long ago. Hmm. But now I visit you again, with a company of dwarfs and a soddit, in the middle of a great journey to the east. We have suffered in our travels, and many of our fellows have – by their own idiot negligence it is true, but nevertheless – got themselves killed. We were hoping for some of you fabled hospitality.'

'For sure,' Biorn replied. 'Come inside.'

They stepped through the wide doorway into a huge timber hall, with planed and polished wood beams, square-cut columns of darker wood, and everywhere a pleasant piney, honey-sweet smell. Many items of attractive wooden furniture were neatly arranged about the place. The dwarfs lined up with Bingo at one end, nodding politely and pointing out the more attractive furnishings to one another. Gandef sat himself in one of Biorn's chairs. He seemed, to Bingo, a very nervous wizard.

'And do you like my house?' asked Biorn, with his odd, up-and-down reverse-camber intonation.

'Very nice,' said the dwarfs, more or less in unison.

'Nice,' agreed Bingo, 'is precisely the word.' It did not seem to him to be the house of an arm-ripping, leg-pulling-off maniac. But then again, the man's torso was unfeasibly crammed with muscle, and his neck was thicker than his head.

'This chair,' said Biorn, grasping a chair with his enormous, tanned, blond-downy hand. 'It is tinted clear lacquered solid beech with Wharg skin green-woven seat.' He held it so that everybody could see. 'I have many chairs.'

'So you do,' said Mori.

There was a pause.

The blank expression on Biorn's face did not change. 'I call my chairs my four-legged friends,' he said. Then, after a two-second pause, he laughed a series of precise laughs, *Hü hü hü hü*.

Everybody joined in, their eyelids more widely separated than was usually the case when they laughed. 'Ha! Aha! Yes, very good. Ha-ha. Excellent.'

Biorn put the chair down.

'And over here,' he added, stepping to one corner of the interior space, 'is what I call Biorn Central. I mean by, of course, that, the kitchen. It all happens here: meals, playtime, a bit of wolf-skinning work brought home. Family life revolves around here, and so I have designed it practical and also with durability, but with adult taste into the bargain.' His blond eyebrows, like strips of yellow felt, sagged a fraction. 'Although, as I have no family, it is only I who occupy the Biorn Central.'

'No family?' asked Bingo.

'No. I am Biorn, the bear-man. I am man in day, and bear in night. I have yet to find woman who will *bear* with me.' He waited two seconds, and then laughed at his own joke: *Hü hü hü hü.*

'Excellent,' everybody said, squeezing grins out of their faces with all the vigour they could manage. 'Aha! *Awfully* good. Ha-ha. Ah.'

'I use the word "bear",' Biorn said doggedly, 'in the two-way sense of large shaggy-pelted wood-dwelling animal, and also endure. This is punning. Sometimes a woman comes, sits and eats with me at my Lokka dining table, which is solid oiled beech, with one extension leaf stored underneath the table surface. Maybe we eat, she and I, meat, bread, or drink a honey beer. But then the sun will be sinking, and I will be turning into a great roaring bear, and she will not usually be staying longer than it requires to exit through the main door – Markör antique-style sap-stained solid spruce, handles included.'

Biorn's face seemed blandly untouched by the poignancy of his own tale.

'Perhaps,' said Bingo in a slightly squeaky voice, 'you might find a bear-woman . . . ?'

'Bear-woman, for sure,' said Biorn, nodding. 'Of course, this is my dream. But I need not only bear-woman, but – since I cannot join my life with hirsute female – a bear-woman who will be contented to depilate. She may use the bees' wax, or she may use my specially sharpened dining knife, with wooden handle and flower pattern twenty-seven – I do not mind.' He looked from face to face. 'I have many bees here,' he added. 'I am the Wolf of Bees.'

'Right,' said Bingo, dwelling on the *i*.

'It is woman that I am waiting for, for sure,' said Biorn. 'Sometimes I feel I would be doing all right, if it wasn't for the nights.'

'Nights,' agreed Mori, 'can be a bugger.' He laughed nervously.

Biorn stepped over to the far wall. 'This shelf,' he said, 'in bi-ply laminate with silver brackets, I was putting it up yesterday. I was doing this putting-up the day before you came.'

'It's,' said Bingo, 'very good. Very, uh, shelvy.' His hunger got the better of his fear. 'You got any, you know, food?'

'Ya, for sure,' said Biorn. He stepped over to a free-standing larder unit, and gestured towards it with his open palm.

Biorn brought out some honey, or as he put it, 'honey, honey'. He brought out honied loaves. He served a dish of tripe, and the dwarfs tucked in with an appetite that seemed to wane within seconds. 'Biorn,' asked Mori.

'Er – don't misunderstand me, but – er, this is *super* tripe, er – but does it have *honey* in it?'

'For sure,' said Biorn.

'Gracious,' said Mori in a low tone.

At first Bingo was so grateful to have something to eat that he was oblivious to the physical proximity of Biorn, his enormous flesh-shredding muscles, his tediously monotonous voice. But as sunset darkened the skies outside, and Biorn lit a log in his Arås stone-block fireplace, Bingo started to feel the dreary weight of the bear-man's presence press down upon him again.

'I have known your wizard,' Biorn was saying, pronouncing the word 'wheezer', which Bingo thought rather appropriate, 'for many years.' He put a musical kink into 'years', such that the '*y*' started on a low E, the *ears* slipped up to an A#.

'Have you really?' replied Mori. 'How interesting.' The dwarf, although he wore an unnaturally wide grin on his face, looked rather uncomfortable on his chair, leaning forward stiffly and pressing his legs together tightly like a man desperate to go to the toilet for several simultaneous and pressing reasons. 'How interesting.'

'Ah yes, he is friend of animal, he is famous Raddledghastly the Ragged, for sure, and all animals – such as I am myself an animal, as I have been saying – know him as friendly.'

Gandef, smiling manically, leant towards Mori. 'He

thinks I'm Raddledghastly,' he hissed through set teeth. 'Play along with it! Don't let him know the truth! We mustn't upset him, or he could flip into his bear state. That would be a disaster.'

He stopped, and turned his head to see Biorn staring at him.

'You are whispering,' observed Biorn placidly.

Everybody was silent.

'I,' said Gandef, looking around him, sweat appearing on his forehead like diamond studs, 'was,' he concluded lamely.

'Please to share,' said Biorn, sing-song.

'I was – ah, telling Mori how, ah, lovely your roof beams are.'

Biorn looked steadily at Gandef. He tipped his massy blond head backwards through ninety degrees and looked up at the ceiling. Then he levelled his gaze and looked at Gandef again for one long minute. Eventually he said: 'For sure.'

'I wonder if it would be all right,' asked Gofur, 'if I used your privy?'

'Bathroom, ah, yes, for sure,' said Biorn. 'Outside in the yard, you will be finding a shed. You will be finding the sophisticated appeal of free-standing design inside, the privy clad in the pale beauty of smooth birch veneer, teamed with sleek cherrywood handles and legs to achieve a stylish simplicity.'

Gofur dipped his head and positively rushed out, almost tripping over his beard.

'As I was saying,' Biorn said. 'Animals are good. My chickens are most special chickens. They came flapping from far away. Now I'm under their spell.'

'Really?' said Gandef. 'Fascinating.'

'I speak frivolously, but they are charming birds. Sometimes – and I am being fanciful, for sure, but – I dream I'm a chicken. I dream I can squalk' (he pronounced every single letter of this strange word) 'and flap, spread my wings, and go to anywhere that I please. But, you are welcome also, I am pleased to have visitors.'

He pondered this last word for a while, as if it reminded him of something.

'Still,' said Gandef, suddenly sprightly, 'we wouldn't want to keep you up past your bedtime. Don't you, you know, turn into a bear soon?'

'Tonight,' said Biorn, 'I shall remain in my man shape, to be hospitable to my guests. But be telling me, please, where your journey takes you?'

The dwarfs breathed a silent but visible sigh of collective relief.

'Ah,' said Mori, in a jollier tone of voice. 'Well, we're off to the Only Mountain. Do you know it?'

'For sure,' said Biorn. 'Strebor, the Only Mountain. For sure. And for why are you going there?'

'Gold,' said Mori, with a quick glance at Gandef.

'Gold!' repeated Gandef, in a loud voice, fixing Bingo with a significant stare.

'Ah,' said Biorn. 'Your quest, then, is for money?'

'Money,' agreed Gandef.

'Money,' echoed the dwarfs.

'Must be,' muttered Bingo. 'Why else would you keep saying so?'

The fire cackled to itself.

'You will be fighting Smug the Magic Dragon for this gold?' Biorn queried. 'The winner will be taking it all?'

'That's,' said Mori, 'the idea.'

'Dragons are great beasts. Great means big, you know.' He stared at the fire for a long time. An unnatural stillness settled in the great hall. 'Greater,' Biorn added, after a long time, 'than bears. And more evil.'

He appeared to be brooding.

'Well, perhaps it's time we all turned in,' said Gandef hurriedly. 'Sleepy sleep time, I think. I say, Biorn, it's awfully courteous of you not to shift into your bear shape when we're under your roof. I think I can speak for all of us when I say that we consider that a sign of a *truly* hospitable, um, hospital. Um hostel. A truly hospitable place of hospitality.'

His voice faded from strong to feeble as the sentence progressed, and had petered out completely by the end. All eyes were on Biorn.

'You are knowing already, perhaps,' said Biorn, his voice for the first time registering an emotional tone, 'of the tale of the Great Bear of the North?'

Nobody stirred.

'The Great Bear of the north . . . ?' prompted Gandef gingerly.

'A good friend of me. A mighty bear. The dragon Smug,' said Biorn, his eyes fierce, 'was fighting with him, and was burning and scorching him, and his pelt caught on the fire. He was burnt. His glorious blue house was burnt.'

'Dear me,' said Gandef.

'Shocking,' said the dwarfs.

'Shockling?' said Biorn vehemently. 'Shockling? Indeed it *is* shockling, dwarfs!'

'Shock-*ing*,' corrected Mori, but in so quiet a voice that it is likely Biorn did not hear it.

'It is *worse* than shockling,' said Biorn, standing up. 'It is tragedy. It is crime against all bearkind. It is being typical of dragons, for sure, that they use this fire. It should ought not to be. It should ought not. Dragons!' His eyes had taken on an alarming intensity, like blue ink being stirred in a pair of white ceramic pots. His hands were jerking up and down. 'Dragons? Do I not like dragons? No I do not. Dragons? I have strong feelings of dislike for dragons.'

'Of course you do,' said Gandef, trying to conciliate. 'Of course you do. Only natural.'

'To be using the *fire*?' Biorn thundered. 'On the furry and the dry? To burn the majestic Blue House of the North? To turn the soothing simplicity of modern design and blue paint mixed from natural fibres and spring water to *char*? To *dust*? To,' he added, with especial if mysterious emphasis, '*bur*?' He strode up and down, shaking his head with mighty, muscles shakes. 'No, no, it is not right. To use no fire on bears, this is necessary, for fire is against the protocols of the ursine. For Smug to do this? The dragon must be punished. Punished! You must kill Smug! Kill Smug! Kill! Kill!'

'Absolutely,' said Gandef, trying to calm the giant man. 'We absolutely intend to. Let's talk about something else, why don't we? Shall we have some more honey beer? A few more cutlets of your excellent honey-roast liver? Or one more pot of your delightfully honeyed caviar? Come, Biorn old friend, don't get yourself – ah – overstimulated. It's funny,' the wizard went on, reaching into the pocket of his poncho for his smoking paraphernalia, 'you should talk of burning dry animals in that way, actually, because – you'll laugh at this,' he said, illustrating the procedure by laughing a little himself, 'this'll amuse you. On our way here we encountered some wolves. Wolves who ate one of our fellows, in fact, nasty beasts, devoured Failin —'

'Wombl,' corrected Failin.

'Just so, and they were about to eat *me*. We were, you see, in a sticky spot, but this'll amuse you, especially in the, eh, ha ha ha!, especially in the light of what you've just been saying. This'll amuse you. They were about to *eat* me, you see, *eat* me, and I used a little fiery spell of my own, and – well, the *first* wolf caught fire, you see,' Gandef chuckled. 'The *first* wolf caught fire, and he leapt about, you see, and he bumped into the *second* wolf . . .'

Biorn, who had stopped pacing, was staring at the wizard with an unnerving fixity. Mori was making little circular motions with both hands, palms outward, in front of his chest, as if polishing a pane of glass immediately before him and shaking his head back and forth. But he did not seem to be able to catch Gandef's eye.

'. . . and – ha! ha! ha! – and the *second* wolf,' Gandef was saying, 'he went up like a torch, and he bumped into this *third* wolf – it was really something of a sight, they made such a noise.'

He glanced up at Biorn, and his voice faltered. 'Made,' he repeated, in a less hilarious tone, 'such a. Noise.'

There was silence for the space of a full minute.

Biorn, motionless throughout this time, began to moan. The moan grew to a groan, thence to a growl, and so to a howl. His huge hands gripped his own clothing and pulled it apart with a skeetering noise of ripping cloth.

'Oh,' said Gandef, in a subdued voice, sprinting nimbly over to one of the sofas and hiding behind it, 'dear.'

The rest of the company scurried to join him.

'Ågh! Årggggh!' bellowed Biorn. 'Ø! Ø! Ø! Ø! Ø! Uh! Uh! Uh! Årggggh!'

'That *may*,' said Gandef, looking from dwarf face to dwarf face, 'have been the wrong tack.'

'Maybe,' agreed Mori.

Biorn was marching up and down the whole length of his hall now, howling and growling and generally making the sorts of noises one might associate with an angry bear. He had torn off his woollen shirt, and was trying to rip the tougher canvas of his trousers. But tearing trousers is no easy task, even for the most muscular of individuals, and in the end he had to content himself with tearing off the button at the waist and half dragging, half hopping out of them. 'Ågh!' he bellowed. 'Ågh!'

'Oh, Þróinn,' swore Mori. 'Now what are we going to do? Trapped in this wooden house with a raging bear!'

'Stay calm,' advised Gandef.

'Perhaps if we rushed to the door?' suggested Bingo.

'Waaaah!' yelled Biorn, his head rearing up over the top of the settee. 'Waaah!'

Gandef raced the dwarfs and Bingo to the behind-side of the other large sofa. Biorn kept making noises of intermittent fury and rage stomping back and forth.

'I couldn't help noticing,' said Mori, 'that he's – ehm, smooth all over.'

'Smooth,' said Bingo.

'I wish he'd stop yelling,' said Gandef. 'It's amplified by my spell and it's making my head hurt.'

'No body hair. Shouldn't a bear have body hair?'

'No body hair?' queried Bingo.

'Some body hair,' Mori modified. 'But, from a dwarf's point of view, look you, *very* smooth. Still smoothly chinned, la, for instance. His chest smooth as sea-sand.'

Gandef was muttering to himself, 'Infernal *ringing* noise now—'

'Röär!' bellowed Biorn. Accompanying sounds to the effect of *smash! Smash! Crash!* were also audible.[3]

Mori popped his head above the top of the sofa, and ducked back down again. 'He's pulling things off one of his shelves,' he reported, 'and roaring.'

---

[3] These words have been translated from the original Middle Earth-ian into an English idiom. They were, in the original text, *furmash! Getsmash!*

'Yes, we can hear him roaring,' Bingo observed. 'Is he a bear now?'

'He's, frankly, just a nude man.'

'Not a bear?'

'Not.'

'Not even a little bit?'

'Well,' said Mori, 'no. All smooth. Look you.'

'That doesn't sound very bear-like,' said Bingo.

He took his courage into his two hands, and stood up. His head reached, just, over the top of the back of the sofa. He peered at Biorn. As Mori had said, the tall man was completely naked, naked with a completeness that only an adult of full muscular development without clothes on can be. The fellow was storming up and down at the far end of the hall, roaring.

'I don't understand,' said Bingo. 'When does he turn into the bear?'

'Röär!' yelled Biorn, stampeding up the hall towards them. '*When*, you say? *When* do I turn? I *have* turned! I *am* a bear! I am Biorn, the mighty bear! Röär!'

As the smooth and nude man reached the sofa, the fully clothed and hairy dwarfs backed against the wall behind them.

'Röär!' insisted Biorn. 'Röär!' He raised his hands in front of him with his knuckles out, as if grasping an invisible iron bar that was suspended horizontally at nipple-height. He opened his mouth and showed two rows of impressive but undeniably human teeth. 'Röär!' he said.

'You,' said Bingo, sweeping his crumbs of courage together internally to produce an, if you will, imaginary biscuit of valour. 'You aren't actually a bear at all, are you?'

'Miserable liar!' howled Biorn. 'For sure I am a bear!'

He made a rush at the soddit, who ducked under Biorn's sandstone-pillar legs and scrambled away. 'You're not though,' he called behind him, panting as he ran. 'Not *actually*, are you?'

'Röär!' called Biorn. 'I shall for *sure* eat you with my great beary teeth.'

'Ya,' Bingo returned, this being the most sophisticated taunt he could think of under the pressure of the moment. He was at the door, and hauled with all his might at the elegantly carved door handle.

'Feel the rage of the great pelty—' Biorn howled, hurling himself at Bingo. He may have been intending to conclude this statement with the words 'man-bear', or possibly 'mighty Biorn'. Maybe 'animal'. We can do no better than hypothesise at this juncture, because what Biorn actually said moved the sentence in a wholly new direction, concluding his utterance with a startled-sounding 'uuu*uu*!' (inflected from E flat up to G). The soddit had ducked and shimmied again, and instead of grabbing him Biorn had fallen through the open door and landed chin-first on the cold doorstep outside. There was a thud, and then another thud, as he progressed on his stomach further beyond the doorstep into the mud.

Bingo put all his weight behind the door, and swung it shut. Instantly six dwarfs were at his side helping him lower the beam of sanded wood into place.

All seven collapsed. It took them a full minute to regain their breath.

'Well,' Gandef said from across the room. 'That went fairly well, all things considered.' He was lighting his pipe.

Outside the door, a slightly muffled voice could be heard. 'Excuse me?' it called. 'Are you, now, locking the door?'

'Ignore him,' said Mori, picking himself up and smoothing the creases from his dwarf garb.

'Hellu?' came the voice. 'Hellu? Can you be unlocking the door, please?'

'Go away,' Bingo called.

'It is cold here outside,' came Biorn's voice, rather mournfully.

'Go find a cave to hibernate in,' called Mori.

'Please, not with the mockery,' keened Biorn. 'It is highly cold. If you allow me inwards again, I am promising to retain my man shape for the rest of the evening.'

'You're a loony,' Mori opined in a clear, strong voice.

'Never mind him,' said Bingo. 'You – Gandef. Don't put away your hearing spell for a moment. I've a bone to pick with you.'

'Eh?' asked Gandef, his hearing magic hovering near his hand. 'What's it?'

'You told us he *actually* was a bear,' pressed Bingo. 'All those stories of ripped-off arms and piles of quivering flesh. Do you realise that you terrified us?'

'Well,' said the wizard, chomping the end of his pipe, 'that's what I heard.'

'That's what you *heard*? I thought you knew him.'

'Oh no, oh no. Never met him before.'

'But you said—'

'A simple strategy to get inside and get some food, which worked, I might add. No, he mistook me for Raddledghastly the Ragged, my fellow wizard. But it worked out all right in the end. And we've learned not to trust uncorroborated stories of ursine metamorphosis.'

'Hellu?' Biorn's voice came from outside. 'My teeth are bouncing up and down against one another. Excuse me! Hellu!'

They slept well that night, and broke their fast with honey cakes with honey and honey mead. Only after they were fully rested and prepared did they open the door. Outside Biorn was lying curled under a hastily scooped pile of leaves. His extremities looked blue.

Gofur was sitting glumly on the doorstep. 'Spent the night in the privy,' he grumbled. 'Is there any breakfast left?'

As Gofur gathered some of the house's supplies for himself, Biorn stood up, shaking off some of the damp leaves and looking very sorry for himself indeed. 'Highly cold it has been,' he told them. 'With the chills, and the frost and the creeping-crawlings. Can I go in again?'

Bingo stepped aside and allowed the large man to scurry through his own doorway. 'And thank you,' he called, as Gofur came out, his coat stuffed with cakes, 'for your hospitality.'

Spider

Chapter Six

SPIDERS AND FLY! FLY!
RUN FOR YOUR LIFE!

ᏆᎵᎵᎭ

They set off in good spirits from Biorn's house, depriving the now moody and withdrawn man of nine stout ponies and a number of his prize chickens. Biorn seemed content to sit in the corner looking gloomy and sorry for himself. 'Ta-ta now!' the dwarfs called to him as they left. 'Bye!'

He didn't reply.

After a night warm under Biorn's thick-weave blankets and an easy day's ride on the plump ponies, they arrived at the expanse of the mighty River M. Across the smoothly flowing waters, reflective as polished stone, could be seen the edge of the great forest. The sky above, a perfect blend of midday blue and metal grey, spoke of amplitude and possibility. The air was fresh in the company's mouths, like pure water.

'How do we get across?' asked the soddit.

'Coracles, boyo,' said Mori, unstrapping the dwarfish breastplate from his chest. 'Aren't you wearing yours?'

'Well,' said Bingo, 'I'll confess, no, I'm not.'

'So,' said Tori, poking his corduroy waistcoat.[1] 'Look you, we did wonder how you expected to keep that watertight.'

'It's not designed to go in the water at all,' Bingo explained. 'Except when it gets washed.' It had not been washed in a long time.

'Oh!' said the dwarf. 'Not designed to go in the water, you say? Gracious. What use does it have then?'

'It keeps my torso warm.'

'Well we can take that as read, like,' said Tori dismissively. 'That goes, see, without saying. But what *secondary* use does it have?'

'None.'

The dwarfs muttered amongst themselves how foolish it was to wear clothing without a secondary use. They took the packs from the ponies and slung them on their backs, then slid their shallow metallic coracles into the water, leapt into them with remarkable grace and they were off, paddling with stubby dwarfish hands and powerful dwarfish arm muscles into the distance. A sizeable lateral transfer was imparted to their journey by the current, and they drifted far downstream as they travelled. Bingo found himself alone with the wizard and the ponies on the near-side bank. 'Hey!' he called. 'What about us? Hey!'

---

[1] A word pronounced, incidentally, 'wsct'.

Shortly, though, he saw two dwarfs reboard their tiny, tinny crafts, and make their way back towards the near shore, carried even further downstream as they went. They were lost to Bingo's eyes before they reached it, but twenty minutes later they came jogging along the bank carrying two spare breastplates.

'There you go, lad, bach,' said On, the first of the dwarfs to arrive. 'You hop into that, and paddle with all your might.'

Tori was endeavouring to coax Gandef into the other spare coracle. 'What about the ponies?' Bingo asked, as he tried to hold the breastplate steady in the water whilst leaning over the edge of the bank.

'They'll have to make their own way home, see,' explained On. But Bingo barely heard, because he had half fallen into the shallow craft and was now several yards offshore, drifting rapidly downstream. He tried paddling, but the arching of his back the action required hurt his spine. He tried lying on his back, and doing a sort of behindways underarm paddling, but it was rather ineffectual. He tried lying on his front, but the sharp rim of the breastplate jagged into his throat. In the end he forced himself to endure the pain in his back, and laboriously paddled and paddled until he was at the far bank. There was nobody around. There was water inside his boots, and his clothes were sodden. He hauled the coracle on to the bank and trudged for an hour upstream with the coracle pulling in the mud. Finally he found the party, settled round a campfire, wizard and all.

The following morning, after another filling breakfast from Biorn's store – honey-glazed smoked kippers, honey on toast and honeyed orange juice – Bingo felt a little better. 'Where now?' he asked. 'Into the forest, is it?'

'That's right, laddo,' said Mori.

They packed and marched two abreast, towards the line of trees. But Bingo's jaunty spirits evaporated as they walked into the wood under a tangle of branches that served almost as a gateway, and along a mossy, chilly path. It was very dark. This forest was nothing like the brittle but sunshiny forest of Lord Elsqare the elf. This was gloom in tree form. Fungus grew in broad-peaked clumps beside the pale, speckled tree trunks, looking like nothing so much as old cheese. Everything that Bingo's fingers or face touched, or that touched *him*, felt slimy.

'What a horrid place!' he declared.

'Truly,' agreed Mori, who was walking by his side. 'This is the evil Mykyurwood. You see those elms over there?'

'Yes.'

'They're oaks.'

Bingo examined them. 'They look quite like oaks,' he said. 'Have they taken the form of elms?'

'Partially,' said the dwarf. 'Enchanted, look you. And those ash trees?'

'Oaks,' said Bingo.

'Good guess,' said the dwarf.

'Not really. When you look a little more closely you can see they're not really ash. They're oak.'

'It's true,' said Mori, 'that it's not a very effective enchantment. But a shape-changing enchantment it is, nonetheless. The wood is filled with mystery and danger.'

'And must we go through? Cannot we go round?'

'It's the most direct route,' said Mori morosely. 'Besides, I thought – that is,' he added hastily, looking around to see if any of the other dwarfs had overheard him, 'that is, our King *Thorri* thought – ahcm – that we'd enjoy the sensation of something over our heads. Almost like being underground I, he, thought. 'Course, it's not so pleasant inside, is it? And there are spiders.'

'I don't mind spiders,' said Bingo haltingly. This was a lie.

'I don't mean *little* spiders,' Mori clarified, 'not knuckle-sized ones, or fist-sized ones. I mean spiders as big as you. Twice as big.'

'Should I have to face that peril, I'm confident that

my hobbld courage will see me through,' Bingo replied.
This, also, was a lie. A rather bigger lie, in fact.

They walked for the rest of the day and in the evening
they camped beside a sluggish, gooey-looking stream
that bisected the path. 'Best not get wet in that water,'
Mori advised. 'Enchanted, I daresay, boys, see. We'll
find a way over tomorrow.'

That night they slept uncomfortably, and in the
morning Mori stood beside the little stream and pondered how they might cross. 'We could hew a tree,
p'raps,' he suggested. 'Make a bridge? Or should we try
our coracles again?'

But Tori was a scoffer. 'Are you kidding, boyo?' he
demanded. This was, presumably, a rhetorical question.
'The stream's an inch deep, if that. You can't float a
coracle in an inch of water! And what would be the
point. 'Let's just wade out and walk over. Wasting time
chopping down a tree? Ap-surd. Ap-*surd*.'

'No no no, Tori boyo,' insisted Mori. 'This is the
Mykyurwood, see, and its precincts are enchanted.'

'Its *what*?'

'Precincts,' Mori repeated warily, and with a slightly
questioning inflection.

Tori laughed scoffingly.

'Its,' said Mori petulantly, searching for a better
word, 'its grounds, its demesne, its general area – it's

all enchanted, see. You don't know what might happen in that stream! It might put you to sleep, bach. It might be a magic stream.'

'And it *might* be just an ordinary, piddling, inch-deep little dribble that we can walk through,' said Tori.

'I invite you,' Mori said hotly, 'to try.'

'And try I will,' said Tori.

He stood at the side of the stream, placed one foot in the water and paused. The water wetted his sole but barely touched the side of his boot. When nothing happened, he turned a victoriously leering face back at the party, and stepped his other foot into the stream. In a trice he was on his back thrashing and kicking his legs up, and before anybody could react he was travelling rapidly downstream, disappearing between the trees. The tiny brook seemed, impossibly, to have become many feet deep, the water much blacker and much, *much* more rapidly flowing. 'Help,' gurgled Tori. 'Help!' But he was disappearing into the distance between the lowering trees, and his voice was soon obscured by the roaring of the great and, now, foaming torrent. Boulders flicked past the party, from left to right, caught in the spate.

And then they were standing in the silent gloaming once again, and the stream seemed to be nothing but an inch-deep dribble.

'Axes,' said Mori, after a long silence. 'Axes, everybody.'

'Should we go after him?' Bingo asked in a worried voice. But the dwarfs assured him that it would be a foolish business leaving the plain forest path in search of anything at all, even a valued comrade and brother. 'We'd all perish, you see,' Mori said. 'Perhaps Tori has drowned, or perhaps he'll be washed out of the forest into the River Sprinting that flows through the eastern lands. Either way he is beyond our help.'

They tried chopping down one of the trees that grew alongside the path, but it was an awkward business. The bark was extremely tough and leathery, and it put out some disgusting slimy extrudence, so that the dwarfs' axe blades slipped and skidded instead of cutting into it. After two hours of exhausting and futile swinging, the dwarfs sat in a gloomy circle.

'Could the wizard help us?' Bingo wondered.

But Gandef seemed to have entered a sort of senile fugue state. He smiled and waved when they yelled at him, but nothing they could do – not loud noises, not mimes, not drawing in the ground with a stick – could make him reply.

'His deafness is much worse now,' said Mori. 'Almost complete.'

'Complete?' asked Bingo.

'Indeed,' said Mori. 'What did you expect? It's hardly going to get any better now, is it?'

'That doesn't mean it's going to get worse, though. You're acting as if you've always expected him to go completely deaf.'

Mori looked at the soddit as if he were a moron, and then seemed to recollect himself. 'Of course, you don't *know*, la. See! I'd almost forgotten you weren't a dwarf! Funny that. Familiarity, I suppose. Got used to you, I have.'

'I don't know what?' Bingo pressed. 'What is it I don't know?'

'Never mind that,' grumbled Mori.

'No – seriously. What? You lot have been keeping something from me the whole way along. What is it? Why precisely *are* we trekking to the Only Mountain?'

'Gold,' said one of the dwarfs in a desultory tone.

'But it's *not* gold, is it?' said Bingo. 'Come along, I'm not a complete fool. I know it's not gold, I just don't know what it *is*. Why are we going?'

'Gold,' grumbled Mori. 'Just gold.'

'Uh!' said Bingo in despair, and he got up and marched to the edge of the enchanted stream. The trickle looked so inoffensive. The distance from bank to bank was no more than ten feet. Could they not leap over? No, of course they could not.

He returned to the group. 'If we cannot build a bridge of wood, then we must build a bridge of something else. There are boulders embedded in the mud alongside. Why not roll those out and use them as stepping stones?'

'An idea,' said Mori, rousing himself. The six remaining dwarfs and the soddit hauled and heaved and pushed one of the boulders out of its position, and rolled it tortuously until it sat in the stream. Nothing changed.

'You two,' said Mori, to Failin and Gofur, 'hang on to my arms.'

They got into position. Gingerly, Mori reached out with one leg and placed a foot on the side of the large stone. Everybody held their breath. But nothing happened. 'Here goes,' said Mori, and pushed off with his other foot. But as soon as this foot left the mud of the streambank there was a great rumble and the boulder shifted position. Foam curled up on its leading edge. Failin and Gofur hauled back and Mori sprawled on the dirt.

The stream was quiet once more.

'I suppose,' said Bingo, 'that we need to cross the stream without anything being in contact with the water.'

'I suppose so,' said Mori glumly.

'What now?'

'That creeper,' said Bingo. 'Do you see it? Hanging down from that branch over the stream. Could we reach it?'

'With one of these sticks maybe,' said Mori, picking up a soggily dead branch lying beside the path. 'We could hook it, draw it to us. You're thinking we could swing across?'

'Yes,' said Bingo.

'You go,' said the dwarf. 'You're lighter than any of us. If it won't hold your weight, it won't hold anyone's. But if you get across, I'll give it a go.'

Bingo wasn't happy with this plan, but he couldn't deny its basis in the physics of mass and weight.

The dwarfs caught the creeper easily enough, and pulled it towards the nearside bank of the little rill. 'I'll take a run-up,' said Bingo nervously. He paced back along the path, turned, and started running towards the stream. Or, to be precise, not really running. It was more *hurrying*, a little frenzied scurry. He grabbed the creeper, swung through the air with a wail, pulled up his legs so that they didn't trail in the water, and found himself rising through the air on the far side.

'Let go, boyo!' shouted the dwarfs behind him. 'You're over! Hurrah! Let go! Try and *roll* with the landing when you come down.'

'Right you are!' squealed Bingo.

But he couldn't let go of the creeper. His hands seemed glued to it. The stick the dwarfs had used to fetch it was still attached, lower down. Nor, as his trajectory reached its highest point, did he swing back down again. The leaves that brushed against his body seemed unpleasantly gooey. He found himself almost horizontal, wedged in a mass of adhesive foliage many feet above the ground.

'Help,' he cried.

But there was no help. From where he was Bingo could see little: the dark dappling of the forest canopy overhead, his own hands glued to a strand of what, now, he was less prepared to call 'creeper'. There was a rustling sound beside him.

'Hello,' said a snide voice in his ear. 'What have we here?'

Bingo turned his head.

Squatting on a taut grey thread amongst the leaves sat the biggest spider he had ever encountered. Its fat woolly body sprouted legs at jagged angles, thick leathery black legs, eight of them. It's worth dwelling on that fact for a moment. Not *two* legs, mind, like normal beings; nor even four after the manner of some of the mild-eyed beasts of the field. But a wholly superfluous and frankly alarming eight. That's right, *eight*. Nasty, eh? Oh yes. The creature's abdomen curved at the end. Its pinched face wore two twitching mandibles over its v-shaped lips, like a surreal moustache improbably and unpleasantly alive and moving. It had eight eyes, although six of these were small and clustered to the left and the right of the face like pimples. But the two main eyes were huge and red, like glass globes filled with claret, and light played curious spiral effects on anything reflected in their spheres. The spider's face had, despite all of this, a peculiarly human cast, as if a tubby person were wearing fat red glasses.

'Come visiting, have you?' sneered the spider. 'How pleasant of you. Or perhaps you've come colonising, eh? Trying to occupy and exploit the territory of honest working spiders?'

'Not at all,' said Bingo, trembling. 'No, no.'

'Which is what an imperialist would be bound to say. And speaking of being *bound*, are you cold there? Shivering? Let me wrap you.'

With dexterous movements of its great fat body the spider hurried round and about Bingo's body, spooling thick thread from its hindquarters and manipulating this with its two hind legs – which were spindlier and knitting-needlier than the other six. In a moment Bingo was swaddled all about. Only his right arm, still stuck to the strand (which wasn't, it seemed clear, a creeper after all), was outside the spool.

'Let me go!' he squeaked.

But the spider had no intention of letting him go. Tutting to himself, the spider smeared a secretion on to Bingo's hand to release the glue, and then tucked the free arm down at his side and swirled it around with another loop of cable. Luckily for Bingo – as it turned out – he did this hurriedly, and as he picked up the little soddit and started transporting it through the treetops the cable sagged and Bingo got his arm free. But the canny soddit kept it at his side, for fear that the spider would bind it again if he noticed it was loose.

Bingo was carried a long way into the forest. All through this bumpy, unpleasant journey he was racking his brains to think of a way of signalling to the dwarfs – to warn them of the danger, and to prompt them, perhaps, to rescue him. But he could think of nothing, and as they arrived at the spider's commune he saw it was a needless task. Seven figures were dangling from a branch, each of them wrapped tightly in spider cord: six of these were dwarfs, and one was a wizard.

'Good grief,' said Bingo.

'Hello, boyo,' said the dwarf nearest him. It was Frili. 'You here?'

'What happened to you?'

'We saw you getting stuck, see, and Mori shouted that the best plan was the one with axes in it. We dwarfs tend to prefer plans if they've got axes in them. So we hurried to our packs, only these here spider boys had spread sticky thread across the path, about six inches up. We all fell, got our shins and our boots caught in it. We might have ditched the boots and got away, but beards is a different matter. So then they were all over us, see, and here we are.'

'At least,' came a voice from further along the dangling line – Bingo recognised it as Mori's – 'at least we're over the enchanted stream. Carried over by the spiders, see.'

Bingo found it hard to take much comfort from that particular development.

The spiders were scurrying about from branch to branch, from fibre to fibre. They were an imposing-looking bunch. Where most people are content to grow beards from their faces only, spiders enjoy growing beards from all of their many legs. In addition to which they had bristles, thick black stubble, sharp-looking lashes, and other forms of shorter hair all over their bodies. They produced a great deal of silk, strands thick as wool which they wove into a number of things, only some of them liable to kill. Their scarves, for instance, were quite highly sought after: warm, if slightly creepy personal adornments. Sweaters, socks, blankets, furniture, roofing tiles, boots, wigs, farming implements and swords, all were knitted by the tireless spiders. Some of these products, frankly, worked better than others; but they were all traded by the spiders with the glum, rather deprived peoples who lived east of the Mykyurwood. The spiders also undertook special jobs for customers who were prepared to pay over the odds

– they might, for example, go to people's houses and cover everything with gossamer cobwebs as an April Fool's joke. Or if a woman were abandoned at the altar by her shiftless groom, a spider would be called in to cover the bridal chambers and the bride herself with cobwebs, so that she could feel properly miserable.

But their trading life had not endeared them to the populations of the open plains. Rather the reverse, in fact. People, not to put too fine a point on it, hated them. Not all people, but most people. Worse, the few people who actively liked the spiders were – there's no other word – weirdos.[2] All the reasonable people hated the spiders with a reflex hatred. They flinched, they shrieked, they ran away, they said things like, 'Eee! Ugh! Ugh! Ugh! Rachel! Rachel! Can you get in here and help me, there's an absolutely enormous spider in the front room—' People traded with them, of course, because people will trade with anybody and anything if the anybody or anything has something they want. But people thought them flesh-creepingly horrible.

Which they were. Even the nicest of them.

This climate of opinion had wrought its work upon the spiders' souls. The spiders of Mykyurwood were bitter. They had been non-specifically bitter for many

[2] I don't care what you say – people who like spiders are weird. Weird. WEIRD I SAY.

years, until one of their number had returned from his travels with a number of socialist tracts and keyworks,[3] and the whole commune had become politicised. The spiders had changed from being simply bitter, to becoming envious, chip-on-shoulder lefties.[4] They were sharply aware of the general anti-spider prejudice of society, the oppressive ideological construction of spiders in Upper-Middle-Earthian culture in which 'spider' occupies the position of hate-figure, the 'other' by which the fascist state defines its own social identity – and why? Why? Let me *tell* you, comrades, *only* because spiders are archetypal proletarian individuals, tireless workers whose exploited labour benefits every-body – pest control, weaving and textiles – make no mistake, comrades, it is rampant imperialist legism, that's what it is, unreconstructed hairy fangism. Well, comrades, it's time spiders banded together, formed a union, took their protest to the streets. Spiders of the

---

[3] Amongst which were *Das Web-Kapital*, *The Attercopmunist Manifesto* and *Condition of the Eight-legged Working Classes*. To quote the famous Karl Marachnoid: 'All the great events and personalities in world history reappear in one fashion or another; the first time as tragedy, the second time as running desperately round and round the sink like a roulette ball in its wheel. Philosophers have only *interpreted* the world; the *point* is to wrap it in silk and sting it to keep it from wriggling.'

[4] A spider can have four times as many chips on its shoulders as a human being. They're efficient that way.

world unite! We have nothing to lose but our sticky threads.

Bingo's first thought when he realised the serious-ness of his predicament was to be thankful that his right arm was free of the binding. But a long and unsuccess-ful attempt to unpick his cords left him with nothing but broken nails. The cord was too strong, and too sticky. He cast about, but all he could reach with his free arm were handfuls of leaves.

Bingo decided the thing to do was to negotiate his and the dwarfs' way out of captivity.

'Hey!' he called. 'Hello! Excuse me!'

One of the fatter spiders broke off from the general spider mêlée and brought his glistening spider face close to Bingo's. 'Yes?'

'Sir, I was wondering, O mighty spider,' said Bingo, his voice warbling a little, 'if I might be permitted a brief word with your mighty and dread monarch – king or queen, I, alas, do not know, but whichever power-ful ruler leads your folk. If that's all right with you, sir.'

This is entirely the wrong way to speak to spiders.

For a long time the spider's huge red eyes simply regarded Bingo. The soddit could see his own face, smeared through a weird arc, twice over, looking back at himself.

Then the spider said: 'Well, in the first instance, I

might question your automatic assumption I am a man
– I might, I say, ask that, were it not patently the case
that your assumption is grounded in a gender essential-
ism, an unreconstructed masculinism and phallogo-
centric privileging of the male. As it happens I *am* a
male, but my gender is of no political relevance.'

Bingo didn't really follow this. 'Ah,' he said. 'Good.'

'And in the *second* instance,' the spider continued,
'your whole statement is premised on the idea that our
collective is hierarchically governed by a fascist-style
dictatorial monarchical individual, and would be insulting were it not so patently an archaic hangover from an
exploded ideological practice to become almost post-
modern in its irony.'

Bingo tried to digest this, but it sat uncomfortably in
his mind like raw eggs in a queasy stomach. 'Exactly,'
he said uncertainly.

The spider, far from mollified, seemed to become
more furious. 'If that isn't *typical* of your pin-eyed,
scrawny, running-dog, web-destroying imperialistic
lackey-mentality enemies of the eight-legged working
classes,' he said, and lumbered away.

'Where's he going?' asked Frili.

'Off to get his leader,' said Bingo chirpily. 'I think. I'll
do a quick parley and get us out of here.'

But one hour turned to two, and Bingo came to the
conclusion that the spiders were going to leave the

party dangling there until they died. 'Do you suppose,' he asked Frili, 'they intend to eat us?'

'Unless they intend using us as festive decorations,' the dwarf returned.

Bingo pondered.

'Mori!' he called. 'Mori! We must get through to Gandef. He can save us with one of his magic spells! He can save us.'

'Your optimism is touching, my lad,' returned Mori. 'If misplaced. But, bach, I'll have a go.'

The wizard was sleeping. How he could sleep at a time like this was beyond Bingo's comprehension. But sleeping he was. Mori shouted and yelled, but no sound penetrated the wizard's ear. 'It's as I said, boyo,' the dwarf called. 'He's deaf as a rugby ball.'

'Wait a mo,' said Bingo.

He stretched out his free right hand and grasped as many leaves as he could. Using his muscles in ways he had not used them before, he pulled with all his might, and slowly his bound pendant body began to move in an arc, a little away from the proximate body of Frili and a little into the air. He hauled. Sweat came. He moaned with the effort, and hauled some more. When he was perhaps forty degrees from the perpendicular, he let go. Swinging back to his former position he collided, breath-removingly, with Frili. Frili grunted in surprise but did not move; nor did Failin, On, Thorri,

Gofur nor Mori. But Gandef, at the far end of the row, was propelled suddenly into the air.

'Eh?' he said, popping awake. He swung up, paused, swung down and Bingo felt himself jerked up again. 'Quick,' he squealed. 'Gandef! Help!'

Swing up, pause, swing down, clack.

A moment later Gandef's crotchety voice could be heard. 'Liberties! Hey! Wo-oh!'

Swing up, pause, swing down, clack.

Bingo's third swing upwards attracted the attention of the spiders. They came nimbly hurrying over branch and thread to stop the motion. 'What are you doing? Stop that!' they said, grabbing both Bingo and Gandef with their powerful forelegs and halting the swinging motion. 'Dangle good,' they abdured.

'We demand to speak to somebody in authority,' squealed Bingo. 'Or it'll be the worse for you! One of our number is a mighty wizard – he will enchant you! Let us go, I warn you.'

The nearest spider's great red globe eyes were unreadable. They stared at the soddit, and all the party. 'Which of you is the wizard?'

'What?' shouted Gandef, abruptly and crossly awake. 'What was all that commotion? Why can't a wizard have a little nap?'

'Gandef!' shouted Bingo. 'Do something!'

'Your hearing spell!' yelled the dwarfs.

'Why can't I move my arms?' the wizard complained. 'Why is everybody mumbling? Is this some kind of dumb show?'

Several spiders clustered around the wizard.

'Ah!' said Gandef, fixing one with a stern glance. 'Is that you, Mori?'

Bingo's heart sank.

'A pie, I think,' said the wizard meditatively. 'A liver pie. And for desert, a cherry pie. In fact, to save time, just bring me a liver and cherry pie.'

'So,' said one of the spiders. 'This is your wizard, you say? He seems a little blind. And a little deaf.'

'A little,' Mori conceded. 'But you don't want to get him riled, believe me.'

'We have,' this spider announced, retreating to a slightly higher bough to address the whole group, 'had a discussion concerning your fate in the Committee Ordinary, which requires a simple majority for its decision, although the final motion may have to be ratified in a higher forum with a two-thirds threshold.'

The dwarfs and the soddit had fallen silent. All except Gandef, who was singing, '*Fair and fair, and twice so fair, as fair as any may be, the fairest shepherd on our green, a love for any lady*' in a warbly voice.

'Our dilemma,' the spider announced, 'has to do with an earlier motion of solidarity with the bearded-oppressed of the world, passed during the spring session

of the General Council of Working Spiders last year.
Clearly your wizard, and you dwarfs, fall into this
category. Can we assume that you too have experienced
oppression and struggled under the hammer of anti-
beardist antagonism?'

'Oh yes,' said the dwarfs.

'And that you have never been tempted, basely, to
remove you beards and ape the imperialist decadence of
smooth skin?'

'Oh no,' said the dwarfs, in unison.

'It may be possible,' said the spider, 'to rehabilitate
you. Our workshops may be able to knit you artificial
limbs, four for each of you, to wear about your torsos.
And we do have certain ocular accessories, fashioned
with red glass, that you could wear. But your eighth
member, the beardless one . . .'

Everybody turned to look at Bingo.

'. . . his clothing and his lamentably smooth face
would condemn him, even if his crypto-feudal vocabu-
lary had not already done so. *Is* he a dwarf? We've not
seen his like before.'

There was a certain amount of confusion amongst the
dwarfs at this. 'No,' cried some. 'Yes!' cried others.
'Certainly he is!' bellowed Mori.

The spiders conferred.

'We are not convinced,' said the lead spider. 'It seems
to us that either he is the odd one out, and that the rest

of you are comrades-in-beards (perhaps he is a ninth-columnist,[5] a spy sent amongst you), or else – and this is as yet undetermined – you are all of the same party, pin-eyed insurgents, enemies of the workers, and that all your beards are false.'

'Nonsense!' bellowed Mori, his tightly wrapped body twisting a little on its thread. 'None of our beards are falsies, look you! Tug away, tug away on any of our beards, and you'll find nothing but good working-class facial hair. None,' he added, 'of your bourgeois false beards here.'

A smaller spider, with a slightly speckled belly and back, twitched forward. 'I'll take you at your word comrade,' he said, and scurried sideways until he was directly in front of Gandef.

'Ah, Bongo,' said Gandef, his eyes twirling. 'You know what I hate? "Howdy doody". Ridiculous phrase.'

'What,' said the spider, 'is it saying?'

'Nothing,' said Mori hurriedly. 'He – eh – had a knock on the head, and his wits are a little disordered.

---

[5] This is the equivalent of what a cockroach would call 'a seventh columnist', and a centipede a 'hundred-and-first columnist'. That humans call such individuals 'fifth columnists' has led many in the animal world to argue that we have, deep down, simply not accepted our bipedalism, and secretly we want to crawl around on all fours.

But they're still to-the-core proletarian wits, even in their disarranged state.'

'If you cut a hole in the top of a turnip,' observed Gandef, 'you can put a candle in there.'

'Test his beard!' called the spiders further back.

The spider in front of Gandef reached out a forelimb, and grasped Gandef's luxurious grey beard.

'Oi!' objected the wizard.

The spider yanked down. Gandef's beard came away in his claw.

Bingo gasped.

The bald, liver-spotted chin of the old man waggled in the breeze. 'Chilly,' he declared. 'What happened to my beard? Is that it there?'

The spiders had huddled together in a conference. One of them scurried along the length of the bound and dangling dwarfs, tugging on each of their beards in turn. None other instance of dwarfish facial hair was removable. After further discussion the lead spider turned to address the group.

'We have decided on clemency,' it announced. 'We shall eat most of you, and lay eggs in the beardless ones.' With this they scurried away.

'Oh dear,' said Frili, after a while.

'I don't understand,' pressed Bingo. 'What happened? Why was Gandef wearing a false beard?'

'He wasn't wearing a false beard,' snapped Mori.

'Then why did his beard come away in the spider's claw? Was it magic?'

'No,' said Mori. 'Simply a sign of ageing, look you.'

'I don't understand,' repeated Bingo.

'When you get older,' Mori explained wearily, 'sometimes you lose your hair. Humans and soddits sometimes lose their head hair. Wizards – eh, um, they sometimes lose their beard hair.'

'But all at once? In a great clump?'

'They're strange that way,' Mori mumbled. 'Wizards.'

'This is daft,' said Bingo. 'Something's wrong. This doesn't make sense. There's something you're not telling me. In fact, there's a whole range of things you're not telling me.'

'It hardly matters now,' said the dwarf. 'We're to be eaten. You're to have eggs laid in you. And so we come to our sticky end. Dew.'

Bingo was silent for a while. He was trying, with his free hand, to force apart the thick strands of spider silk at his waist and flip his fingers inside his waistcoat pocket. 'Things may not be beyond all hope,' he announced. 'When I was underneath the Minty Mountains, I – chanced – upon a Thing®. A magic Thing® in fact. Perhaps it can help us.'

This caused a great stir amongst the dwarfs. Or, to be

precise, it caused them to stir as much as was possible, which, given that they were all bound extremely tightly by spider silk, was not very much.

'Why didn't you tell us about this before?' Mori demanded.

'I was shy,' said Bingo.

'Shy*ster*,' retorted Failin, 'more like.'

'Shy – like a fox,' opined Gofur, with disgust in his voice.

'I wanted to keep it to myself, that's all,' insisted the soddit. 'But it is definitely a magic Thing®. Sollum was awfully keen to get it back. Murderously keen. Maybe it can help us out of this pickle.'

'Can you get it out of your pocket?' asked Frili, wriggling to try and rotate himself so as to see Bingo better.

'It's tricky,' said Bingo, squeezing his fingers into a spike and thrusting them between the tight cables. He could, just about, get his forefinger and middle finger through. Indeed, he was a luckier soddit than he knew: his spider captor had freed him from the sticky thread that he had mistaken for a swinging forest creeper by smearing a chemical desolvent over his hand and arm. Some traces of this remained on his skin, or else his right hand would have stuck fast to the threads and he would have been trapped. As it was, the tightness of his bonds meant that he could barely reach inside his pocket with two fingers, and could tantalisingly only *just* touch the Thing® inside.

'Wait a mo,' he said.

'Hurry,' said Mori. 'I can see the spiders through the leaves. I think they're gathering their eggs.'

Bingo scissored his two fingers, and felt the Thing® jiggle around at the bottom of his pocket. He tried several times to cup his forefinger nail underneath it and scoop it round, but it kept slipping away. A grotesquely obese purple-grey spider clambered past them on his way somewhere else. Bingo's heart was thudding.

'Almost,' he said.

He tried bending one of his fingers in line with the normal action of a knuckle, and bending the other finger in the opposite way, so as to produce a finger pincer. But such finger distortions are achievable only by guitar players, and Bingo was no such person.

'Almost,' he said.

Then, with another little tip of luck, the Thing® slipped into place between his two fingers. He drew it out very slowly, easing it past the confining threads, and when it was clear he closed it into the palm of his hand.

'Let's have a look,' urged Frili.

Bingo held up the Thing®.

'Ooo!' said the dwarfs. Even those who couldn't see it. 'Ooo!'

'Do you know how it works?' Bingo asked. 'Do you know what it is? When I was trapped under the Minty Mountains it helped me orient myself. I don't know how, but it seemed to help me run faster, and helped me run in the right direction.'

'This is one of the famous Things® of Sharon,' said Mori, in a hushed voice. 'The feats you speak of are the least of its accomplishments. The Evil Sharon made it in the mighty workshop of Dumb, and it has been long lost to—'

'Never mind that now,' interrupted Bingo. 'Do you know *how it works*? They'll be back to lay eggs in me any minute now. Is there something I can do with it?'

'All right, boyo, all right,' said Mori in a sulky voice. 'I was only giving you some of the background, la. It's a powerful Thing®, is that. Powerful magic.'

'Do you know how it *works*, though?'

'Well,' said Mori, turning the word from something uttered in a brief moment to something spoken over several seconds. 'No,' he concluded finally.

'I do,' said a small voice.

'Well that's no use to us, is it?' snapped Bingo. 'Why didn't you say so right at the beginning instead of — hold on, hold on, who said that?'

There was silence.

'Me,' said the small voice.

'Who?'

'Thorri,' said the voice, even smaller.

'You know how it works?' asked Mori incredulously. '*How* do you know how it works?'

'It'th jutht one of the thingth that we Kingth have to know about,' said Thorri.

'Well?' prompted Bingo.

'It hath many functionth,' said Thorri. 'The evil Tharon who forged it built many magic athpects into the devithe. But the motht important one is itth powerful magic of oppothed reverthibility.'

'Of what?'

'Of,' Thorri repeated in a still smaller voice, 'oppothed reverthibility.'

'OK,' said Bingo. 'Never mind what it's called. How does it work?'

'You thpeak your wordth *through* the Thing®,' said Thorri. 'And it will make the *reverth* of your wordth the truth.'

'The reverse of my words?' asked Bingo.

'But it mutht be a thtatement!' urged Thorri. 'Don't uthe the Thing® to make a conventional wish – it will only reverthe the wish and make it the thing you wish for *leatht* in the whole world. A thimple statement. The thpiders are coming!'

'The spiders are coming,' echoed Bingo. But Thorri was only speaking the truth. The spiders were indeed marching towards them, and with them were some egg-stocked females with uncomfortably determined expressions on their spider faces.

'Well, here goes,' said Bingo. He brought the Thing® up to his mouth, and spoke directly through it. 'The spiders are coming,' he said.

And, as soon as he finished saying it, the spiders were marching in exactly the opposite direction, determinedly hurrying away from the party.

'Blimey,' said Bingo.

But this was a weak spell. As soon as the spiders realised they were going in the wrong direction they stopped, slightly puzzled, turned their fat bodies around on their eight legs, and started making their way back towards them.

This – although Thorri didn't have time to explain the point – is the other important thing about the magic Thing®. Its magic does indeed consist in reversing the truth value of statements spoken through it, but its magic *also* depends on the subtle balance of all the magic force in the whole world. It is not infinitely capable. If one were to speak something huge enough through the device – say, 'The earth goes around the sun' – it might very well exhaust its magic in trying to make the reverse true. As it happens, in the many thousands of years since it was made its magic had waned considerably. When it was fresh from Sharon's workbench, it might, just perhaps, have had the magic power to spin the sun around the earth, with all the cataclysmic consequences of that action. But now, separated from its creator for so long, it could come nowhere near achieving so massive a reversal. Instead it would do the best, or the worst, it could. It might reverse the direction of the earth's orbit – such that the earth *comes* around the sun – or it might (if even that required too much magic power) simply fuse, close down, break, and its magic would drain out of it. Accordingly it was to be used with extreme caution: the unwary user might break it, or might do themselves, or the whole world, great damage.

Bingo, of course, did not realise any of this.

The spiders were now hurrying back. They did not look happy.

Bingo lifted the Thing® to his mouth a second time.

There is one final quality of the Thing® which it is worth mentioning, and that is the way it embodies the perverse wickedness of its creator's imagination. A statement usually has several possible opposites. The Thing® tends to choose the one most likely to do mischief, in accord with its creator's particular and warped perspective of the world.

Had Bingo spoken the sentence, 'I wish I were free' through the Thing®, it would have made the opposite true, such that Bingo did not wish to be free, was happy to be a captive and welcomed the fate the spiders had in store. Had he said, 'I wish I were a captive', then he would have found nothing changed – the Thing® would have been happy with the world as it found it, a world in which Bingo did *not* wish he were a captive. But let us assume that Bingo was wise enough to follow Thorri's advice, and to speak only declarative statements, rather than wishes, through the Thing®. Let us say he had uttered the phrase, 'We are captives'. Then the Thing® could have chosen to free the dwarfs, the wizard and the soddit. But it could, just as well and more likely, have chosen to interpret 'we' as meaning all the captives in all the prisons of the world; or as meaning only Bingo and the spiders; or as meaning anything its perverse magic imagination liked. It is a truth that applies to all magic devices, and applies to the Thing® above all: one must phrase one's wishes *very carefully indeed* when one uses such objects.

In the event, Bingo's imagination dried up at the vital moment. He saw the approaching spiders. He racked his brains to think of a sentence that, reversed, would have meant the spiders were permanently moving away from him, but he could not. And the beasts were almost upon them.

'Thay what you thee!' urged Thorri.

Bingo spoke. 'Spiders,' he said, 'are eight-legged creatures.'

All the approaching spiders collapsed. Many fell

from the trees to the ground far beneath. Some happened to fall upon tangles of boughs, or net-like webs; but they could not rouse themselves.

It took a while for Bingo to see what had happened. The giant spiders that had threatened them in so dire a fashion were no longer eight-legged creatures. They were now single-legged creatures with eight bodies. Their eight bodies were linked together at the neck and the abdomen but were otherwise distinct, with eight separate stomachs, blood supplies and other internal organs. The creatures looked like monumental clusters of grapes with a single, flexing leg, helplessly stuck in the position in which they fell.

It was in this fashion that the Thing®'s magic worked.

'Hurrah!' called the dwarfs. Bingo cheered.

'Now, boyo,' urged Mori. 'Use the device to get us out of these bonds.'

'Be very careful *indeed*,' insisted Thorri. 'If you allow any loophole at all, any leeway of interpretation, then the Thing® will uthe it to our detriment. Believe me, it ith an *extremely dangerouth* devithe.'

'Why don't I just say,' Bingo suggested, clutching the Thing® tightly in his fist, ' "We are tied up"? That might release us.'

'Or it might rethult in uth being tied *down*,' said Thorri. 'No. Thay thith: "The cordth binding mythelf, the thix dwarfth and the wizard to my left are *thticky*." '

"The cords,' repeated Bingo, speaking through the Thing®, 'binding myself, the six dwarfs and the wizard to my left are sticky.'

The cords flew off them, imbued instantly with a powerful repulsive power. It was so fierce that several of the dwarfs suffered nasty rope burns. And the suspending cords leapt from their branches, dropping the party through the canopy of leaves to the forest floor beneath. Most of them fell on the prone octo-bodies of fallen spiders and bounced clear. A few of the dwarfs landed on the forest floor, but dwarfs are tough creatures and none of them suffered permanent damage, except Frili who landed awkwardly on his ankle. Gandef went limp as a baby in the fall and was unhurt, if rather annoyed. Bingo landed on a comfortable pile of dead leaves.

The eight-bodied spiders spat thread at the party, and tried to reach them with their single remaining leg, but good luck was on the side of the dwarfs, and they mustered and hurried away from the spiders' territory in quick order, hauling the complaining Frili after them.

They passed many multi-bodied spiders lying on the ground, and took care to skirt round the creatures. Some of the prone beasts called after them pitiably, speaking in weird, eight-tracked voices, 'Hhhhhhhhelp! Helpppppppp!' But the company hurried on.

Finally, when they had left the mass of deformed spiders far behind, they paused and gathered together in a group.

'Give me the Thing®!' urged Frili. 'Give it to me – just for a moment.'

'And you'll do what with it?' asked Bingo.

'I'll use it to stop my damn leg hurting, boyo,' said the dwarf.

But Bingo was starting to become wise to the ways of the Thing®. 'And how will you do that?'

'I'll say "my ankle is hurting",' snapped the dwarf. 'It's nothing but the truth, see.'

'And then it'll stop your ankle hurting,' said Bingo. 'Or, maybe, it'll make every part of you hurt *except* your ankle.'

Frili grumbled, but said nothing more.

'I took a chanthe,' said Thorri, 'in formulating thuch a long thentence, back there. The betht polithy is to keep it brief and thimple. The more wordth there are for the Thing® to work with, the more mithchief it can wreak.'

'Well let's think it through,' said Mori. 'Why don't we, look you, say something like "we are in the forest". That's plain and easy, don't you think? Then the Thing® would make it so that we're *out* of the forest.'

'I think I begin to understand how it works,' said Bingo, looking at the device. 'Yes, it might do that, but if it did it would surely put us outside the forest on the wrong side, just to be cussed. Or, if it wanted to, perhaps it would reverse the statement in a different way – it might make it that instead of us being in the forest, the *forest* was in *us*.'

'Pff!' said Mori. 'That doesn't mean anything, bach.'

'Perhaps,' Bingo continued, 'by ripping us to a million bloody fragments and positioning them in an unbroken line all around the forest perimeter.'

Everybody was silent for a while.

'We should use this Thing®,' Bingo said, 'only as a very last resort. A *very* last resort.'

'Well thpoken,' said Thorri.

And, indeed, it was. In fact, although Bingo did not know it, the Thing® had used a great deal of its magical potency up. When the soddit had said, 'Spiders are eight-legged creatures', it had made *every single spider in the world*, large or small, into eight-bodied, single-legged creatures. This had required a great deal of magic, of course, and was to have dire consequences for much of Upper Middle Earth in the years that followed – flies breeding unchecked, locusts ravaging crops, infestations everywhere. But this is in the future, and it is not the business of this tale to relate it.

Drunk Dwarves

Chapter Seven

BARRELS OUT FOR THE LADS

ᏒᴍᴍᎧ

Fortunately for the party, the Thing® had a number of other features built into it in addition to its power of reversal. Amongst these was a compass, and this told them which direction was due east. They struck off, taking turns to carry the complaining Frili.

'I'm worried about Gandef,' Bingo told Mori as they trudged along. 'He's not as coherent as he used to be.'

'Difficult to deny that, laddo,' said Mori.

The wizard was waving his hands through the air in front of him as he walked. As Bingo watched, it became apparent that the right hand had acquired, in Gandef's mind, the ability symbolically to represent an eagle, and the left hand a dragon. These two imagined creatures were, it seemed, engaged in an aerial fight. When the 'eagle' swooped, Gandef made swooping eagle noises, 'Wheeh! Ach! Ach! Neeeaaoow!' When the 'dragon' turned and flew, the wizard went, 'Ggrrrrr!'

'What's happened to him?'

'Like I said in the forest,' replied the dwarf. 'He's getting older.'

'But he's useless like this,' Bingo pointed out. 'He's supposed to be coming along to guide and protect us, isn't he? But he can't do either of those things in his present state. Do you think he'll get better?'

'I think he'll get,' said Mori, peering through the trees ahead, 'different,' he concluded. 'Let's camp here tonight.'

They were all ravenously hungry, but despite an hour's foraging in the woods for mushrooms or tasty small creatures, they could find nothing to eat. The whole group sat in a circle and debated whether it was safe to use the Thing® to try and conjure up some food. Bingo opposed the whole idea, but his stomach was so empty it was mewing. He felt as though he had spent a month eating nothing but ozone. The dwarfs were insistent that food was a necessity, not a luxury, right now, and that the Thing® was the way to create it, and eventually they began to wear down Bingo's opposition. 'We'll pick the phrase carefully,' they said, and proposed and rejected several drafts before deciding on, 'There is not a small pile of food in front of me.'

Steeling himself, Bingo spoke the sentence through the Thing®. Nothing happened. He examined the device closely, wondering if it were broken, or its magic exhausted, until Mori, making what seemed an obeisance at the soddit's feet, reported that there was indeed a small pile of food on the forest floor. 'We might serve it on the head of a pin, la,' he said.

'I really, really think we shouldn't use the Thing® any more,' Bingo announced, tucking it away in one of his waistcoat pockets. The dwarfs immediately started complaining. 'What about,' suggested Gofur, 'trying, "there is not a large pile of food in front of me"?' But – as Bingo observed – this phrase might very well result in the appearance of a pile of food large enough to crush them all to death. 'And given the choice of being squashed to death by fried eggs and pineapples and mangetouts on the one hand,' he declared, 'and going to sleep hungry on the other, I choose the latter.'

Grumbling, the dwarfs agreed.

The party settled down to sleep.

Bingo was woken by shouting.

'Hey!' Mori was calling, scrambling to untangle himself from his own beard (in which, of course, he slept). 'Hey! Frili! Put that down, boyo!'

Blurry-eyed, it took Bingo a moment to realise what had happened. Frili had not been sleeping. Presumably infuriated by the pain in his ankle, he had pulled himself over the ground to where Bingo lay, and had prised the Thing® from the soddit's pocket. Now he was sitting a little way away, hunched over the device.

'Bingo-boy,' Mori called. 'Stop him! Double quick!'

Bingo lurched forward, calling out, 'Frili! No!' But it was too late. Frili was speaking into the Thing®.

'My ankle hurts,' he said, 'and *nothing* else.'

Instantly it was true to say that Frili's ankle no longer hurt. At the same instant it was the case that *something else* was true. The something else was hideous, ghastly, and – over a period of thirty seconds or so – fatal to the gasping, writhing dwarf.

It was unspeakable.[1]

The group was silent for many minutes.

'Nobody,' said Bingo fiercely, snatching the Thing® from Frili's cold and deformed hand, 'is to use this device any more. Do we understand one another? Is it understood?'

They all mumbled their agreement. Except, that is, for Gandef who declared that 'Seed cake is never the tastiest unless there's owt to wash it down'. Nobody asked him what he meant by *owt*.

They buried Frili, digging a shallow dint in the forest floor with their breastplates. By the time they had finished, dawn was seeping through the forest canopy. Nobody felt like sleeping anyway. They gathered themselves and trudged east again.

❀

[1] Which is why I'm not speaking of it. You'd probably worked that out for yourself, hadn't you?

~ 186 ~

Within a few hours the trees began to thin. The sound of flowing water became audible. Half an hour after that the group came to a clearing, which is to say a ring of clear ground with a fat oak tree in the middle. Gandef started trotting round and round this tree, laughing, but the remaining dwarfs and Bingo were too weary and hungry to chase him. Past the last singleton trees, the group trudged over open fields, drawing the beardless wizard after them by tugging on his poncho.

Soon they came in view of a large rectangular-faced building standing beside the rushing river. Its large gateway was shut and barred, and a painted sign hung above with the legend 'Sottish And Brewcastle', and beneath it in smaller letters, 'Wheer's Beer? Near!'

'A brewery,' announced Mori.

'A dwarf,' Bingo said, 'stating the bleeding obvious.'

The two of them scowled at one another.

'Now, now, ladth,' said Thorri, stepping between them. 'Let'th not fight. Where there'th beer there'th corn and barley. Where there'th corn and barley we can eat something. Pluth, jug of foaming wouldn't go down badly either.'

'Sire,' said Mori. 'You speak the truth.'

'Thertainty I thpreak tho. Thince I'm thaddled with the crown. It'th thevere, but it'th no more than'th ecthpected,' replied Thorri.

Mori looked at him, with a tired and vaguely puzzled

expression, but then shook his head as if to say he couldn't be bothered to work that out. Instead he stepped to the front door and hammered on it with his fist.

After a while a small portal slid open at man height. 'Who's there?' came a clogged voice. 'Wha'? Who's that?'

Mori summoned Failin and On rapidly, and had them lift him on their shoulders. 'Sir!' he called. 'Here.'

The face that peered through the slot in the gate was coloured a kind of sunset purple-red, and its nose was lumpen and coral-like. Little eyes, like lower-case letters '*o*', flicked from side to side, up and down, and finally registered the dwarf. 'Oh,' said the face. 'Who are you?'

'Dwarfs,' said Mori.

'Are you the glee?' asked the gatekeeper.

Mori didn't hesitate. 'Certainly we are,' he declared.

'Hold up, I'll let you in.'

The portal slid shut, and the noise of somebody with a slight cough shuffling about on the other side of the gate was audible. A noise suggested that a timber beam was being slowly withdrawn from some boltish location. 'Why did you say we were the glee?' Bingo hissed as this went on. 'What's a glee anyway?'

'I've no idea, boyo,' said Mori. 'But it's getting us inside, isn't it?'

The gate creaked open about a yard. 'In you come then,' sniffed the gatekeeper. He was, now that all of him was visible, a creature who could have with justice declared to the world, had he been so minded, 'Behold the man that beer made'. His belly was almost perfectly spherical; his legs as thin as creepers; the skin on his hands and neck was florid, and the skin of his face was florida.[2] He sniffed repeatedly as he spoke, a sort of *whhsht* noise made on an indrawn breath.

'Come on, I haven't *whhsht* got all day,' he said. '*Whhsht*.'

The dwarfs and the soddit scurried inside, drawing the wizard after them.

'Thank you, good sir,' said Mori.

'We was beginning to wonder,' the gatekeeper said, pushing the great door shut behind them, 'if you lot was, *whhsht*, coming. Derek!' he shouted. 'Derek! The glee's here.'

'About time,' returned a bellowing voice from the darkness.

The dwarfs lined up, turning their broad smiles upwards at the gatekeeper. He was, in turn, looking down, although without a smile. Indeed, his face was bulbous with suspicion.

'So this is the glee, is it?' he said. 'Six dwarfs and some old codger?'

'I assure you sir,' said Mori, tugging the hem of the

---

[2] Sorry. This should be 'florider', obviously; the sense being 'more florid' rather than, say, 'resembling a man's member'. But these errors will creep in.

gatekeeper's shirt, where it depended from the curve of his moon-shaped belly. 'I assure you that we are indeed the glee of which you speak. Glee is us. We are glee. Oh yes. If it's glee you want, then we're the dwarfs to give it you. Glee glee glee.'

The gatekeeper stared down with his disconcertingly umlaut eyes.

'Glee,' Mori added. And then, 'Oh yes.'

'You'd better, *whhsht*, come through,' said the gate-keeper, turning and falling into a loping gait.[3] The party trailed along behind him. They passed through the wood-ceilinged entrance room, and into a much larger hall behind. Large copper vats lined both walls, and a yeasty, soapy, gunky, gooey sort of smell was very evident. Another man, of similar stomach proportions and with a similarly purple-red face, was standing on a little stepladder at one of these vats.

'Derek,' called the gatekeeper. 'Here's your glee.'

Derek stepped slowly down the ladder and shuffled over the floor towards them. His eyes, in contrast to the gatekeeper's, were large and enormously protuberant, like two white boils with blue heads. He wiped his nose in a distinctive manner, by rubbing the palm of his

---

[3] You won't believe this. In the first edition the printers misprinted this as 'loading gate', which gave the sentence an, I feel, unnecessarily slapstick feel. Printers? Misprinters, more like. (Not you Gerald 'the Type' Weedon, you're all right. It's all the rest of them.)

hand directly upwards over the nostrils, moving it from chin to crown in one smooth movement, something like a salute. Years of this practice had bent his nose snub, like a fat tick marking approval of his face.

'A bunch of dwarfs and an old geezer?' he said, with a thinly veiled incredulity.

'I'm not a dwarf,' said Bingo.

'This is not what the agency promised,' said Derek. It seemed as if his eyes could swivel through a surprisingly wide range of movements: they looked at the wall, the ceiling, the other wall and back at the party again. 'A load of dwarfs? What kind of glee is that?'

'The best kind,' said Mori firmly.

'Dancing girls,' said Derek, 'is what they promised. Dancing girls and a prestidigitator. You lot aren't girls.'

'He is,' said Mori, pointing to Bingo. 'And he,' indicating Gandef, 'is the greatest expert at pressing digits in the world today.'

Derek looked unconvinced.

'No, really,' said Mori. 'Surely you've heard the name? Gandef the digit man?'

'Never heard of him,' said Derek. 'And never heard of you lot neither.'

'*Whhsht*,' added the gatekeeper.

'Now, don't have a *go*,' said Derek, turning on his fellow.

'I didn't say anything,' said the gatekeeper.

'I know what you're thinking,' said Derek in a hurt tone. 'But I tell you, I'll organise this glee *proper*, if it's the last thing I do.'

'And it will be the last thing you do,' observed the gatekeeper, 'if Al the Ale finds out you've messed it up.'

'Messed up what?' Derek asked, casting his eyes about. 'Nothing's messed up. Here's the glee, just like I was deputised to organise. Come on lads, and, uh, miss.' He wiped his hand over his nose again. 'Through here.'

'We were wondering,' said Mori, as he trotted beside Derek. 'Are refreshments included in the, eh, perquisites? Of the, the, the glee, you see?'

'Refreshments,' said Derek. 'Beer.'

'Ah, excellent. And – food?'

'Beer,' said Derek, 'is food. How do you think I got this belly?' His perfectly spherical eyes swivelled down to look at his perfectly spherical stomach.

'Excellent,' said Mori. 'Excellent. So there isn't any, I don't know, chicken? Bread? Potatoes?'

'Beer,' said Derek.

'So,' concluded Mori. 'To sum up. Just beer, then?'

'Beer,' said Derek. 'Here you go.'

They had arrived in a long hall. Great stacks of barrels were stacked along the walls. Other stacks of barrels were visible, neatly stacked, just behind these stacks.

'I'll go get Al the Ale,' said Derek. 'And the rest of the lads. You do your turns here,' he added, indicating a vague area of floor. 'We'll be over there.' He nodded at

~ 192 ~

two long, benched wooden tables. On each table stood a line of tapped barrels. Empty jugs and earthenware beakers were littered everywhere.

Mori hurried to one of the barrels and knocked it with his fist. Then he tried another, and another. 'Beer,' he said. 'They're all filled with beer. There's not *one* filled with soup.'

The dwarfs were running around the hall, examining the tables, rapping barrels with their knuckles. 'Isn't there any solid food?' Gofur asked. 'Not, see, that I *mind* a quick beer, but I could do a chicken stew, la.'

'Or a beef stew,' said On.

'Or a vegetable stew, even,' said Gofur.

'Or jutht,' said Thorri, 'a vegetable. Even a thmall one.'

But there wasn't so much as a crumb. It began to dawn on the party that the employees of this brewery ate and drank nothing but beer.[4]

---

[4] There are, of course, three stages. The first is when you finish a half-pint of lager with your lunch by smacking your lips and saying, smugly, 'Very nice'. The second is when you're out to the pub most evenings of the week, and you find yourself admiring a fellow drinker because he can open his throat and drop a pint in seconds where it takes you a dozen gulps. The third stage is the final one: you drink nothing but beer; you brush your teeth at night and rinse your mouth afterwards with beer; you keep a glass of beer on your bedside table in case you need to moisten your mouth in the night; you replace the tea in your teabags with hops, and you start saying things like, 'We have nothing to beer but beer itself' and 'Beer – beer is my ally'.

'I'm ravenous,' complained Bingo. 'And what is a glee? What are we supposed to do?'

'Play along with it,' said Mori. 'Follow my lead. Is that sawdust on the floor?'

'Yes.'

'Only I wondered if it was oats or something.' He sighed.

'Is there any food under that trapdoor?' asked Bingo.

Everybody looked at the trapdoor.

Mori went towards it and pulled on its metal ring, opening it a few inches and peering through the gap. 'It leads down into the river,' he reported.

'There might be some fish —' Gofur started saying.

The noise of a large group of middle-aged men could be heard approaching from the far end of the hall. Mori dropped the trapdoor, and the dwarfs hastily arranged themselves into a line as a motley crowd of brewery workers entered. Bingo recognised Derek, and the sniffling gatekeeper. A dozen, or more, men in similar states of physical decrepitude surrounded them: bellies on stilts, ragged purple jowls, high lumpy foreheads and strands of hair plastered over their flaky scalps.

At the front was a larger man. Bingo assumed that this was Al the Ale. Where the others had pot bellies, his was more of a cauldron belly. Where the rest had purple faces and bulbous noses, his face was a deep crimson, overlaid with scarlet broken veins inset into the skin as if in parody of crazy paving. His nose was so enormous, so misshapen and swollen, that it looked as though he had pressed his face against a muslin sack containing several mouldy potatoes, and come away with it as a permanent piece of face furniture. His nose looked like one of Bingo's feet.

'Right,' he said, his voice gravelly to the point of boulders. 'Where's this glee that Derek's organised?'

'Here they are, boss,' said Derek, scuttling alongside him. 'First-class glee, as promised.'

Al stopped and examined the party. 'Dwarfs?' he said. 'And some old geezer?'

'That one's a woman,' said Derek, pointing at Bingo.

Al raked his stare up and down the line of them.

'Right,' he said suspiciously. 'If you've organised it, Derek, then I'll take your word for it. But it'd better be a bloody good glee, or you're in trouble. Hop knows we need some bloody glee around here.' He turned to his men. 'You lot!' The brewers shuffled and looked shifty. 'Get yerselves around that table there. Get yourself comfortable, and *get drinking*.'

A groan rose from the brewers.

'What?' bellowed Al. 'What? Groaning, is it? Get yourself good and proper drunk – I'm not paying you to sit around sober. How can we have a glee if you're sober? Eh? How can we? Larry, I'm looking at *you*.'

'We can't, boss, you're right, boss,' said Larry in a

sulky voice. 'I was drunk at breakfast, boss,' he added hopefully.

'Breakfast?' boomed Al the Ale. 'What you talking about? Boasting, is it? *Twice* as much beer for Larry, everybody, you hear? You'd do best to button your lip, Larry, and concentrate on the drink in hand. Nobody likes a smart-ale,[5] laddo. Breakfast is breakfast, it's in the past and long gone. This, here, is the glee. Derek's organised it, and glee we'll have or it'll be the worse for you. You'll have fun, or I'll bloody well flay each and every one of you.'

Miserably, the brewers sat at the two tables, filled their beakers with beer and started drinking. Foam dribbled down their chins. Some of them gasped after each draught, a sound that resembled the lip-smacking sound a beeraholic makes on finishing his drink, only more despairing.

'Come on, you lot,' shouted Al at the dwarfs, as he manoeuvred his prodigious stomach in between table and bench and reached for a jug of beer himself. 'Let's have it then.'

The dwarfs looked at Mori. Mori looked at Bingo. Bingo tried to look at Gandef, but the wizard had fallen asleep against a barrel behind them.

'Glee!' shouted Al, banging his fist on the table. It

---

[5] Like a smart-alec (or in Wales, a smart-aled), but in a brewery.

was a fist extremely well suited to the business of banging on tables. A meaty and solid fist. 'What are you waiting for?'

Mori stepped forward. 'Good, eh, afternoon, good sirs. We *are* the glee – and I was just wondering – it's a question, see, I ask at all the functions, wherever we're booked in, and the question is: what *kind* of glee would you like? We have so many varieties of glee on offer, you understand.'

Al the Ale stared at Mori. 'What do you mean?' he said, with force. 'What on earth are you talking about? Just *do the bloody glee.*'

'You're the boss, you're the paying customer,' said Mori hurriedly. 'In that case, allow me to introduce the champion glee-er, the most gleeful boyo in the history of glee . . . Binglee Grabbings.' He stepped back into line, and Gofur (standing next to the soddit) gave Bingo a shove.

Bingo stumbled forward. All the brewers were eyeing him, some of them over the rims of their tankards.

'Right,' said the soddit. 'Some glee. Here goes. A justice of the peace,' he said, ratcheting his voice into a more comical tone by pulling his lips tighter and talking more nasally, 'did ask an old man how old he was, and the old man did reply, "My Lord I am eight and fourscore," to which the justice replied, "Why not fourscore and eight? 'Tis more the customary expression," to which the old man replied, "Because, forsooth, I was eight before I was fourscore." '

He opened his mouth in mock surprise, widened his eyes, threw his arms wide and put his right foot forward.

There was no sound in the hall, except the mournful slurp of somebody drinking beer.

'What,' said Al, his brows contracting like an approaching thunderstorm, 'the *bloody hell*—'

'What's the difference between the sea and vinegar? One's,' Bingo gabbled, 'a beautiful ocean for ships and the other's a beautiful lotion for chips, ta-daa.'

'Songs!' roared Al the Ale. 'Songs, Not Jokes, You Twits!' When he yelled in this manner, the words he spoke were unmistakably capitalised.

'Songs?' asked Bingo.

'Of *course* songs! What kind of glee are you anyway?'

'Oh *songs*,' said Mori. 'Songs! Of course. Of course songs. You want a *singing* glee. Of course you do.'

'What other kind of bleeding glee is there?'

At the far end of the table, one of the brewers belched. He belched again. When he belched a third and fourth time, Bingo realised that he was, in fact, laughing. 'Fourscore and eight!' he said, chuckling lugubriously. 'Eight and fourscore!'

'Shut it, you,' snarled Al. He turned back to the dwarfs. 'Now look, you lot—'

'Certainly we have songs,' said Mori, stepping forward and elbowing Bingo back. 'A song – why not?' He cleared his throat, and began warbling in a strained falsetto.

> *Buttercups and daisies,*
> *Oh, the pretty flowers;*
> *Coming ere the springtime,*
> *To tell of sunny hours.*
>
> *The something-something-something*
> *And something in the trees, um,*
> *Something of the trees, shadow of the trees,*
> *Or – hang-on.*
> *Hang-on.*
> *The dappling, I think it is, from the trees,*
> *And all the summer singing*
> *And sighing in the breeze.*

'That should be,' Mori clarified, 'and all the *springtime* singing, of course. Not summer, see. That was a slip of the tongue.'

Al the Ale was staring at the dwarf open-mouthed.

'I know another,' said Mori hopefully.

'No!' howled Al. 'No! No! No! What kind of miserable, twittering, bleeding song is that?'

'Now,' said Mori in a warning tone, 'there's no need to get personal, boyo.'

'A *drinking* song. A song we can sway our tankards to – you morons, berks, fools. You idiots! You teetotallers! What – who – *Derek!*' This last word was expressed with such volume and such vehemence that even Bingo shut his eyes and screwed up his face. 'Derek!' screamed Al, banging the table repeatedly, making those cups and tankards not in brewers' hands bounce up and down in time to his blows.[6] 'This is the last drinking straw, Derek. You've had your last drink in the last-chance saloon. You've gone too far this time.'

'Boss!' squeaked Derek.

Al the Ale was trying to haul himself up and out of his seat, but his belly seemed to have wedged itself beneath the tabletop. 'You stick where you are, Derek. I'll wring your neck in a minute. Meanwhile, you—' He gestured angrily at the dwarfs. 'I'll wring *more* than your necks. I'll wring your *heads* – one by one.'

He stood up with a loud pop, his belly swooping up and slapping down on the tabletop.

'Each and every one of you,' he bellowed, pointing a fat finger at each of the dwarfs in turn. 'You're done for. That's it. Trying to pass yourself off as a glee? Lads –

[6] If I'm completely honest, these cups and tankards bounced up a fraction of a moment *after* the blows rained down, but there's no point in me being prissy or pedantic about a thing like that.

take them and drown each of them in a barrel of beer. Starting,' he added, rotating his pointing arm so that it indicated Bingo, 'with *her*.'

'Now wait just a *moment*, boyo,' said Mori.

But Derek, eager to ingratiate himself with his angry employer, was already halfway across the floor to the soddit. Several other brewers were behind him. The dwarfs, glancing at one another with wild surprise, their hands on their axe shafts, were grabbed by a second cohort of brewers. In a moment the whole party was disabled.

Bingo, squealing and kicking his legs, was carried over to a barrel and held aloft. 'Wait!' he gasped. 'Stop a minute! I know a drinking song! I do!' But it was too late. The lid was off the barrel, and the beer inside, slopping at the very topmost lip, promised a beery death. The soddit was thrust down. Ale spilled over the edge of the barrel and foamed down the side, and in a trice the lid was being nailed back down. Pitiful thumps came from inside, and the barrel rocked a little on its base. Then it went very quiet.

The mass of brewers turned, as one, to deal with the dwarfs.

'Really, boys,' said Mori, 'you don't have to do this—'

'Actually,' said the brewer with his arm around Mori's neck (or thereabouts), speaking directly into the dwarf's ear, 'to tell you the truth, it makes a nice change, drowning people. Normally we just have to drink all day. At least, if we're drowning you lot then we're not drinking.'

'Stop!' said Mori. 'Wait! I've an idea.'

But a second barrel was being prepared, its top levered off. Mori was hoisted up and held over the barrel.

'Stop,' he whimpered.

'Stop,' said somebody else. It was Al the Ale.

The brewers all turned. Al was standing next to the barrel in which Bingo had been drowned. 'There's something fishy about this,' he said. 'Put that dwarf down a mo. Listen to this.' He reached out with a knuckle and rapped the side of the barrel.

It returned an empty noise.

'Get the lid off this,' Al commanded.

When the nails were pincer-squeezed out and the lid removed, Bingo was discovered sitting in the bottom of a dry barrel. His clothes were not even moist. The soddit smiled.

'Lord Hop above,' said Al. 'Malt things bright and beautiful. Blimey.' He peered in again. 'Do you mean to tell me,' he growled, 'that you drank all that beer?'

'Ah,' said Bingo, standing up. His forehead appeared over the lip of the barrel. 'Yes, that's it. That's what I did. Ye-ee-es. Drank it all, that's right. Rather than drown, you see. Besides I was thirsty.'

Al put his head back and laughed. It was a scary sound. He laughed and laughed. 'Now,' he said, when he had his diaphragm under control again, 'that's drinking!' He reached in and lifted Bingo out, hauling him over to the table and pouring him a beaker of beer. 'I have to work with these ninnies, these teetotal beer-avoiders. This dwarf girl could drink any of you under the table!' He laughed again.

'Really,' said Bingo, in a small and slightly nervous voice. 'It was nothing.'

'Nonsense!' bellowed the brewer. 'Lads, release those dwarfs. Have them round this table. Something to celebrate at last. Beer!' he called. 'Beer!'

They drank for hours and hours. They sang many beer songs, amongst which were 'Be-ee-ee-e-eer Is Love?', 'Hit Me Baby, One More Tun', 'Shine On You Crazy Double Diamond Works Wonders' and 'Beer! Beer! Beer!' At one point in the proceedings Mori grabbed Bingo's arm and hissed into his ear, 'I thought you said *no more use* of the *you-know-what*?' and Bingo hissed back, 'It was a life-or-death situation, a risk worth taking', before they were yanked apart by over-affectionate brewers and made to drink more beer. They drank a light wheat beer. Then they drank a beer that tasted like a large jar of Marmite diluted with half a cup of dirty dishwater. Then they drank a beer with a higher alcohol content than whisky.

In a very short time they were drunk.

Despite the fact that only an hour earlier the brewers had tried to drown him, Bingo was now moved to hug these large-bellied men, and tell them the story of his travels in particular detail. The brewers might have become suspicious at how quickly the little soddit became inebriated if they didn't think that he had already downed an entire barrel of beer. When they congratulated him, he grinned stupidly and patted his waistcoat pocket.

In fact, early on in the binge, he thought of a plan: he would wait until the brewers were dead drunk; then he would use the Thing® to sober himself and his comrades up (telling himself, *I'll use it one more time, and that'll be the end of it – no more after this*). Then he and the dwarfs and the wizard could creep away. It seemed, after two jugs of beer, a good plan. After ten jugs of beer it seemed the most brilliant plan in the world, a plan of such cunning and genius that only a super-hobbld, a hobbld of all hobblds, could have come up with it. At the same time, he could not remember what the plan was. He could barely remember what his own name was. Nor did he care. In fact his recklessness was dangerous.

'Lemme lemme show you a liddle something,' he told

one of the brewers as they leaned together on the
bench. 'Liddle-liddle-something.' He brought out the
Thing®.

'What's?' asked the brewer, too drunk to complete
the question.

'Issa Thing®, iss.'

'Like,' said the brewer, 'like the Thing® that the Evil
Sharon made?'

'Precisely,' said Bingo, after three or four attempts.

The brewer looked at it.

'What's it do?' he said.

'Lemme, lemme show you,' said Bingo, and raised
the Thing® to his lips. And there his brain stalled.
What had his plan been? It had been a good plan. It
had been the best plan. He couldn't remember what the
plan was.

'What you doing?' asked the brewer.

'I don't remember,' said Bingo, the words drifting
through the Thing®.

And he did remember.

'I am drunk,' he said, slurring the words a little. And,
instantly, he was sober.

For a moment, now that he was sober enough to
know what he had done, he held his breath. The risk
he had taken! Had the Thing® woven some ghastly
sting into his sobriety? But moments passed, and
everything seemed normal – except that he was as

sober as a stone[7]. He was not to realise it until many weeks later, but his physiology had indeed been changed by Sharon's malign magic. He could never be drunk, no matter how much he imbibed. His wished-for sobriety was absolute. He could still have hangovers if he were to over-indulge alcoholically, but he would never again experience inebriation. But this grim revelation was in the future.

He looked around at the slouching or snoring figures. The dwarfs were starting to drift off into a drunken sleep (and dwarfs can take a lot of drink). The brewers were mostly snoring, including the one Bingo had just been talking to. Al the Ale was lying on his back like a model of a mountain.

Bingo was acutely conscious of a sense of terror. In face he had been feeling that all the way through, but the beer had obscured the sensation. Now that he was more sober than he had ever been, he felt a desperate urgency to get out of this place. They had tried to drown him! Because they hadn't thought his jokes were very funny! And they were classic Soddlesex jokes, too.

He hurried over to Mori, who was asleep in the arms of Thorri, their beards trembling like seaweed in a

---

[7] Stone-cold sober. Which is to say sober as a *sober* stone. If you've ever seen a drunken stone, for instance at a rockslide or avalanche, you'll know how important the distinction is.

gentle current as they snored. 'Mori!' he hissed in the dwarf's ear. 'Mori! We've got to get out of here! Mori!'

Nothing.

It was the same with the other dwarfs. Gandef too seemed dead drunk. Bingo scurried from supine body to supine body, his anxiety eating at him. He had never felt so acutely aware of the world around him, so anxiously prescient. Any one of these brewers – hardened by a lifetime of drinking – could wake up at any time. Grumpy with hangovers, could they expect mercy from them? Of course not, of course not. He couldn't afford to leave it until the dwarfs woke naturally from their beer slumber. And he couldn't think of a way to wake them sooner.

He took out the Thing® and examined it. But, in his new sober-anxious frame of mind, he could not summon the courage to use it. What if it backfired? What if awful consequences followed?

There was only one thing for it. Bingo examined the stack of barrels closest to the trapdoor. Wooden rails were nailed against the floor planks to guide these barrels to the hole, once a foot-tall wooden wedge was removed from the base of the stack. Thinking fast, and fidgeting as he did so, Bingo tied the beard of Failin to Gandef's ankle. He tied On's beard to Failin's ankle, Gofur's to On's, Thorri's to Gofur, and finally – lugging the bodies of the sleeping dwarfs about, he tied Mori's beard to Thorri's ankle. Then he hauled open the trapdoor. The water whooshed past beneath. They had been drinking all afternoon and all night, and now the pewter-coloured light of dawn tinkled chillily on the fast-flowing water.

'Sorry about this, guys,' he said, hauling the dwarfs and the wizard into a rough pile beside the lip of the trapdoor hole. He sat himself on the top of the snoring, grumbling, breathing mass of dwarf bodies, reached forward with his foot and kicked aside the wedge.

He shut his eyes, but he could hear the tremble of the tumbling barrels as a sort of thunder before the first struck the pile of bodies. There was a sense of jarring movement, a weightless split-second, and then the water was all over him with a great splash. He barely had time to swear before he was tugged under by the flow. Bubbles swarmed around his open eyes, and then he was bobbing on the surface and moving swiftly beneath a grey-glass sky.

Raving, the Insane Bird

Chapter Eight

ON THE DOORSTEP, NOT LITERALLY A DOORSTEP, IT'S A MOUNTAINSIDE ACTUALLY, BUT IT'S A DOORSTEP METAPHORICALLY SPEAKING, IF YOU SEE WHAT I MEAN

ᚱᚢᚢᛡ

They bobbed and floated down the River Sprinting amongst a slick of wood. Barrels twirled and knocked against one another in profusion and great confusion. Even as deep a drunkenness as the dwarfs had acquired was loosened from their consciousness by the sheer chill of the river, and the shock of their sudden immersion; not to mention the surprise and chagrin of discovering themselves chained together by their beards. Mori, with a little more self-possession than the others, scrambled on to a barrel, and the others grabbed passing floats. Bingo himself swam for a while, and then managed to balance himself half-sprawled upon the top of a barrel that was bobbing, iceberg like, mostly underneath the waves. The fact that these barrels were full of beer meant they floated very low in the water.

In this fashion the party proceeded downriver for several hours, as the sun rose ahead of them finding diamonds and splinters of gold in the ever-crinkling wave tops and warming Bingo's face. The landscape on either side reminded the soddit, somewhat, of home: broad fields, wheat and barley on either side of the river, and a deep-breathing wraparound sky above.

'Soddit!' called a dwarf, rolling a barrel under his body like a hamster in a hamster wheel, and not, to judge by the expression on his face, deriving much satisfaction from the exercise, 'Bingo! Help!' It was Gofur, slapping the wood with his hands in increasingly rapid patterns as he struggled to stay above rather than beneath the barrel.

Bingo swam over to him.

'Untie my beard,' Gofur said, 'and my ankle, glub glub glub.' These last three words may not have been attempts at communication, for Gofur had slid off his barrel.

Bingo fished him out of the water, unknotted his beard and untied his ankle. The dwarf was still not happy, but he was able to thrash out and find another barrel. Bingo, feeling like a mother duck, went from dwarf to dwarf, freeing them from their bondage. Finally he swam out to the wizard, but found him perfectly happy, floating on his back and singing a song about a loofah.

He swam over to Mori, who was grumpier than Bingo had ever seen him. The soddit pointed this out.

'I'm drunk and *freezing cold*,' the dwarf retorted. 'Are you surprised I'm unhappy about it? Drunk doesn't *go* with freezing cold. It goes with nice-warm-fire-toast-your-toes-nicely. It goes with lying under a blanket. Drunk and freezing cold makes for an unhappy dwarf. Look you,' he added, and he clearly meant it to sting.

'All right, all right,' said Bingo. Now that he was in the icy water he was finding it rather refreshing. 'We're probably far enough from the brewery now. We can make our way to the bank, climb out, maybe start a fire.'

But as he spoke he noticed that the banks had risen around them from a few feet of mud to several yards of sheer chalk. There was nothing for it but to cling to the barrels and wait until the landscape permitted disembarkage.[1]

After a few hours in which the soothing effect of the sound of fast-flowing water was counteracted by the

---

[1] I'm *sure* this is a word. All right, my dictionary doesn't include it – but that just shows the inadequacy of my dictionary. I *know* this is a word. I feel it in my gut.

simultaneous noise of multiple chattering, moaning and complaining dwarfs, the riverbanks started to draw away from them on both sides. Soon after this they floated out into a wide and brimming lake.

This was Lake Escargot, whose waters were silver and whose water snails were the most celebrated luxury in the whole of Upper Middle Earth. The famous town of Lakeside sat on timber stilts alongside the shore. And past this, just visible above the haze of the lake's northern shore, was the Only Mountain, the famed Strebor that Bingo had travelled so far to see.

He noticed that the barrels were starting to drift in different directions, and bestirred himself to round up the crotchety dwarfs. Under his direction they swam to a shingly beach to the south of the rivermouth, Mori and Bingo pulling Gandef after them. When they were all out, some tried to roll themselves in their beards there and then and sleep on the shore. But Bingo, who was tired and sober (instead of being tired and hungover), insisted they march to the bridge that joined Lakeside to the land. 'For once,' he told them, 'I intend to sleep in a proper bed and eat proper food. It's been long enough.'

They followed him, complaining but compliant.[2]

---

[2] That's nice writing! I like that. That's almost poetry, that is. 'Complaining but compliant' – two very different words, you see, that sound fairly alike. There's a name for that in rhetoric, isn't there, but I can't bring it to mind.

The guards on the bridge were only too happy to welcome this bedraggled party into their halls. 'Custom has been down,' they said, 'since the dragon moved into the Only Mountain.'

'Really?' said Bingo, fishing out the entrance fee from Mori's leather purse. 'How long ago did he arrive?'

'Seventy years or so,' said the guard.

Inside Lakeside the exhausted party were almost overwhelmed by the profusion of goods on offer. Shop-keepers who had never seen a customer and who had survived on selling things to other shopkeepers, and on tales of actual customers passed down from their grand-parents, crowded around the group, eager to sell them anything and everything. There was a plethora of stalls selling axes, barrels, haunches of venison, wool and such, with extensive boat-parking and mead halls in which the wearied heroic shopper could find refreshment.

'Really,' said Bingo. 'We're just tired and hungry at the moment. Can you direct us to a refreshment house? An inn, with some beds?'

Disappointment was bitter for the majority of shop-holders, but the landlady of the Boing Inn was so excited she almost did a dance. 'Actual guests in the inn!' she kept saying, as she led them between the narrow ways of Lakeside. 'Actual guests!'

There was a fire in the inn's front room, and the

dwarfs huddled round it with pathetic eagerness. They devoured plates of porridge, followed by bread and cooked meats, and then they clambered upstairs to fall into complete and unmitigated sleep on top of their beds. Bingo, the last to succumb, thanked the landlady, paid her in advance with some more of Mori's gold, and finally collapsed into dreamless slumber.

The dwarfs and Gandef slept a total of eighteen hours: the dwarfs because they were each sleeping off monstrous hangovers, and Gandef because he seemed to be sleeping all the time these days anyway.

Bingo woke, feeling indescribably refreshed, during the morning of the following day. A plump, short man was sitting on a chair in the corner of his room.

'At last you are awake!' this man announced. 'Our first customers for seventy years! I greet you, sir. You and your courageous dwarf shoppers! You bring new hope to the town of Lakeside of Thurrock.'

'I am delighted to be of service,' said Bingo, remembering his manners. 'And honoured to make your acquaintance, Mr . . . ?'

'Ah,' said the stranger, standing up and clasping the sides of his expansive belly. 'I am Lard, the Bowman. I am, to be straight with you, Mayor of Lakeside.'

'It is indeed an honour,' said Bingo, scrabbling out of bed to be able to bow.

'No – no – I won't stand for it, if you intend to treat me as a somebody,' said Lard with jocular self-effacement. 'It is not long since I was nobody. I'll not subscribe to the cant of fame. I was a lowman until last year, sir, one of the lowest of the low lowman in this town. I was a poet, a bard – can you imagine it? Can you think of a more disgraceful and untouchable social caste? But I have raised myself up by my efforts, and I put aside the miserable trade of poetry for bowmanship. Now I am Lard the Bowman. And I have come to welcome you all personally – personally – to the shops and stalls of Lakeside. Your companions . . . ?'

'They,' said Bingo, glancing at the other beds, 'may sleep yet awhile. Our journey here has been wearying and long.'

'But you *are* here, nonetheless,' said Lard. 'That is the important thing.'

'Your trade has been depressed?' Bingo asked.

'Oh, woe, woe, woe,' agreed Lard, although still with a degree of complacency, as if he were reciting rather than expressing the sentiment. 'Since the wicked dragon Smug took possession of the Only Mountain, our customers have shied away from us. Steered clear. We live under a terrible threat all the time. These are not ideal trading conditions.'

'Yet you have not been tempted to abandon this site, and move your stalls further south?'

'Abandon Lakeside?' said Lard, in horror, or mock-horror it was difficult to tell which, since the sentiment was delivered with a rather puzzling wide-eyed indolence. 'Out of the question. Besides, our patience has been rewarded with *your* arrival. New custom! May you be the first of many!'

'Alas,' said Bingo, 'we were not planning on staying. We are travelling on, as it happens, to the Only Mountain itself.'

'You don't say,' said Lard conversationally.

'Indeed. But in fact, Sir Lard, it may be we can be of service to you and all of Lakeside.'

'Service?' Lard asked, with the air of a man who understood what the requirements of good service entailed.

'Our quest – perhaps I should not be so free with this news, but I see no harm in your knowing – our quest is . . . to slay Smug.' Bingo had long since decided that this must be at least part of their quest, despite the reticence of the dwarfs.

'Really?' said Lard mildly. 'I say. Is that so?' He sat for a while, as if digesting this news. Then he shrugged, and said, 'To do what, sorry?'

'To slay. To kill.'

'Oh! Kill – I *see*,' the Mayor said, in a much more animated manner. 'Well that *is* fantastic news! Fantastic! Fairytaleous! Marvellous! I can only hope that you are successful. If you were to rid us of our curse, then Lakeside could once again blossom as the well-provisioned and convenient one-stop shopping emporium of the eastern wilderness.'

Bingo and Lard talked long on this topic, and by the time the dwarfs awoke (moaning and clutching their heads) the Mayor of Lakeside had agreed to ferry the party up the river to the foot of the Only Mountain in Lakeside's best transit barges.

'It seems you are proving a useful addition to the party after all, Mr Soddit,' said Mori as he munched, hungrily, on some toasted bread for his late breakfast. He had doused his beard in vinegar and wrapped it around his temples to assuage the thumping there, which gave him a slightly peculiar look.

'They will take us directly to the mountain,' said Bingo, 'and provision us. The rest is up to us, they say. I was thinking: perhaps we should leave Gandef here? He would be well cared for, I am sure.'

'Leave the wizard?' barked Mori, jerking his head up so quickly his beard fell down again. 'What are you saying? Of course we can't leave the wizard. Of course the wizard has to come with us. The *very idea* of leaving him!'

'But why? He's not doing anything now much, except sleeping.'

'He must come,' said Mori. And that was that.

The following morning, the dwarfs made a handsomer group than they had for a long time as they stood on one of Lakeside's piers. Their breastplates had been polished, their beards washed and combed, and the holes in their boots expertly mended. Eager-faced lakeside barge operators handed them down into the boats, and pushed off with their poles.

For almost an hour the party simply sat, watching the sun-tickled landscape sliding past. Bingo let his eyes meander. Beasts of herbage stared from the meadows that overlooked the lake. Cranes flew overhead and wheeled around to land on the lake, their gawkiness folding away as they settled themselves, bobbing in the water, to observe the passing boats. In the zenith a tiny cloud seemed to cap the immense blue dome of the sky.

Before them, the conical peak of the Only Mountain rose slowly. At the northern bank of the lake, the bargemen poled their craft up the narrow river that flowed from the sides of the mountain. Before sunset the dwarfs were able to set out a temporary camp on the first upslope. 'We shall leave you here, heroic ones,' said the chief bargeman. 'You can trek the rest of the way easily tomorrow. Good luck in your mighty quest! May your right arms prove strong!' And they departed.

'What on earth,' said Mori, 'did he mean about "right arms"? What was that all about?'

It was strange to think that they had finally arrived at
the Only Mountain, after their long, varied and
attritional adventures. Dwarfs and soddit breakfasted
on hessian-packed bread rolls and miniature cork
barrels of orange juice (supplied by the burghers of
Lakeside). Afterwards Bingo sat on a broad-topped
rock and simply stared up at the mountain. The Minty
Mountains had been impressive, but this was something else – a gigantic monument in stone, out of which
the morning light was pressing a thousand facets of
grey and white: right to left in myriad planes and curves
from cinder-coloured, ash, fish-scale, iron, raincloud, to
purple and black, streaked and capped higher up with
bone-coloured and cream-tinted snow. Many rooks
circled in the sky overhead, their cawing as soothing a
sound as Bingo had ever heard.

Thorri coughed discreetly at the soddit's side.

'Oh,' said Bingo, who had yet to learn the proper
way of speaking with royalty. 'Hello there. It's a
magnificent mountain, isn't it?'

'Thertainly very big,' said Thorri. 'It occupieth the
eyeth, don't it? It'th a shame, really, thince it getth in
the way of a beautiful view.'

'How can you say so?' said Bingo. 'I think it's
spectacular.'

'More'n a thpec,' said Thorri archly. 'But don't take it

~ 221 ~

perthonally. We dwarfth, we like *down*, not up, you thee. We prefer the inthide to the outthide.'

'But this mountain is hollow, I suppose. Everything's hollow, after all.'

For the first time Thorri looked at the soddit with a twinkle of respect. 'Indeed it ith,' he agreed. 'Tho you have learnt thomething about the way the world workth, young thoddit.'

'I've picked up a few things on my travels. So what do we do now?'

'We go inthide,' said the King. 'That'th why you're here.'

He pulled off his boot and drew out a crumpled scrap of parchment. The other dwarfs began gathering around as Thorri spread the paper out on the rock. At first glance Bingo took it to be a picture of an old cabbage leaf with copious annotation. But he saw, looking more closely, that it portrayed with rather crude delineation the environs of the Only Mountain. 'We can't go in through the front door,' Thorri was saying, pointing to a kink in the side of the mountain, 'on account of it'th locked.'

'Locked front door,' murmured the dwarfs.

'Tho,' said Thorri, 'we need to find the thide door. But, Mr Grabbings, the *thide* door is only wee.'

'Is only what?' asked Bingo.

'Only wee.'

Bingo tried to decipher this. 'I don't understand.'

'It'th wee,' insisted Thorri. 'Wee – wee. And the passage to which it gains accethth, that'th wee ath well.'

'Wee?' hazarded Bingo.

'Wee!' said Thorri, starting to become tetchy. 'You're thmaller than a dwarf, tho you can fit down there. Or tho we hope.'

'Oh,' said Bingo uncertainly. 'I see. And the stuff about wee . . . ?'

'Never mind about that,' said Mori, clapping the soddit on the shoulder with one hand.[3] 'We need to find the door. Come! Gather our belongings! We trek up the western flanks of the Only Mountain at last!'

There were some half-hearted hurrahs at this, and the dwarfs trudged off to collect their things. 'Thorri,' said Bingo, as he hopped off the rock. 'Can I ask you something?'

'Mm?' replied the dwarf King.

'You're King, aren't you?'

Thorri sighed. 'I'm afraid tho,' he conceded.

'So why is it you allow Mori to boss you about? Couldn't you silence him with, I don't know, one royal command?'

'Oh,' said the dwarf. 'It doethn't *do* to be in the front

---

[3] Incidentally, and in case you're interested, *this* is the sound of one hand clapping.

line all the time. Ethpethially,' he added, 'if one ith King.'

A rook flapped its wings, landing on a boulder some way distant, regarding them with inkily intelligent eyes. It put its pointy head on one side.

They made good progress at first, but the way became harder and harder as it became incrementally less horizontal. Soon they were picking their way from boulder to boulder and resting every quarter of an hour. Matters were made considerably less agreeable by the necessity, which devolved upon two of the party at any given time, of dragging the sleeping wizard behind them on a blanket. 'I only wish I knew,' complained Bingo, '*why* it is we have to bring him along. He never seems to wake any more. He sleeps through everything. He's completely deaf. He's lost his beard. He's lost his mind, as far as I can see. And yet we're pulling him up a bloody mountain.'

None of the dwarfs enlightened him.

By late afternoon they had reached a little plateau littered with curiously shaped rocks that had clearly fallen from the nearly sheer slopes above. The group sat regaining their breath, and ate a little food. Thorri was poring over the map. 'It ought to be hereaboutth,' he announced. 'From what I can thee.'

'Look at those rooks!' said Bingo. 'Perching in

amongst the crannies and crags of the slope above us. They seem to be watching us.'

'Watching us, they are,' said Mori. 'The rooks of Strebor. They are a great and wise race.'

'Wise?' asked Bingo, whose experience of birds was limited to the robins and occasional off-course seagulls of Soddlesex. 'They're just birds, though, yes?'

Mori shook his head thrice, which caused his beard to shake five times. 'They are intelligent and cunning,' he said. 'They live long, and their memory lasts many generations. They play chess you know—'

'Chess?' asked Bingo, frankly incredulous.

'Oh yes. For what other reason is it the case, do you think, on a chessboard, that rooks are called rooks?'

'But rooks on a chessboard look like castles.'

Mori hissed at him in a shocked voice, 'Tush, soddit! *Never* call them that! It is forbidden! They are rooks – rooks is their name. Tut! Pshaw! You'll be calling the pawns *prawns* next.'

'I just find it rather hard to believe. Birds play chess? How do they play?'

'They, eh, nudge the pieces around the board with their beaks.'

'But how do they set the pieces up in the first place?'

'You're splitting hairs,' snapped the dwarf. 'The fact is that these rooks are not to be trifled with. They can speak, you know. They have a King.'

'What's he called?'

'Eh?'

'What's his *name*, this King of rooks?'

'Well,' said Mori, 'the rooks have long been friends of the dwarfs, and thus it so happens that I can tell you. His name is Caaw. Caaw the Mighty.'

'Funny-sounding name.'

'In fact,' Mori admitted, 'all their names are Caaw. They only have the one name between them. But they are very bright folk, these rooks, believe you me.'

Bingo craned his neck to look up at the rooks, wrinkling his eyes into crow's-feet. 'I'm not sure I'm convinced, Mori,' he said. 'I'm not so easily gulled.'

'Suit yourself,' said the dwarf.

They searched for the rest of the day but found no sign of the door. 'Is it like the door of the Coal Gate that led underneath the Minty Mountains? Is that it?' Bingo wondered. 'Should we wait until moonlight?'

'No, boyo,' said Mori. '*That* was an entrance into the great dwarfish halls of Dwarfhall, mighty Black Maria. This, look you, is more of a portal.'

'Portal?'

'Exhaust.'

'For?'

'Smoke.' The dwarf looked around him shiftily. 'And such.'

'So?'

'So it opens easily, see, but from the inside. We have to find it and try to, you know, prise it open from the *outside*.'

'It's a chimney, in other words,' clarified the soddit.

'Ay.'

'So you want me to crawl down a *chimney*, to come face to face with a terrible dragon from a *fireplace*?'

'Wasn't that made clear to you at the start?'

'Not,' said Bingo, 'really.'

'Ah. Well there you go, there you go.'

The party broke off its search to have supper, sitting around a small and rather mournful fire. Crows, rooks and ravens cawed and swooped overhead through the thickening light. To the west, the sun dropped red as a cherry tomato, painting the ragged stretches and bars of horizontal cloud through which it passed purple and orange and gold.

Shadows lengthened.

'Look at him there,' said Bingo, pointing to Gandef, who was sleeping peacefully wrapped in a blanket. 'He's been asleep now for, what? Four days? He looks so peaceful.'

The dwarfs mumbled their agreement, nodding.

'His cough seems to have cleared up,' the soddit said meditatively. 'Odd that. It used to be so severe, didn't it? Disabling, sometimes.'

'That stage is past,' said Gofur in a low voice.

'Eh?' said Bingo. 'What?'

'Nothing, nothing,' said Mori. 'Let's get some sleep.'

Bingo pressed them for a while, but they all clammed up. 'We clearly haven't come here for the gold,' he said. 'Or at least not just for the gold. I can believe that you'll happily take the gold if, when, you've done what you really came here for. Why won't you tell me what that is? What's the story?'

'Time for sleep now,' said Mori, as he wrapped his beard around himself.

They were woken at dawn by the cawing of the rooks, which seemed to Bingo's ears louder than ever. It was cold. Light shone on the lands to the north and south of the mountain making the fields and the plain bright, but the dwarfs and the soddit were in the mountain's huge shadow and it was dark all around. There were numerous little patches and puddles of ice in amongst the peak's shadow, reaching up the mountainside like dandruff. Bingo stood up and vigorously embraced himself a dozen times or so, repeatedly slapping both of his palms against their opposite shoulder-blades to try and warm up. Gofur tried to get a fire going, but there was rime on the twigs and the flame wouldn't take.

'So,' said Bingo, sourly. 'Another day of fruitless searching for this chimney pot, is it?'

'We'll find it,' replied Mori, 'if we only persevere.'

'I could be of some help there,' said a voice from behind them. 'Yo.'

It was an enormous thrush, yellow-white with pale freckles, half as tall as Bingo himself. It had settled on a boulder and was eyeing the group of them. Its eyes were pale, and its beak was of an almost pink hue. It was wearing a gold-thread jacket with ridiculously long sleeves that dangled, empty, from the front. The bird had ripped, or cut, two large holes in the armpits of this coat through which its wings poked out. A gold tag rattled on the creature's spindly left leg. A tiny cap was squeezed over the crown of its head. This headgear was too small for even that small head, and seemed to be pinching the top of the bird's skull into a nubbin.

'Good morrow, Master Bird,' said Mori, bowing low.

'Yo,' said the thrush. 'You havink a bit of bother?'

'Bother,' repeated the dwarf. 'Well, I suppose you could say that.'

'Visitors don't often come to this hood,' said the bird. It flapped one of its wings out, a strange and jerky gesture that ruffled the feathers at the end, and then folded the wing away again. It gave the impression of a one-sided St Vitus's dance. 'Hood – you know?' it added as it surveyed the non-comprehension on the faces of its audience. 'It's a word, it's short, innit, for "place-of-the-hooded-hawk", or somefink. Bird slank.'

'Slank?'

'Yeah,' said the bird, shuffling on its asterisk-shaped feet. 'Slank.'

'Oh,' said Gofur, realisation dawning. 'Slang.'

'Yeah.'

'Sir Thrush,' said Bingo, bowing civilly to the bird. 'We are delighted to meet you.'

'Ca-aaarcg!' shrieked the bird, flapping both its wings in a positive conniption of anxiety. 'Nah! Nah! Nah! I'm no *frush*, innit. I *am not* a frush. I'm a raving — a raving, I tell ya.'

'A raven,' said Bingo.

''Sright,' said the bird. 'Wired,' it added, emphatically if mysteriously.

'It's just that you look, at first glance, rather thrush-like,' said Bingo.

'Certainly *not*. Not a frush, me. I'm *down* with the ravens. Well, I'm up there with them, actually,' it said, its accent momentarily slipping up the social register. It tossed its beak towards the mountain peak. 'But down at the same time. If you follow.'

'Right,' said the soddit, who didn't. 'I must say, though, without meaning any offence, that you don't, exactly, look like a raven. Not like a conventional idea of a raven, at any rate.'

'What you mean?'

'Well — your colour, for instance.'

'Good raving colour, this,' said the bird. 'Innit.'

'Aren't ravens usually a bit blacker than — ?'

'Ca-aaarcg!' shrieked the bird again, becoming quite fiercely agitated. 'Yo! Ba-ka-ka-ka-ba! Wheeh! Polly want a cracker cocaine! Birdy bling-bling!' It flapped so fiercely it lost its footing, and skeetered around on top of the stone for several seconds before recovering its balance.

'Best not annoy it,' said Mori to Bingo, sotto voce, 'Sir Raven!' he declaimed loudly. 'Sir Raven!'

'Mornink, vicar,' said the bird, settling itself down again. 'I am a raven, you know.'

'Of course you are,' said the dwarf in a conciliatory voice. 'We all thought so when we saw you.'

'Really?' said the bird, looking pleased.

'Certainly. I said to my comrade, Gofur the dwarf here, I said, is that a mighty raven settling on to that rock? I do believe it is. Nobody would ever mistake it for a thrush, I said. Clearly.'

'Like the hhhat?' the bird inquired, aspirating the word prodigiously and leaning its head forward for everyone to see. It had the words 'Tomtit Hilfeather' written round it. 'It's wicked, innit.'

'It's very,' said Bingo uncertainly, 'tight. How did you fit it on?'

'Weren't easy,' said the raving. It plocked around in a little circle on the rock, three hundred and sixty degrees, and ended where it began. 'Ca-aaarcg!' it said, loud and sudden. '*I'm* a raven! *I'm* a raven! *I'm* a raven! See-eed*cake*. Ca-aaarcg!'

'Mighty bird,' said Mori, 'we accept your kind offer of help, for we have need of assistance. We have travelled far—'

'Cup o' tea!' shrieked the bird. 'Nice juicy snail! Booba-booba-booba!'

'. . . travelled far through many perilous adventures—'

'Re-*speck*led!' Re-*speck*led! Egg!'

'. . . far under mountains and through the forest of—'

'Tu-whit, tu-woo. She told me to squawk this way-yy! Ca-aaarcg!'

'We have *travelled far* . . .' Mori persevered, 'and now we are searching for—'

'Have a nut?' the raving suggested.

This, for some reason, seemed to take the wind out of Mori's sails. There was silence for the space of thirty seconds.

The raving put its head on one side. Then it put its head on the other side.

'What it *is*,' said Bingo, 'is a sort of chimney. Like a little doorway. Do you know it?'

'Cup o'tea?' said the bird, in a more considered voice. 'Blimey. Boiling-boiling. Two sugars and gold je-*well-*

ery. Did you ever notice that the clouds got no wings, yet they fly? Funny that.'

'But do you know where this chimney can be found?'

'Chimney,' said the bird. 'Ca-aaarcg!' it shrilled. 'I seen a horse fly, I seen a crane fly, I seen a bird fly, I seen a fly fly, but have I ever seen a chimney door-way?'

'That is indeed the question,' pressed the soddit.

'Lil-bow-wow-wow,' said the bird. 'Crac! And *they* diss *me*? I tell you, they call me just a trash-nest white flapper – but I'm *real*, I'm street, ca-aaarcg! I work with real raven flappers all the time. This is what my critics don't understand. Blimey.'

'Flapper,' said Bingo, trying to steer the conversation back to the hidden entrance, 'yes, well *clearly* we can all agree on that. That's plain as the noses on our faces. But about this chimney that we're looking for—'

'Listen to this,' said the bird, and began squawking tunelessly. 'Now *I'm* a raven, yes *I'm* a real raven, all you *other* non-ravens are just *im*itating so *won't* the real bling raven *please fly up*! *Please fly up*! *Please fly up*!' He accompanied this recital with jerky flaps of both wings together.

'Sir Bird?' said Bingo.

'What?'

'The chimney?' He pronounced these two words in his sternest voice.

The bird looked abashed. 'Chimney? Opens on to a shaft? Down into the mountink, is it?'

'Yes.'

'You know,' it said, becoming conspiratorial, and looking at them from underneath its right wing, 'that there's this, like, dragon down there? Don't you?'

'We'd been led to believe so,' said Mori.

'He's a scary old boy,' said the raven. 'That dragon. Just so's you know.'

'We'll take your comments under advisement,' said the dwarf. 'And if you could indicate the exact location of the doorway, we will be forever in your debt.'

'Sure,' said the bird. ' 'Sover there.' It leapt up and flapped into flight, oaring its way across the little plateau to the rock face. The dwarfs and Bingo hurried after it. At a place where the smooth mountain wall rose at an angle at forty-five degrees, the raven settled on the floor and tapped sharply at the rock, once, twice, thrice.[4]

A hatch, barely large enough for even a soddit to crawl through, swung in towards the mountain's innards an inch, and then swung slowly the other way, opening outwards on creaky stone hinges until it was

---

[4] This is the archaic mode of counting, of course, which has been largely superseded in modern times by one two three and so on. But in the olden days we all used to count this way: *once, twice, thrice, tvice, tgice, tmice, tjice, hethera, tethera, many*. This schema served all human counting purposes for many centuries.

gaping wide. A few strands of smoke drifted out of the hole.

'Thank you, thank you, Sir Thr, um, Raven,' cried the dwarfs.

'We owe you a great debt, Sir Bird,' said Mori. 'What is your name?'

'My real name, or my street name?' asked the bird.

'We dwarfs never forget a kindness done to us,' explained Mori. 'I ask your name that we may remember it, and repay your good deed at some point in the future.'

'You probably want my real name, then,' said the raving. It squawked uncomfortably a few times. 'Lovely bird! Beautiful plumage! Cup o'tea! It's,' it added, in lower and much more sane-sounding tones, 'Gavin Dembrell, of Mountain View Nest, the Glades – my mum and dad's nest, that,' it continued, its voice even lower. 'I'll be moving out, soon as I find my own crib, but when that happens they'll, you know, have the forwarding address.' It leapt away from the dwarfs, flapped and flew around their heads for a while. 'Bling-bling!' it shrieked. 'Ca-aaarcg! Have a nut!' And with that it flew away.

The dwarfs huddled around the smoky opening in the mountainside. Bingo elbowed them aside and peered down.

'You really expect me to go down there?' he said. 'There's smoke coming out of it. There's probably a fire at the bottom. It'd be suicide.'

'You'll be all right, boyo,' said Mori. 'It's not so slanted. Almost horizontal.'

'It's tiny,' said the soddit. 'And it's pretty slanted – it goes down at a sharp old angle.'

'Never mind about that for now, boyo,' said Mori. 'We need to have a little chat first. You and we, we and you, we need to have a little talk about what you're to do when you go down there.'

'Does this mean,' asked Bingo, 'that you're finally going to tell me why we're really here? No nonsense about gold?'

'Patience, boyo,' said Mori, clapping him on the shoulder. It was an unfortunate blow, catching the soddit slightly off balance. His foot slipped through the gap and over the lip. He threw his arms forward to try and grab the sides of the opening, but it was too late. The next thing he saw was a square of light receding rapidly, and he was plunged in darkness. And not metaphorically plunged, either: literally plunged. Oh yes.

Smug

Chapter Nine

INSIDE, IN FORM

෬෩

Down went Bingo, his arms above his head. He spoke. 'Aaaagghh!' he said. The shaft narrowed as it descended, and soon it was chafing violently at the soddit's belly and shoulders, and scraping his sore feet. 'Ow! ow! ow!' he said. 'Aaaagghh!' he added. Friction increased. There was the sound of cloth ripping. His descent slowed, painfully, as the skin around his middle felt as if it were being grated.

He had stopped.

'Dear me, dear me,' he said to himself, panting a little. It was utterly dark. He was wedged uncomfortably in the chimney with his arms up. The faint sound of dwarf hallooing was just audible somewhere far distant above him, but he couldn't make out the words. 'Dear me, dear me,' he said again.

He sucked his gut in and breathed out as far as he could. Then, turning a little blue (not that you could have seen his colour in the dark) he wriggled and wriggled. He shifted an inch downwards, then half an inch, and then with a jolt he began falling again. He said: 'Dear.' He did not say this, however, because the experience was especially dear to him. Rather he intended to say 'dear me' one more time, but was interrupted by his downward movement. Instead of saying 'dear me' he found himself saying 'dear aaaarrgh', which is – I hardly need to point this out to you – not the same thing at all.

And then he dropped out of the bottom of the shaft and, with a soft crash, fell into a great pile of old ashes and bits of burnt timber. Everything was instantly obscured by a cloud of grey, and Bingo started coughing. He thrashed about in the cool talcumy pile and staggered out, sore and startled but upright. He felt stone flags under his feet. Dust was in his eyes and he could see nothing, but he heard a deep, deeply rumbling voice, say:

'Gracious.'

Bingo stopped where he was. He tried wiping the ash out of his eyes, but the hands he was wiping with were also covered in ash, and his wiping proved a zero-sum game, smearing as much dust in as he smeared out. He was still trembling from his fall, and a deep terror was growing inside him. His stomach seemed to shrink to nothing and the roots of his hair shivered. He was acutely conscious that the deep rumbly voice almost certainly proceeded from the throat of Smug the

Dragon. Whilst his eyes were closed, he told himself that – since he lacked ocular evidence – it was still possible, just, that it was not a fearsome fire-blowing dragon that had spoken, but (say) somebody with a large chest and a bad cold. Although he knew the chances of this were rather small, he clung to the hope.

'Are you,' rumbled the voice, 'all right?'

Bingo put one hand in his waistcoat pocket, and closed his fingers around the Thing®. This gave him some small solace. He wondered whether, should Smug decide to blast him with a great wave of fire, he would have time to speak any reverse wish through the device. Probably not. But it was better having it than not.

Several blinks, and copious tears, were washing some of the ash out of his eyes. He opened them very cautiously.

There was Smug the Mighty in all his enormous and terrifying magnitude. He was stretched on his back over a large pile of gold and jewellery, his belly out and his long head resting on his own chest. His wings were spread to either side of his enormous body, and his hind legs were crossed one over the other. He was not naked; in fact, he wore several layers of tough cloth over his torso, a dark inner coat, and a brown-green fine-checked outer jacket. His snout was long and his head lumpy, but his dragon eyes glinted with a fierce intellect. In his left claw, Bingo saw, something was clutched – at first the soddit thought it a canoe, or something of similar proportions. As he blinked again, and as the dragon lifted the thing and placed it to his mouth, Bingo could see that it was a tobacco pipe, a pipe of gigantic proportions. The dragon took two deep puffs, and laid the pipe at his side again.

'Dra,' said Bingo. 'Drag. Dra. Dragon.'

He stumbled back, but there was nowhere to hide, and nowhere to go. The beast's eyes were fixed upon him.

Bingo looked from left to right with a degree of desperation. The floor of the creature's lair was piled high with gold, and the walls were stacked with enormous and multitudinous books – volumes of ancient lore bound in various leathers. To the right were a number of bottles, with labels that read 'wyrmwine' and 'Dragon's Friend'. Torches flickered behind, draping an intermittent red light over everything.

'Good morning,' said the dragon.

'Good,' said Bingo. Then his tongue seemed to seize up. 'Momomomo,' he added.

'I did not realise,' said Smug, 'that I had an appointment. Pull up a chair, do – that one, yes – just move those papers off it. Put them anywhere.'

Bingo looked around stupidly.

'I'd offer you tea,' said Smug. 'But I'm sorry to say I ran out of tea some forty years ago.'

'That's quite all right, quite all right,' said the soddit. He saw the chair to which the dragon had gestured, and pulled a stack of leathern parchments from its seat. With a little hop he climbed on to the chair. Somewhere in his brain he was thinking, half consciously, *If I'm sitting on his furniture perhaps he'll think twice about burning me to death. If he values his own furniture, that is.* He was still clutching the Thing® in his right hand.

'And what can I do for you?' said Smug.

'I—' said Bingo. He thought for a moment. But he had no idea what to say.

'You'll have to remind me of your name,' the creature rumbled.

'Bingo Grabbings,' said Bingo, without thinking. As soon as he said it, he wondered if he had made a terrible mistake. Giving one's true name to magical creatures, such as dragons, is not advisable. But it was too late now.

'So,' mused the creature. 'So, Bingo Grabbings, is it? At first glance, that would be a burglar's name, now, wouldn't it?'

'I come from a family of respectable gentlehobblds!' squeaked Bingo.

'Of course you do,' said the dragon, 'since the etymological root of *burglar* and *burgher*, or *bourgeois* if you prefer, is to be found in the same word – from the old Brackish **bruh* or **burh*, you know. Being a robber and being respectable are, philologically speaking, more or less the same thing.'

Bingo had got his hands more or less clean of ash now by dint of rubbing them together, and was able to wipe his face more effectively clear. He hadn't really been listening to this. 'Fascinating,' he said nervously.

'But,' the dragon continued, 'I'd say that Bingo Grabbings is a west-country name. Am I right? There's a Grabesend, isn't there, on the coast up that way? I'd hazard – this is mere conjecture, of course, please don't note this down – I'd *conjecture* a root for names like bingo is from **beo-wing*, "he who flies from bees". Are you afraid of bees, Mr Grabbings? No? They do have a nasty sting, don't they? It is probably a good idea to get out of their way.' He chuckled at this, and clacked the fearsome claws of his empty right hand together, making a dry, drumbeat noise, *cloc, cloc, cloc*. 'As for Grabbings—' the dragon said.

'Please don't kill me!' shrieked Bingo, unable to contain himself. He fell from the chair on to his knees. 'I'm sorry! Sorry! I'm sorry I fell down your chimney! It was their idea! It wasn't my idea!'

'Dear me, dear me,' rumbled the dragon, not unamused. 'Do calm down, little chap. Really. Kill you? Why should I want to kill you?'

'We've travelled all this way, hundreds of leagues,'

the soddit burbled, 'to slay you and steal your gold, and I'm sorry I'm sorry I'm sorry.' He sucked in a shuddering breath, and was only prevented from more unfortunate disclosures by the fact that he chanced to inhale a lungful of the fine ash that was still drifting around the lair, provoking a short soddit coughing fit.

'Dear me,' said Smug, when the coughing had stopped. He took another few pulls on his pipe. 'This is a serious development. I'm sorry to hear it. Might I ask *why* you have come all this way to slay me?'

Bingo sat back on his knees. 'I'm not sure,' he said. 'I assume – I don't know. I assume you've done some great wrong to their people?'

'And *they* are . . . ?'

But Bingo was, finally, learning some circumspection. He had already given far too much away. 'My travelling companions,' he said. 'I'm sorry, but I didn't realise that one needed a specific reason for slaying dragons. Isn't that – slaying dragons, I mean – just something people do?'

'My life would be terribly uncomfortable,' said Smug, 'if that were so. Dear me. This is a very disagreeable development. I'm trying to think,' he added, 'whom I may have offended. I really can't think of anybody.'

Bingo was still terrifically nervous, which may have been why he blurted: 'The Lakesiders have seen no customers for seventy years – you've scared their customers away.'

'Dear me,' said the dragon, sounding genuinely contrite. 'Have I? How dreadful. It really wasn't intentional. I don't see, though – to be fair – that it's *exactly* my fault if people find me scary. I don't go out of my way to be scary.' He puffed on his pipe for a while.

The conversation was not going the way Bingo had anticipated at all. 'I am sorry,' he said, 'if I startled you, falling into your fireplace like that. And I'm sorry about – you know, the talk of slaying you.'

'Perhaps,' said Smug, 'if you were to tell me the identity of your travelling companions, I might be able to remember if I had done them any wrong. Are they, perhaps, hobblds, such as yourself?'

'Mighty Smug!' said Bingo, scurrying behind the chair and peering out. 'Pardon me! I have said too much already! If my friends knew what I have revealed they would be sorely angry with me.'

'Oh well, oh well,' said the creature in a mournful voice. 'Of course, if you'd rather not say, I understand perfectly.'

There was silence in the lair for a while.

'I do apologise,' grumbled the dragon, 'about the lack of tea.' He hoomed and hummed for a while. 'Interesting word, tea,' he said, as if talking to himself. 'Derived, I'd argue, from *tyr*, a variant of *þyrs*, the old Eastron word for *giant*. Because it is a drink that makes one feel like a giant.' He hoomed some more. 'Wonderful drink,' he added.

It was starting to dawn on Bingo, despite his fright, and despite the various aches he had sustained coming down the chimney, that Smug was wounded in his feelings. The soddit had not expected that. Rage, fire, destruction, yes. Cunning and guile, yes. But a hurt look in the eye and some defensive puffs on a pipe, not at all.

'Sir Smug,' the soddit said cautiously. 'I fear I have offended you.'

'Not at all,' murmured the dragon. 'Don't mention it. Only, you see, it is a *little* disconcerting to discover that a group of people have travelled such a long way to kill one.'

'Surely you have many enemies,' said Bingo. 'I mean,' he added hurriedly, anxious that his words had come over as merely insulting, 'one so, eh, magnificent and terrible as you.'

'Enemies?' said the dragon. 'I don't believe so. Let me have another think. No, no. I had a bit of a ding-dong with Blaze the Dragon from the Ice-Plain of Gungadin – over, it was, the correct derivation of the term *wodwo*. But that was settled amicably. Yes, amicably. He's a good old worm, that one. Modest, too.'

He shuffled on his bed of gold, and scratched his

stomach with the claws of his right foreleg. 'Hmm,' he said.

'I must say, you don't seem, sir,' said Bingo in a tiny voice, 'you don't seem very *smug*, if you see what I mean.'

'What? What's that? No, you're quite right, you're quite right. Smug is not what my friends call me, you know. Although it is, philologically speaking, quite an interesting word.'

'Really?' said Bingo weakly.

'Certainly. It's a west-land variant of the east-land root-word *Smýk*, which has, in fact, come down into modern language via another branch of the linguistic tree, as *Smoke*. The vowel shift, you see. Smoke is a perfectly descriptive name for a dragon.' He lifted his enormous pipe in his left claw and puffed on the stem for a while. Billowing quantities of smoke poured from between his teeth.

'Is that then your name, sir? Smoke the Dragon?'

'No, no, Smoke is what *people* used to call me. People aren't very original with their names for dragons. Hmm. They tend to name dragons, in man-speech, on a merely literal level: Smoke, Flame, Puff, things like that.' He shook his great head. 'No, that's not the name I call myself.'

'So what is the name you call yourself, mighty sir?'

'Ah. When I was a young dragon, fighting and

rushing around, I was called Rashbold. But it's been an age and an age since anybody's called me that. An age and an age since I've been rash, although I hope I'm still capable of a little boldness.' He chuckled, and took another draw on his pipe. 'It sounds as if I'll need a little boldness, indeed, if your friends are genuine in their intentions to slay me.'

'I'm sorry for my friends' intentions,' said Bingo.

'Well, well,' said Smug. 'I'll try not to get too huffy. A dragon's huff is, you see, rather more destructive and fiery than a regular person's.' He chuckled at this, as if he had made a joke. 'There's a great deal of mis-conception about dragons, you know,' he added mildly. 'A great deal. People tend only to see the smoky and the fiery side of dragons. They don't see the *creative* side at all.'

'The creative side?' said Bingo, interested.

'Oh yes. I hate to boast – that goes against the grain, boasting – but it can't be denied that dragons made all this.' He gestured with his right claw, and his leathern wings rustled beneath him.

'This room?' said Bingo. 'These books?'

'What? What? No, no. Well, yes, strictly speaking. But I meant the world as a whole. Everything.'

'Dragons,' said Bingo, uncertain he had heard cor-rectly, 'created the world?'

'Well,' said Smug, as if embarrassed, 'yes. Brought it

to life, breathed fire and smoke into it. That's what caused the sun to shine, what filled the upper sky. That's why the sky's blue, it's smoke – high up, I mean, *aither*, hot and dry. The lower air isn't blue, it's clear, of course. And,' he added, 'that's why the mountains and the hills are hollow, because dragon breath puffed them up into the landscape, like glass-blowing. But I don't mean to brag. Dragons can't take all the credit.'

'No?'

'No, no. Some of the houses are, you know, made by later people. But anyway, anyway. I don't mean to bore you. It's been a pleasure speaking to you.'

Bingo came out from behind the chair. 'I can't believe, sir,' he said, abashed, 'that it has truly been a pleasure.'

'Well – perhaps pleasure isn't the right word,' conceded Smug. 'Perhaps not pleasure, exactly. But it has been edifying. Edifying. I'm sorry I have to draw it to an end. But I think I'd better *pop*, you know, *pop* down to Lakeside. There's clearly been a misunderstanding between us, between the Lakesiders and myself. I'd better flap down there and try and sort it out. Drive away their trade? Nothing could be further from my thoughts. I'll have a chat with them, and I'm sure we can arrange some kind of compromise. Dear me, dear me, what an unfortunate situation. What a disagreeable situation. Well, Mr Grabbings,' Smug continued, stirring on his pile, 'goodbye. I'll show you the main gate – I don't suppose you'll fit back up that chimney.'

'No, sir,' said Bingo. 'Yes, sir.'

It was clear that the dragon had finished talking. He reared up from his pile, and stood for a moment on his hind legs with his huge wings unfolding behind him, as tall as any of his tall kin. The edges of his wings were lined with sharp claws, and the aerodynamic whole was perfectly designed – a tool for flying, but a tool keen and sharp for cutting the air. Bingo felt fear return to his gut, and he staggered against the wall. The dragon fell forward, and stalked into a corridor just high-ceilinged enough for him to stalk in, although it seemed a mighty cavern to the soddit as he scurried along at the creature's heels. With earth-jarring strides the beast covered the whole length of the corridor in minutes. Bingo had to run to keep up, passing many side rooms and archways leading through to other lairs, rooms, caverns, although the soddit had no time to look in. He was running too rapidly for that.

'Sir Dragon!' he gasped.' You go too fast!'

'Oh,' said Smug, turning his long face over his shoulder. 'I do apologise. Don't feel you have to run at my speed. I'll leave the door open for you.' And with that he leapt forward like a tiger, a mighty leap, landing in the air outside the mountain and spreading his wings.

Bingo sat on the floor until he had recovered his breath. Then he got up and trotted down the remainder of the great corridor. The massive front doorway, tall as twenty soddits, grew as he ran towards it. He was almost outside again in the clean air but, at the last minute, his eyes were distracted by something glittering, something precious-looking, sitting on the floor next to the door: an enormous gem. Other precious flotsam and jetsam was scattered about, pieces of gold and jewel-encrusted cups, but it was this huge diamond, as large as Bingo's fist, that caught his eye.[1] Eager as he was to get outside the mountain, he could not pass by so magnificent a gem. As he bent over it he thought he discerned a gleam shining out of the heart of the jewel. He cradled it in both his hands and lifted it before his face.

'Woof,' said the jewel.

'You are fairer than any jewel I have ever seen,' said Bingo. 'I shall . . . borrow you. Perhaps Smug won't mind. What do you think?'

'Wooah! Wooah!' said the stone.

But Bingo ignored its warning and slipped the great jewel into his coat pocket, where it settled with a gentle 'woof'.

---

[1] The earlier story of this gem is told in the famous tale *A Diamond As Big As The Fist*.

This, although he did not realise it at the time, was the famous, enchanted Barkingstone, a gem with a long and special history. It was as valuable a gemstone as existed in Upper Middle Earth, and a very great find for a burglar to make.

Bingo trotted out of the main entrance to the caves of Strebor with a sudden gaiety in his heart. He had survived his fall down the chimney, had come away from his interview with the dragon with his life intact, and to boot had discovered a gem of fabulous wealth and beauty. All in all, he told himself, it had not been a bad day. The sunlight prickled on the fast-flowing stream that led out between the two arms of the mountain, and the land to the south looked yellow-brown, fresh and warm. The sun was still climbing, and Bingo realised that he had spent only a few hours inside the mountain.

It took him more than a few hours, however, to make his way back to the dwarfs. First he had to clamber over a spur of the mountain, and down into the valley on the other side. Then he had to circle the flank of Strebor until he recognised the place where the party had climbed up two days before. Then he had to retrace that arduous and difficult climb.

But when he hauled his puffing body on to the plateau, as the sun sank red in the west, the dwarfs were delighted to see him. 'Bingo!' cried Mori. 'You're alive!'

They clustered around him.

'How glad we are, see, that you're all right, boyo,' said Mori embracing him. 'We'd almost given up on you.'

'We were debating what to do next,' said Gofur.

'We weren't at all sure *what* to do,' said On.

'My dear friends,' said Bingo. After he had refreshed himself with some water and a bread roll, whilst the dwarfs lit a fire, he settled himself and told them the sequence of his adventures – omitting only the part about finding the Barkingstone. But instead of becoming more and more congratulatory as he proceeded, the dwarfs became more and more dismayed.

'You told him,' said Mori severely, '*what*?'

'You said we were here *to kill him*?' said a horrified Failin.

'Well, yes,' said Bingo, faltering. 'That is why we're here, isn't it? I understand that to be the purpose of our quest.'

Five dwarf faces stared at him aghast.

'I know you *said* it was gold,' Bingo told them, becoming a little annoyed himself. 'I mean, I know you said that. But clearly that wasn't it. Or wasn't the whole story. There is lots of gold down there, by the way,' he added. 'Just lying around. Seems a shame to leave it.'

'You idiot,' exploded Mori. 'Id! i! ot!'

'I beg your pardon?'

'You told the dragon we were going *to kill it*? *Why* did you tell it that?'

'I was in a tight spot,' said Bingo, growing heated.

'And it flew off towards Lakeside?'

'Yes.'

The dwarfs looked to the south. In the darkening sky, nothing could be seen except a series of shadowed vaguenesses in the landscape and the emerging stars over the horizon.

'At least,' said Mori, with hope in his voice, 'you told him you had travelled with a troop of dwarfs?'

'No,' said Bingo proudly. 'I managed to stop myself before I blurted that out.'

The dwarfs stared at him. It was actually possible to see their mouths, so far had their jaws dropped.

'Look—' Bingo began.

'Idiot! Idiot – idiot – idiot – sheep-for-brains,' exclaimed Mori. 'You *should have told him* we were dwarfs. He'd have *never* believed we were coming to kill him if he'd known we were dwarfs.'

'Wouldn't he? Why not?' Bingo looked from face to face. 'Why wouldn't he? I don't understand,' he said.

'Oh,' said Mori, 'that's *perfectly* plain.'

'Well,' said Bingo, his soddit anger roused, 'don't you

think you should explain it to me? Don't you think I've been blundering about in the dark for long enough? Maybe you should have told me at the beginning, instead of spinning these yarns about gold and gold and gold. Eh?'

Mori, in the firelight, looked at the ground. 'If we'd told you,' he said, 'you'd never have come.'

'I *wish* I'd never come!' Bingo declared.

'It's not the kind of thing a dwarf, or a wizard, can just – tell,' said Mori, after a while. 'It's private. It's not something we'd want the rest of the world to find out about. We thought, see, that we'd wait a while, see how you shaped up. We always planned to tell you sooner or later,' he added.

The other dwarfs nodded.

'Tell me what?' Bingo demanded. 'Tell me what? *Why* have we come all this way, to this mountain, past all these dangers? Eh, Mori? What *was* the reason?'

'The reason,' said Mori. Then he stopped. He turned his gaze to the sleeping figure of the wizard. The whole party looked at Gandef. '*There's* the reason,' said Gofur. 'He's why we came.'

Bingo stared at the wizard.

There was a silence for a several minutes.

'Things are not always as they first appear,' said Mori in a low voice.

'I thought he came along as a guide, as a sort of

protector,' said Bingo. 'Protecting us. Like he did with the Gobblins. Or the wolves. But you're saying it was actually the other way around. We were bringing him, not him bringing us?'

'Of course,' said Mori. 'Couldn't you read the clues?'

'What clues? What – what is happening to Gandef?'

'He's turning,' said Mori in a low voice, 'into a dragon, look you.'

Bingo digested this for a while. 'I don't understand.'

'Where did you think dragons came from?' Failin asked.

'I'd never really thought about it,' said Bingo. 'I assumed that a mummy dragon and a daddy dragon got together and, I don't know, laid an egg.'

'The processes of life are much richer than you realise, la, and much more closely interconnected,' said Mori. 'You know an insect egg becomes a grub, and a grub becomes a caterpillar, and a caterpillar a moth. You know this is how nature works. If it is so complex, so interconnected, at the level of moths, how much more so for the larger winged creatures?'

'You wanted me to read the clues?' said Bingo. 'That wizards are the larval form of dragons? How on earth was I supposed to deduce that? Why couldn't you just *tell* me? I can't even think what the clues might have been that I was supposed to read.'

'Well,' said Mori. 'There was the smoking.'

'Plenty of people smoke,' Bingo pointed out. 'Not just wizards or dragons.'

'There was the deafness.'

'Deafness?'

'He was losing the use of his ears. Dragons don't have ears – they hear through the membranes of their wings. Didn't you know that?'

'And Gandef has *wings*, does he?' said Bingo snidely, to cover his ignorance.

'They're growing now. Whilst he sleeps.'

Everybody looked at the supine wizard again.

'I still don't see,' insisted Bingo, 'how I was supposed to guess.'

'There's the magic. Wizards and dragons are the two great magic creatures in the world. Didn't you know *that*? There was the fire.'

'The fire?'

'The time Gandef breathed out fire and burnt those wolves. Didn't you think that was a strange thing?'

'I assumed it was a spell,' Bingo said.

'Then when his *beard* came off, we thought that was the giveaway,' said Gofur. 'You've never seen a dragon with a beard, have you? Dragons don't have beards.'

'This,' said Bingo, 'is a lot to take in.'

He sat for a while, listening to the sounds of the fire. It was as if the long red fingers of flame were cracking their knuckles.

'So we were in fact bringing Gandef to Smug for him to – what? Complete his transformation?'

The dwarfs nodded in the darkness.

'So why were *you* doing it? Why does it matter to a load of dwarfs what happens to one old wizard?'

'Perhaps,' said Mori, 'you'd like me to enumerate the many points of similarity between dwarfs and wizards – not counting, of course, the difference in sizes. There's, one, the beards—'

'You mean,' said Bingo, understanding striking him suddenly, 'that dwarfs are an *earlier form* of wizards? Grubs to caterpillars to moths, you said. Dwarfs turn into wizards?'

'Well, if they live long enough,' said Mori. 'As you've seen, the world is a harsh environment for us. But yes. Dwarfs are quickened in the rocks, and we emerge much as you see us, only smaller, in caves and caverns. We grow slowly, and many of us perish, but eventually some small number change, metamorphose, shoot up in height and acquire our adult magic, and then we are wizards. A wizard's life is long, and not without peril, and few survive as long as Gandef here – *Mithrandwarf*, to give him his proper name. But, for those few, eventually, the second great transformation begins. He senses it, last year. We brought him here to Smug for the change to be completed, and so that he will have a mentor when he emerges. *You* were supposed to slip down the chimney, and get Smug to open the front door. That's *all.*'

'But,' said Gofur sourly, 'you have instead sent Smug down to Lakeside to pick a quarrel with the men who live there. And even if he has survived that encounter, he now thinks we have come to kill him! A pretty pickle.'

'Pickle,' murmured the other dwarfs in sorrowful agreement. 'Pretty. Hmm, hmm, hmm.'

All eyes turned south again, trying to pick out the shapes of the lake and the town in the increasing darkness.

Lard the Bowman

Chapter Ten

FIE! AND WATER

ᏬᎧᎧᎧᎧᎩ

And so we must, if you desire to know what happened between Mighty Smug and the marketing men of Lakeside, move our imaginary point of view southwards to the slow waters of Lake Escargot. For that was the direction in which the dragon wended.

Smug flew with easy, lolloping strokes of his broad wings through the midday sunshine. In a brief time he was circling above Lakeside, blowing great gusts of wind up and down the narrow wooden streets with his leathern[1] wings. The Lakesiders scurried to and fro crying out, variously,' The dragon is come! Woe! Woe! Woe!', and, 'Ichabod and alas, the glory has departed from Lakeside!', and, 'Who'll buy my lovely apples, *lurvely* apples? Ten a penny, come buy.'

'Now,' boomed Smug from the air, his voice sounding like a hundred thunderstorms.[2] 'Let's not get

[1] I checked with the copy-editor whether this shouldn't be 'leather', but she insisted that the extra 'n' makes all the difference.
[2] Well, technically it sounded like ninety-eight point three thunderstorms. But for the sake of the metre I rounded up.

carried away down there! I have only come to talk!'

Lard the Bowman stood, his belly proud. He was the only stationary person in the milling throng, his strong longbow in his hand. 'Dragon!' he called up, his voice almost lost in the wind made by the beast's wings (although, luckily, dragonic hearing is unusually acute). 'Fie Dragon! Beware!'

'Now, now,' said Smug. 'I mean no harm. Can we not *simply* talk, dragano-a-mano? Just thee and me?'

'I have my bow!' called Lard, brandishing it above his head.[3] 'And I'm not afraid to use it! Be warned!'

'Eeek!' called the crowd. 'Alas! Disaster! The dragon is come!'

'Apples, apples!' called the deaf appleseller.

Smug circled again. 'I'm going to land on that bridge,' he said, pointing down with one of his mighty claws. 'Then we'll be able to chat. I don't suppose,' he added, as if in afterthought, 'that you've any *tea*, have you?'

'Woe, woe, woe!' called the people of Lakeside.

Smug curled the ends of his wings in and beat in slightly circular motions, creating a down-draught that enabled him to land. People scattered beneath him as he settled on to the town's main bridge. Lard ap-

---

[3] 'Brandishing' in Lakeside is a slightly different process from conventional heroic brandishing (which is to say, 'shaking'), and involves instead a logo and a series of careful product placements.

proached the great beast, running with his head down in the accepted human manner (if there is a draught from above). The timbers of the bridge creaked under the creature's weight.

'Ahh!' said Smug, as he folded away his wings and reached to the breast pocket from which his enormous pipe protruded. 'That's better. I'm not as fit as I used to be, you know. I used to go for a constitutional, a quick flap around the mountain, after every meal. But I've been neglecting my exercises latterly. Dear me! So you must be Lard? Delighted to meet you. Delighted.'

'Fearsome worm,' shouted Lard, brandishing his weapon again. 'Begone back to your hole of vileness! Fie!'

'Well,' said the dragon, a little nonplussed. 'Eh. Quite. Yes, I must say, you've done a *lovely* job with the lake town here. A lovely job. Is that pine cladding on the oak beams of the main hall? Lovely, lovely.'

'Creature of darkness!' yelled Lard. 'Spawn of Malcorm! Ye shall not pass!'

'I see,' said Smug, unable to keep a certain crushed tone out of his voice. 'Ah well. It's nice to see you. I thought I'd pop down —'

'Grrrr!' said Lard.

'— pop down,' said Smug, in a more subdued voice as he tamped tobacco into the tub-sized bowl of his pipe. 'See if we can't sort out this little difficulty.'

The beams that held the bridge groaned again under the great weight of Smug.

'I understand,' said Smug, puffing on the stem of his giant pipe, 'that some of your customers have been a bit – shall we say? – shy, since my arrival in the Only Mountain . . .'

'Fie! Bah!' called Lard, fitting an arrow to his bow. 'Grr! Evil wyrm! Fie!'

'. . . I really *must* assure you I had *no* idea. It's a most unfortunate situation. I feel obliged to try and find a solution, and restore your trade. Now, I was wondering if—'

Lard lifted his bow, and aimed his arrow.

But the supporting beams beneath Smug could take the weight no longer. With a series of splintering crashes, they gave way, tipping the whole fifty-yard stretch of bridge into the water. With a grumbling 'oh, my' the dragon toppled backwards and disappeared into the lake with an apocalyptic splash.

Spray leapt a hundred feet in the air. Waves surged and rose between the timber legs on which Lakeside stood clear of the water, the swell pressing against the underside of the town and water squeezing through the planks to flood up into many streets and houses. When the first waves had subsided, a wreath of moisture lingered in the air, scattering myriad tiny rainbow sparks as the bright sun shone through.

It took the people of Lakeside many moments before their collective relief found expression in a shout of joy. 'Hurrah!' they cried. 'Lard has slain the dreadful beast!' 'The dragon is no more!' 'Apples! Apples! Only slightly bruised!' and, 'All hail Lard the Deliverer! Lakeside is saved!'

Lard stood at the extreme edge of the wrecked bridge and stared out over the water. The waves were settling now, the surface resuming its snail-like placidity, and closing over the sunken body of the dragon. He stood motionless for a long while, half expecting the creature to rear up from the lake in fire and tempest. But nothing broke the surface of the waters. It began to dawn on Lard that Smug was truly dead. 'For is not a dragon,' he said, more to himself than anybody, 'a creature of fire? Is it not truly said, to kill a dragon, drown it?' He turned to his people. 'The waters have swallowed the beast! The curse has been taken from Lakeside!'

'Hurrah!' they cried.

A dozen strong men swarmed around their mayor, and grasped him to carry him, shoulder-high, amongst the rejoicing people. They abandoned this ambitious plan after half a minute of grunting and heaving, and instead Lard consented to walk amongst the throng. 'If only I were still a bard,' he said to himself. 'What a lay I would compose about this adventure!' And, thinking of lays, he passed about the town.

The celebrations lasted for the rest of the day and into the night. The sun set in gaudy red splendour, and the waxing moon shone clear.[4] Torches gleamed over the still waters. Everybody sang, everybody danced. Troths were plighted, and in some cases (in dark doorways and behind packing cases) more than plighted. Healths were toasted, toast was consumed, consumption cured, and cured ham taken from the storerooms to be put on the toast. It was a celebration to remember.

The bridge that linked Lakeside to the shore had been destroyed, but the Lakesiders went to and fro in their numerous boats. Nobody was surprised, therefore, when a number of boats pulled up at one of the landing berths, and two dozen tall figures jumped out. Indeed, there was hardly anybody still conscious and adequately compos mentis to be surprised.

'Where's the lord of this town?' the leading figure called. 'Take us to the lord of this place!'

These newcomers moved, swiftly but gracefully, up and down the streets of the town, before meeting again by their boats. 'Dear me,' said one. 'They all seem to be asleep.'

'A little over-indulgence, I fear,' said a second.

'I asked one of them for directions,' said a third, 'and

---

[4] 'Waxing': becoming more like wax – which is to say, acquiring a yellow hue and building into a plug-like ball.

he replied in Gobblin-talk! All ugly gutturals and plosives! I assumed the Gobblins had already arrived, and had taken over the town. But then I realised that this chap wasn't actually replying to me at all. He was just throwing up.'

'How distasteful,' said a fourth.

'Well,' said the first, 'it seems they're all drunk. This makes our job easier, I suppose. Elstree, go and fetch the rest of the army. We'll rebuild the bridge in the morning, link the town and the water's edge again. But until then, let's just consolidate what we have.'

'Righto,' said the figure who had been addressed as Elstree. He hopped back down into one of the boats, his cloak flapping apart as he dropped to reveal a glint of elvish armour beneath.

By morning, Lakeside was under new management. The elves had dragged or pushed the sotted inhabitants into a central hall and locked the gates. Then they quartered their men – several hundred, dressed in the most elegant armour – in the best rooms of the place. Finally the elves strapped together a long line of Lakeside rowing boats and barges to make a pontoon bridge to the shore.

This was finished before breakfast. As the elves munched their delicate weybread and sipped their gray tea, the original inhabitants of Lakeside were beginning to regain their now battered and aching consciousnesses. Elsqare gave orders that the lord of the town be brought to him, and twenty minutes later Lard himself was standing in front of the elf.

'Good morning,' said Elsqare. 'How are you today?'

'What?' said Lard forcefully, with a cross expression.

'Are you well?'

'What?' He blinked, glowered, looked around. 'What's going on?'

'I am Lord Elsqare, the elf,' explained Lord Elsqare the elf. 'At the moment, and much to my chagrin, I find myself at the head of a mighty army. We don't mean to inconvenience you, you understand, but my men must be billeted somewhere.'

'What?' said Lard a third time. 'Who are you?'

'Give the chap some tea,' said Elsqare.

'You've invaded!' said Lard suddenly. 'You've invaded Lakeside!'

'Not in the least. Our presence here is only temporary, I assure you,' said the elf lord. 'Allow me to explain. We understand that a party of stout dwarfs has travelled here, on their way to the Only Mountain. We understand that they had some business to settle with the dragon who lives there . . .'

'Smug!' blurted Lard. 'I killed him!'

There was an elegantly shocked silence amongst the elves at this news.

'Really?' Elsqare asked eventually.

'Indeed, he came yesterday to threaten Lakeside,' said Lard, hoisting his belly up and standing prouder. 'I confronted him with my trusty bow – I am a bowman, you know. He settled upon the bridge. It collapsed, and he drowned in the lake.'

'My, my,' said Elsqare. 'How interesting. So Smug the Mighty is dead?'

'Yes,' said Lard. 'And did you say something about tea?' He waddled over and sat himself beside the elf lord. 'And some breakfast, perhaps?'

Elsqare motioned to his followers to provide the necessary. 'Well,' said the elf, 'if, truly, the dragon is dead that places a very different complexion upon events. Are you sure he has perished?'

'Certainly,' said Lard, through a mouthful of crumpet. This is not an easy word to say when one's mouth is full of food, but Lard had a bold stab at the pronunciation anyway.

'Have you recovered his corpse?'

'No,' said Lard, with a slight hesitation.

'If he's in the lake, then surely it would be an easy matter to drag the water for his body. Don't you think? To be on the safe side?'

At this, one of Elsqare's followers burst into song.

> *When they drag in the Dragon*
> *And bring back the corpse of a monster so monstrous,*

And lay it out dead on a pontoon so ponstrous
Why then we'll be sure he really has gone.

Elsqare silenced his minion with a severe look. 'Mr –
Lard is it? Lord? – are you, Lard?'

'Mayor,' said Lard.

'Mayor, excellent. Believe me, the elves have no
interest in *invading*, as you put it, your delightful lakeside town. We are here as your allies, not your enemies.'

'Yet you have locked all my people in the great
central hall.'

'A precaution,' said Elsqare, making a dismissive
gesture with one hand in the air. 'When they're properly sobered, and properly apprised of the situation,
then they'll be let out.'

'Apprised of what situation?' asked Lard, his mouth
sagging open to reveal half-mushed scone.

'So you *don't* know? Dear me. Well, I'm afraid I come
as the bearer of bad news.'

'Bad news?'

'Yes. You see, an enormous Gobblin army has assembled.'

'Gobblins?' repeated Lard, with a catch in his throat.

'I'm afraid so. A simply enormous army. They've
recruited Gobblins from the whole length of the
mountains. And they're a day's march, at most, from
here.'

'Here? Why should Gobblins want to come here?'

'The dwarfs I mentioned. It seems they made rather a *mess* when they went through the Minty Mountains. They stirred up a tremendous fuss. And – I see no reason why you shouldn't be told this – there's something else. Amongst the Gobblins is a creature not Gobblin-shaped: something else, a philosopher of doleful countenance called Sollum. From his lips the Gobblins have learned that an artefact of enormous power and evil – one of the Things® created by the Evil Sharon – is in the possession of these dwarfs. Word of this has spread all over the western lands. The Gobblins have come for revenge, for destruction, for the gold, but most of all they have come to seize the Thing®. Who knows what terror they might wreak, if they can but obtain it! It is time for all the free peoples of Upper Middle Earth to unite and face this dire threat!'

'Blimey,' said Lard.

Through that same night, and into the early hours of that same morning, the dwarfs on the mountainside kept a sombre vigil, watching the lands and the skies to the south, the direction of Lakeside. They were waiting for Smug's return, or for some news of him. 'If there were some big fight,' Bingo said, 'wouldn't we see it? Flame and fireworks?'

'Maybe,' said Mori sulkily. 'Maybe not.'

'What shall we do?' Bingo asked.

'Don't think you're back in our good books so quickly,' snapped the dwarf, and turned his shoulder to the soddit. It was a warm shoulder, literally speaking, because it had been close to the fire; but in metaphoric terms it was a cold shoulder. So, you could say, it was simultaneously a warm and a cold shoulder, which sounds paradoxical I know, but isn't really when you think about it.

'All your fault,' mumbled On.

'A fine pickle you've got us into,' grumbled Gofur.

'Mavis!' gasped Failin. But he was asleep, and his comment had no particular relevance to the situation in hand.

Bingo stared sorrowfully into the fire, watching the glowing logs and the wriggling, writhing, belly-dancing flames that leapt up from them.

'Don't be too dithcouraged,' said Thorri, settling next to him. 'You weren't to know.'

'I feel something dreadful has happened,' said the soddit. His sense of awkwardness and gloom was compounded by the fact that he had still not yet told anybody of the Barkingstone, which lay like a guilty secret in his coat pocket.

'Thomething dreadful,' agreed Thorri. 'I thenthe that too. But we can't help that. It'th a thame we didn't get a chanthe to chat with Thmug before he hurried away, but there you go.'

'What shall we do now?'

'The front door'th open, you thay?'

'Yes,' said Bingo. 'The dragon left it open after he left.'

'Well, when it'th light again, we'll carry Gandef into the mountain. Even if Thmug'th not there to help, we can at leath make the old feller comfortable.'

Bingo looked, for the hundredth time, at the wrapped-up sleeping figure of the beardless wizard. 'He does seem taller,' he said. The wizard's head was six inches closer to a particular pile of rocks than it had been before.

'Yeth,' said Thorri simply.

It was hard to sleep. Just before dawn Bingo managed a couple of hours, but he was woken by dwarfs kicking dirt into the fire and gathering their things. 'Come along, Grabbings,' said Mori in a hostile tone. 'I suppose we can't leave you on the mountainside. Although we're all sorely tempted, look you, to do just that.'

They picked their way back down the mountainside, taking turns to drag Gandef's oblivious body behind them. It was easier than the ascent, but harder than it might have been. The wizard was considerably weightier than he had been before.

They rested for lunch, and then pressed on through the afternoon, keeping the mountain on their left side.

They crested the westernmost ridge flanking the front door as the sun was sinking, and as they climbed that hill they temporarily reversed the sunset for a few minutes, bringing the sun a fraction back above the horizon. It was on that low peak that they made their camp for the night, as the sun set for a second time in fifteen minutes.

They ate in silence. 'It's still hard for me to understand,' said Bingo.

If the dwarfs had not yet forgiven him, then they were at least too tired by their exertions to be expressly angry. 'The world is a stranger place than you realise, little soddit,' said Mori.

'Apparently so. When a female soddit and a male soddit get together, they create something new. I don't understand how dwarfs, or wizards, or dragons – since they're apparently all part of the same creature – how they – how *you* propagate the species.'

'Propagate,' said the dwarf meditatively. 'It sounds strange in my ears, that word. You mean: fill the world up with versions of yourself until the world is overcrowded and the landscapes are made a desert and crowds of the starving sway in time to their own moans?'

'Well,' said Bingo. 'Not that exactly . . .'

'With us,' said Mori, 'we know exactly how many there are. The creator breathed a certain number of dwarf lives into the stone at the beginning of things. These are crystals of the divine, look you, and their coming to life is part of the self-becoming. The great sequence unrolls, and form follows form until the crystals – or those that have survived – achieve their ultimate form. The form of the creator itself.'

'It sounds a little circular to me,' said Bingo sourly.

'Circular? Well, la, perhaps so. Circular like the way spring leads to winter leads to spring? Like the way the sun sets and rises? Circular's not so bad, look you. Besides,' he added, '*this* way the Divine experiences the nature of existence in creation.'

'And the creator can't do that otherwise?'

'The creator's outside creation,' said Mori, as if that were the most obvious thing in the world. 'He can't just poke his nose in, or he'll break it.'

All this metaphysical speculation was making Bingo's head hurt, so he wrapped himself in a blanket and tried to sleep.

The morning burst upon them in glory, muslin-coloured clouds refracting and making glow the yellow-white light of a new day. Bingo woke with the sunlight, squeezing his shut eyeballs and pressing its warmth against his face.

The soddit roused himself to find the dwarfs already awake, and standing in a line. 'What is it?' he asked, rubbing his eyes by punching himself very slowly and very delicately in each eye in turn. He yawned. 'What's up?'

'I'd say,' said Mori, pointing down the valley before them, 'that an army is up.'

Below in the valley that led to the cave-mouth entrance of Strebor the Only Mountain, a great host had assembled. The elegant armour of the elves shone like golden water; their purple banners, carrying the emblem of the purple carnation, fluttered in the morning breeze. Beside them was a host of Men of Lakeside, wearing their lacquer-coated leather armour (which doubled as sportswear) and brandishing their various forms of weaponry.

Bingo looked at the ranks upon ranks of warriors: a thousand men and elves all told. 'Golly,' he said.

Gobblin Charge

Chapter Eleven

CLODS BURST

෯ඏ෯

'Can Smug truly be dead?' said Bingo, in dismay.

The dwarfs and the soddit were gathered in Lord Elsqare's stylish silk tent, which had been pitched between the two hills before the main entrance to the mountain. Men-at-arms and elves-at-arms moved to and fro, entering and leaving the tent. Preparations were being made for the battle to come.

'Indeed so,' said Elsqare languidly. 'Something of a fortunate happenstance, I think we can agree. This Gobblin army facing us is ten thousand strong. If they'd had a dragon with them as well, then they'd have been, well – I don't know let me see – hmm, let's say *unbeatable*. That's what they'd have been.'

'Which shows how little you know, see,' said Mori, bustling forward in fury. 'That dragon, look you, would never have sided with the Gobblins. He'd have been our ally!'

'There's never been friendship or alliance,' said Elsqare, 'between dragons and elves.'

'No,' said Lard. 'Nor between dragons and men neither.'

'Dragons and dwarfs, however,' said Bingo, holding the fuming Mori back, 'is a different matter. I think Mori is right. I think Smug would have fought with us against the Gobblins, and a mighty ally he would have been. But there's no point in fretting over might-have-beens. Might-have-beens,' he added, growing strangely poetic, 'don't help any more, they just lie on the floor 'til you sweep them away.'

Everybody looked at Bingo. He looked at the floor. 'Sorry,' he said. 'I don't know why I said that.'

'As you say, however, Sir Soddit,' said Elsqare, 'whether the dragon would have helped or hindered our cause is moot.'

'Is *what*?' asked Mori.

'Moot.'

'Moot,' repeated the dwarf, as if trying the word for size. 'Moot,' he said. 'Moot, moot, moot.' He walked in a circle around the tent trying variants of pronunciation, drawing out the '*oo*', making the '*t*' more clipped. 'Moot moot moot. I *like* that,' he concluded. 'That's lovely, look you. *Moot*. What does it mean?'

'It means,' said Elsqare, 'that it is something as yet undecided.'

'Moot,' said Mori. 'Grand. What'll you have for breakfast?' he said in a little play-acting voice. '*Moot*,' he added in a basso profundo. 'Which came first the chicken or the egg? *Moot*, moot. Mirror on the wall, who is the fairest dwarf of all? *Moot is fairest. Moot moot*,' he continued, in this antiphonal manner. 'That's good, boyo,' he said in his usual voice, turning back to Elsqarc. 'I like that. I'll try and work it into my conversation, la.'

'Hmm,' said Elsqare. 'Anyway. Putting that on one side, we have yet to determine our best strategy. The Gobblins will be upon us in a day and a night. We have a mighty army of elves, and a mighty army of men – a thousand warriors all told. Will the dwarfs join this cause?'

'We will,' said Mori firmly, casting a glance behind him at Thorri, who nodded. 'We will stand beside you.'

'Then we are joined,' said Elsqare, with a glad face, 'by a mighty army of dwarfs! How many warriors are there in your army, Sir Dwarf?'

'Eh,' said Mori, rolling his eyes up as if calculating a rough approximation of the number. 'Five,' he said.

There was silence in the tent for a little space.

'They are mighty though,' Mori added. 'Those five.'

'Very well,' said Elsqare in a heavy voice. 'Sir Soddit. Will your people join in this cause? Death may follow, but glory comes also and we, the free peoples of Upper Middle Earth, welcome all allies in this battle against the evil Gobblins.'

'Sure,' said Bingo, feeling light-headed. 'Why not?'

'Then,' said Elsqare grandly, standing up from his throne, 'our great alliance will be of four armies! An army of elves, of men, of,' he coughed, 'dwarfs, and a great army of soddits! Together we shall stand shoulder to shoulder against the hordes of ten thousand blood-hungry Gobblins!'

Everybody in the tent cheered.

'How many,' Elsqare asked Bingo, as if in after-thought, 'are there in your army, Sir Soddit? You are small, but I'll wager you are tough, strong, thrawn, single-minded folk in battle, slow to anger but terrible when your blood is up. How great is your army?'

'Just me,' said Bingo.

'I see,' said Elsqare, sounding peeved, 'well that's not exactly an *army*, now, is it?'

'Doesn't that depend,' said Bingo, 'on what you mean by an army?'

'No, it doesn't. Ah, but it doesn't matter. I've declared ours an alliance of four armies, so that's what it'll be. The scribes and historians will have to be creative in future accounts of it, that's all.'

The elven scouts had estimated that the Gobblin horde was nearly upon them. The new allies had very little time. 'We must prepare for war,' Mori told Bingo. 'Look you.'

There was still the question of Gandef. 'We hoped the dragon would supervise his transformation, but that's not to be,' said Mori. 'Without Smug's help it is difficult to know what will happen. But it can't be helped. The future is moot. Gandef himself is moot.'

'Mute?' asked Gofur, puzzled.

'No, bach, moot,' said Mori eagerly. 'That's a word I just learned. It means uncertain.'

'Ahh,' said the other four dwarfs.

'Anyway, what I suggest is,' said Mori, 'we move Gandef inside the mountain. He'll be comfortable enough there. Leave him in Smug's old hall. At least he'll be out of the way of the Gobblins.'

'Unless the Gobblins are victorious,' Bingo pointed out. 'In which case they'll swarm into the mountains and kill him.'

Mori shrugged. 'We'll all be dead then, boyo,' he pointed out. 'So that's moot too.'

It took all five dwarfs and Bingo hauling together to drag Gandef's sleeping form. His body was twice as long as it had been before, and although not twice as broad around it was considerably thickened in the torso. Like a sprouting adolescent there was a stringiness to his limbs and torso. His face had elongated, and although it was still recognisably Gandef it had a weird and unnerving quality. The wizard had burst the blanket in which he had been wrapped, and ripped his clothes to pieces in his growth. Bingo took one foot and Gofur the other, and the other dwarfs took up places beside the wizard's six-feet-long legs. Pulling together they dragged him up the valley, through the main entrance and along the corridor within. Bingo, grasping the old wizard's ankles, found himself unpleasantly fascinated by Gandef's toenails. They were black, protruding, and were starting to claw-up at the end. It was not nice. His shoulders had blackened also, and two spikes had grown out of the blades like the tips of furled umbrellas.

'Should we cover him with something?' Bingo wondered as they positioned Gandef's supine form on Smug's pile of gold. 'Won't he get cold?'

'You're still thinking he's got the same sort of body as you,' said Gofur. 'He hasn't. He's in the metamorphosis state now.'

'How long will that take?' the soddit asked.

'Nobody knows exactly—' Gofur began saying, but Mori interrupted him. 'That's moot, see,' he said. 'Moot.'

'I see,' said Bingo.

They left Gandef in the chamber.

The party came out of the mountain again to bright sunshine, and to the sight of elves and men drilling in the valley before the front door. 'We'd better close the gate,' said Mori.

They pushed together, heaving with all their might, first on one of the huge stone leafs, and then on the other. Slowly the pair of hundred-yard-tall doors closed. When the second slammed shut with a great shuddering clunk, they could hear another sound, the clanging of the brass lock inside. 'He's sealed in there now,' said Mori.

'How do we get back inside?' asked Bingo.

'You could always go down the chimney,' suggested Gofur.

The dwarfs laughed together at this. Bingo did not join them.

'Either that,' Gofur added, 'or else Gandef will open the gates when he's ready.'

'Could we not have hidden ourselves in the mountain?' asked Bingo as they stood there. 'Surely we could have hidden from the Gobblins in there.'

'No, bach,' said Mori sadly. 'If they win, they'll batter the gates down and sack the halls within. We stand a better chance meeting them in open war here, rather than being caught like rats in traps inside.'

'Let's hope we win then,' said Bingo. 'For Gandef's sake.'

'Let's hope so,' agreed the dwarfs.

That day, before the battle, seemed to Bingo the longest he had known. The sun moved incrementally over the blue sky. Men and elves cut trees and sharpened them at one end, planting the jagged stakes in several rows beside the river. The archers in the company whittled new arrows and rubbed wax into the bowstrings. The soddit, however, had nothing to do; he felt superfluous, and he didn't like the feeling. He begged a short sword from one of the armourers of Lakeside, paying for it with dragon gold, and for an hour or so in the hot, fly-drony, pollen-dusty afternoon he practised making sweeps with this blade. He cut the tops off long strands of grass that grew in the meadows by the water. He stabbed the bark of old trees, forcing little plugs of wood out. An hour of this was enough for his arm to grow sodden and tired with the practice, and he stopped.

Then he climbed the eastern hill and watched the sun set over the dark sea of trees on the horizon, but his heart was heavier than the sinking sun. An hour of play-fighting and his arm had become too weary to lift, and now it was sore and ache-filled. An hour of play-fighting! Come the morning, he would have a whole day of *real* fighting, and – for all he knew (for he knew very little about real battles) – all night too. He dreaded the thought that he would collapse with exhaustion before the fight had barely begun. He was, by himself, the army of Soddlesex, the Hobbld-Ahoy! battalion. He had never fought before, and he had no relish for it.

That evening, the four armies lit many camp fires, and ate what would be for many of them their last supper, and drank their last wine. Bingo sat around one of the fires with the Army of Dwarfs. The six of them ate in silence, and afterwards sat in silence. 'I was thinking,' Bingo said eventually, although the words felt heavy and unreal in his mouth, 'of a plan. Tell me what your opinion is of this, boys. I was thinking – there is still the Thing®.'

The dwarfs groaned.

'I know, I know,' said Bingo. 'It's served us mostly ill, and if we give it the chance it will bring catastrophe down upon us.'

'That,' agreed Mori, in an emphatic voice, 'is *not* moot.'

'But maybe there's some watertight, guaranteed, win-win spell we can cast through the Thing®,' Bingo insisted, 'that could bring an end to this terrible battle before it's begun. Don't you think?'

'No,' said Gofur.

'No,' said Failin.

'No,' said On.

'No,' said Mori.

'I'd thay,' said Thorri, 'that it'th betht not to uthe it at all.'

Bingo sat in silence for a while.

'So Smug is dead,' he said. 'How and if I were to say

"Smug is dead" through the Thing®? Wouldn't that bring Smug back to life? Then at least he could help us defeat the Gobblins – and afterwards, he could aid Gandef.'

The dwarfs sat in silence. They were, clearly, tempted by this prospect. But Thorri steeled their resolve.

'No,' he said firmly. 'The Thing® ith a magic artefact. Dragonth are magic creatureth. Micthing magic with magic, micthing malign magic like the Thing® with benign magic like the dragon would not be clever. Leave it alone. Just leave it alone.'

'Thorri is right,' said Mori sadly. 'The Thing® would find a way of thwarting us, and bringing disaster through our wish, no matter how carefully we framed it. Let us leave it alone.'

They sat in silence for a long time.

Bingo could not sleep. He tossed and turned, turned from his left side to his right and from his right to his left, but neither side was comfortable. He found himself wishing for a third side on which to lie, and instead of trying to sleep he got up and wandered about the camp until dawn. The fires were burning brightly, and the elvish and mannish soldiers seemed in good spirits.

Dawn came slowly, first with a thinning of the darkness to the east, then in a glory of sunrise gold.

Low horizontal clouds brimmed with brightness, as if they were rips in the sky and diamond-gold illuminations were pouring through from some other place. Bingo watched for long minutes. Then he noticed that the chiefs of the other three armies had assembled, with their standards, on the top of the hill east of the main entrance of Strebor. He hurried up there as fast as his little legs could carry him.

'Ah,' said Elsqare, as the guards let him through. 'Here is the general of our fourth army. Have a look, general.' He gestured to the south.

From their vantage point, Bingo could see for many leagues. At first his eyes confused him. It was as if the grass meadows that lay alongside the river had been overgrown in a single night with gnarled black thickets, with thorn bushes and stark pole-like trees. But then the sight before him resolved, in his mind, to reality. The ground was covered with Gobblin soldiers. Ten thousand or more, armed and armoured, waiting for the order to charge.

'A horde,' said Elsqare. 'Wouldn't you say?'

'A horde,' agreed Bingo.

'Don't let your heart quaver, Sir Soddit,' said the elf. 'Be brave.'

'It's not my heart I'm worried about quavering,' said Bingo. 'It's lower down in my torso. What can we do? That army stretches as far as the eye can see –

ten thousand soldiers, you said. How strong is our army?'

'Our *combined* armies,' corrected Elsqare. 'I lead a force of five hundred elves. Lard commands five hundred men. The dwarfs, fierce and resolute, represent a force of five. And you yourself, Sir Soddit, are a force of one.'

Bingo could do the maths for himself. 'Oh dear,' he said.

'Quite,' said Elsqare. 'Still, can't be helped, can't be helped. Ready the squadrons!' he called. 'Trumpeters, prepare to sound! Fall back upon the mountain if the press is too great!'

Bingo tried to swallow, but his throat no longer seemed to be in working order. A fine time, he thought to himself, for my throat to seize up. How can I beg for mercy if I can't beg at all?

The Gobblins had marched day and night without pausing, all the way from the Minty Mountains, led by their terrible King, Kluk the Bald.[1] A hunger for death and a lust for battle was upon them: battle red in tooth and wattle, as the saying goes. Their soldiers had been inflamed with stories of the wrongs done to Gobblin-

---

[1] Son of Gallopavo the Meagre, who had been slain in the Minty Mountains by Thorri's father, Phwoah the Stunner.

kind by elves and men and dwarfs. 'Kill! Kill! Kill!'
they chanted. 'Elsqare the baster! Lard the waster!'
Above all, they had been fired with excitement by the
tales of the Thing®, and of the great things that Kluk
would achieve once he possessed it. They felt, in their
gobblin innards, the tug of the device: for they had
themselves also been created by Sharon the Evil One,
just as had been the Thing®. Theirs was a like sub-
stance. The soldiers chanted:

> *Bring the Thing®!*
> *Bring the Thing®!*
> *We want the Thing®!*
> *We want the Thing®!*

As the defenders watched from the hill, King Kluk was
carried to the front of the horde on his silver platform.
'Chicken!' called the front rank of elves and men,
hoping to discomfort the Gobblin army with this as-
persion upon their King's courage. 'Chicken!' But the
Gobblins only scowled and hissed, and the Gobblin
King was brought closer.

He was armoured in the most splendid of Gobblin
armour. White parchment overshoes, folded and cut
with harsh curlicues, had been placed over his shoes to
prevent the unclean blood of his enemies soiling the
soles of his boots. His armour presented two enormous

breastplates to the world, one on either side of his sternum, implying that his heroic chest was twice the size, twice as muscled, as lesser beings. The space between his armour and his skin had been crammed with herbage – grasses and herbs that possessed healing properties, such that should a blade pierce his skin their charm would lessen and close the wound. He carried a two-pronged killing pitchfork in one hand and a long-bladed knife in the other, both polished and glinting in the morning sunlight. As the ranks of Gobblins passed to allow his bearers to carry him forward, the soldiers chanted his name in an ecstasy of excitement.

> *Kluk! Great Kluk!*
> *Kluk! Kluk! Kluk!*
> *Kluk! Kluk! Kluk!*
> *Gre-eeat Great Kulk!*
> *Kluk! Kluk! Kluk!*

And so on.

'Archers!' called Elsqare. The hilltop silence was broken by a whittlish sound, as a hundred bowstrings were drawn back in unison.

'Fire,' said Elsqare. And a hundred arrows shot into the sky, and arced their deadly hail upon the Gobblins.

The horde roared, and surged forward.

And so the battle of the Famous Five Armies began.

Bingo's memory of the battle would always, afterwards, have a number of gaps in it. He would never forget that first charge of the enemy, and the burning, desperate sense of panic that it created in his torso all the way from his hips to his throat. Neither would he forget the first of the fighting, as the fore-guard of Gobblins, the fearsome Uruk-Low, came sprinting up the hillside on their ungainly legs. To the right elves brought down their swords in a coordinated sweep, cutting into the advancing wave; to the left, men thrust and parried. In the middle, dwarf axes swept up and down in a pendulum motion, catching little patches of sunshine on their blades at the highest point of the swing until the iron was too blackened with Gobblin blood. And he would never forget his first taste of fighting: running underneath an elvish swordsman's legs, hacking and stabbing with the sword, and cutting into the side of a Gobblin head. Bingo's blade bit deep, and the Gobblin squealed and jerked, but as he fell he drew Bingo down after him because the sword had jammed in the skull. Bingo tumbled forward and collapsed on the corpse, trying to lever the sword out of the Gobblin's bone. After what seemed an age Bingo got the thing free, with a wrench that caused him to stagger backwards. He paused and looked around him, and his heart seemed to fail in his breast. Gobblins were everywhere he looked, jabbing with their pikes, swinging their maces and their notched blades; men and elves fought bravely, but, like outcroppings of rock in a stormy and poisoned sea, they were beset on all sides. A gobblin bounced into Bingo's line of sight, his wicked little eyes glancing left and right, his red wattle swinging from his grisly neck. Bingo swung his sword.

But he could not remember what happened after that. There was a series of disconnected memories: of Gofur struggling with a mass of Gobblins, two hanging on each of his arms, and two on each of his legs. Bingo ran at the mass, trying to cut the creatures away. Then he remembered running in a different direction, trying to keep up with a party of elves. He remembered seeing the blue sky scratched and stitched over and again with ceiling after ceiling of arrows. He remembered seeing decapitated Gobblins sprinting with extraordinary vigour in random directions. He remembered seeing a mannish warrior struck in the small of his back with a long pike, forced along by three Gobblins, and seeing the jagged head of the weapon erupt from the man's chest. Other than that it was all a maelstrom of indistinct memories: the smell of blood, the terrible weariness in his arms that told him he could barely lift his sword again, and the insistent fear in his head that compelled him to lift his sword anyway; the sight of rush and counter-rush, of blade colliding with shield, and always the whizz and thrumming fall of storms and storms of arrows in the air overhead. Bingo thrust his sword into the chest of a Gobblin soldier, and the blade squeaked as it sank home.

The next clear memory in Bingo's head was of himself standing, panting, next to Lord Elsqare and Mori and two dozen warriors, men and elves. They were no longer on the hills flanking the front door. Under the pressure of the Gobblin advance the four armies had retreated, and now they had taken up positions on the mountainside itself, to the west of the main entrance. Bingo could not remember the actual retreat; but now here they all were.

'How goes it, Master Soddit?' Elsqare asked. 'Warm work?'

'Blimey,' said Bingo, which was his way of agreeing.

'My lord!' called a subaltern, a man splattered with blood and dirt, with a deep wound in his forehead. 'My lord, the Gobblins are swarming up the eastern flank of the mountain. I fear they will clamber over the main gate, and come down on us from above.'

'A grim prospect,' said Elsqare. 'If they can establish a position up there, then we are doomed. Archers!' he called. 'The gate!'

Those archers still alive took up position, and began firing arrows at the Gobblins that were scurrying along the mighty door lintel of the front gate. Bingo could see the danger. Once a large enough party crossed this narrow ledge, they would possess the higher slopes of the mountain, and could rain down weapons, boulders, anything upon the defenders beneath. His heart burning in his chest, Bingo watched the archers at work; but although their darts flew accurately, and although many Gobblins fell from above the door to the ground far beneath, yet still there were too many of the creatures to be killed in this manner, and droves of them were reaching the upper slopes.

Bingo's next memory was from much later in the day. He could not say what happened in the intervening time, except that he looked around and noticed that the sun was lower in the western sky, and that he felt much, much more tired – more tired than he had ever felt before. His sword was dented and chipped along its cutting edge, and was smeared with black blood. A huge Gobblin, cleaver-wielding, ran at him, and Bingo half ducked, half fell out of the way, heaving round with his sword, cutting into the creature's neck from behind. His arm was so weary that it burned with a fierce pain. The muscles threatened to disobey his mind every time he ordered them to move. He could hardly grip the handle.

'Bingo!' called Mori. 'Bingo!'

The dwarf staggered towards him, his beard slick with blood – both the black blood of Gobblins, and the red blood of its owner. Several crooked Gobblin arrows poked out of his body. 'You're still alive, boyo!' the dwarf called. As he reached Bingo he tripped and sank to his knees.

'Mori – are you hurt?'

'Oh it's nothing,' said the dwarf. 'Stings a bit,' he added. Then he rolled on to his back.

Bingo dropped his sword as Gobblin arrows plocked into the turf around him to stick up like dead and blackened stalks. Grasping the dwarf's legs, he pulled with all his weary might, hauling Mori to the higher ground. He arrived at a narrow ledge, on which some elves and men stood shoulder to shoulder. The paths were crammed with the dead. Stones and arrow shafts rained down from above. Six men were holding their broad shields in the air to provide shelter from this deadly hail.

'Bingo,' said Thorri, hurrying out to help the soddit drag Mori in underneath this rudimentary cover. 'Good to thee you're thtill alive.'

'And you, sir,' gasped Bingo, close to sobbing with his exhaustion. 'The others?'

'It'th been a grim day,' said the dwarf. He shook his head.

'This is our last stand,' said Elsqare, crouching down to address the soddit. 'We've been pushed back here – sheer weight of numbers. I'm sorry to say that Lord Lard is laid low.'

'Dead?'

'Dead, with many other heroic souls. Ah well,' the elf added lightly, 'some you win, some you lose.'

'Lose?' wailed Bingo. 'Can it be true?'

'They had another army behind the army we could see,' explained Elsqare. 'Twenty thousand soldiers in all. We had one thousand and six soldiers. We never really had much of a chance. See!'

Bingo looked out across the plain south and west of the mountain. The Gobblin dead were piled high, but were still vastly outnumbered by the living. Waves of Gobblins moved back and forth, some surging towards the mountain, others – it seemed – merely going round and round in a meaningless way.

The hail from above stopped. Bingo could see King Kluk processing through the files and ranks of his army, over the foothills and up towards them. As he approached, his troops chanted:

> *Bring the Thing*®!
> *Bring the Thing*®!
> *We want the Thing*®!
> *We want the Thing*®!

'What can we do?' asked Bingo, feeling a terrible and hopeless desperation. 'We can't give them the Thing® –

they'll do unspeakable and terrible wickedness with it!
We can't give them the Thing®.'

'And yet,' pointed out Elsqare, reasonably enough, 'if
we refuse it them, they'll simply kill us and take it from
our dead bodies.'

'What can we do?'

A thousand Gobblin archers had taken up position
around the last redoubt. Elsqare ordered his men to put
their weapons down. 'If we so much as notch an arrow
to a string,' he observed, 'we'll die in a swarm of
Gobblin darts.'

But it was hard to obey, for Kluk was now within
bowshot, and a single well-aimed arrow could have
pierced his head. He drew closer and closer, and his
followers muttered, 'Gobble, gobble, gobble' and
'Kluk! Kluk! Kluk!' as he advanced. Finally the silver
platform on which he was borne came to a halt.

'Elves!' King Kluk announced in his horrid voice.
'Men! Dwarfs! You are defeated!'

A cry of triumph rose from the Gobblin hordes.

'The Thing®,' said Kluk, 'is ours! Surrender.'

'We surrender,' said Elsqare suavely. 'Certainly.
We're not at war any more, and I'd like to remind you
of the terms of the Gungadin Convention—'

'Silence!' barked Kluk. 'You may not be at war with
us, but *we* are at war with *you* – always!'

Another great and terrible shout broke from the ranks of Gobblin troops.

'Gobblins are forever at war with elves and men and dwarfs!' shouted Kluk.

'I think that meanth,' said Thorri to Bingo, 'that they're going to kill uth, dethpite the fact that we've thurrendered.'

'That may very well be the case,' agreed Bingo.

'Give us the Thing®!' howled Kluk, and his army yelled in agreement.

'This is a tight spot,' said Elsqare. 'What do you think we should do, O soddit?'

Bingo fingered the Thing® in his pocket. Now was the time to use it, if ever there had been a time to use it; but his mind went round and round in an empty track and he could think of nothing. He tried to think of a spell, or a form of words, that would save the day, but nothing came to him. He thought of saying 'The Gobblins are victorious', hoping that the device would change the world such that the Gobblins were defeated: but he knew, in his heart, that the Thing® wanted the Gobblins to triumph, and that it would twist his words to destroy *him* if he tried such a trick, perhaps by making their victory imminent rather than actual. Then he thought: perhaps I can use the Thing® to destroy the Thing®. What would happen if I said through the Thing®, 'the Thing® exists', would it cease to exist? But then, since it would no longer exist, it would not have been able to make itself disappear, and surely it would exist again. But then it would exist and would be able to make itself disappear . . . and so it would not exist . . . and so it would exist . . . and the possibilities whirled in Bingo's exhausted brain until he could see nothing proceeding from such a wish except a great *bang* and Bingo lying dead on the floor, and the Gobblins picking the Thing® from his cold corpse.

'Which one of you carries the Thing®?' called Kluk. 'Is it you, elf?'

Bingo saw Gobblin archers draw back their bows and aim darts at Elsqare. 'It is I!' he announced, stepping forward. 'Bingo Grabbings, the soddit. I carry the Thing®.'

The whole hideous army seemed to breathe the words 'Doom, doom', the sound sweeping through the air like thunder.

'Give the Thing® to me!' called Kluk.

'If I do,' said Bingo, 'will you allow us to go free?'

'Ha!' laughed Kluk. 'No, manrunt, no – but I will kill you cleanly, and burn your bodies. If you deny me, I will kill you slowly and eat your corpses.'

'Right,' said Bingo, as if considering this. He could see a thousand Gobblin arrows aimed at his own chest. His mind raced. *The arrows are not marshmallow*, he thought to himself. Would that save them? What evil twist could the Thing® place on such a statement? *King Kluk is alive*, he thought. But if the King died, his soldiers would simply kill them all. *All Gobblins are war-loving*, he thought, and wondered to himself if even the magic of the Thing® were enough to reverse such a statement, to root out the love of war from all Gobblin hearts at once. What better phrase could he think of? None.

'At once!' shrieked Kluk. 'At once! Or you will all die!'

Bingo's hand went into his coat pocket. He drew out the Barkingstone, and it glinted in the dying light of the day. The Gobblin soldiers nearest him went 'Ooo!' and drew back a little.

It occurred to Bingo that the Gobblins did not know what the Thing® looked like. Why should they? It had never been theirs. It had been fashioned by Sharon in the fires of Mount Dumb, and had passed somehow to Sollum.

'Here,' he shouted holding aloft the great jewel. 'Here is the Thing®!'

'Woof,' went the Barkingstone.

Bingo threw the gem. It sailed, sparkling like a daytime firework, through the rays of the sinking sun, and Kluk himself reached out and grabbed it out of the air. 'The Thing®!' he yelled, holding the gem above his head. 'The Thing®!'

Fearful and ugly was the cheering of the Gobblin host.

'Now nothing will stand against us!' cried Kluk. 'All the world will fall before the armies of Gobblinkind!'

The cheer was renewed with even greater and uglier vigour.

Bingo was trying to think. It was his only and his last chance. Kluk would kill them all, sooner or later, and would kill them at once if he realised he had been tricked. *All Gobblins are war-loving*, he thought to himself. *The Gobblins are war-loving*. Would 'the Gobblins' be better than 'all Gobblins'? Or just 'Gobblins'. *Gobblins love war*, perhaps? But 'love'? What might the Thing® make of that? It might take the love of war from Gobblin hearts, yet leave a professionally disinterested dedication in its place. It might twist 'war' in strange ways, such that they loved not war but slaughter – not war but suicidal destruction. It was impossible to tell. But in his heart he knew it was hopeless. It was the wrong statement to make through the device.

Bingo's fingers were around the Thing®. It was hot, and seemed almost to twitch and writhe in the soddit's grip. It was eager, Bingo knew. Eager. It wanted to be taken by the Gobblins, for they would use it for what it had been originally made – for evil – instead of trying, all the time, to pervert the Thing's® usage to good. Bingo felt his tiredness swirl up inside him like a sandstorm. He wanted nothing more than to lie down and sleep. He could not decide.

This was the moment of decision. As with many decisions in Bingo's life, he made it without even realising it.

The Thing® was already in his hand, and his hand was already out of his pocket and up by his mouth. He caught a glimpse of Elsqare's face, bent by anxiety and fear, as the elf saw what Bingo was doing. So much could go so badly wrong.

What to say? How to phrase it?

Inspiration failed at the vital moment.

'War—' said Bingo randomly. And the word drifted through the Thing®.

His heart stopped.

And started again. He took a deep breath. What had he done?

He had done nothing. He was exactly where he was. His few remaining comrades were disarmed, surrendered, surrounded on all sides by savage Gobblins. A thousand Gobblin arrows were still aimed at their breasts. Kluk was still holding the Barkingstone over his head. The Gobblin army was grumbling en masse, a rumbling noise of triumph and pride.

'What did you say?' Elsqare asked, hissing. 'What did you say through the Thing®?'

'I think it may be broken,' said Bingo. And he said it

hopefully, because if he had truly exhausted the magic potential of the device then it would matter less that Kluk had won the battle of the Famous Five Armies, it would mean that the Gobblins could do much less damage. 'I did say something through the device, but nothing has happened.'

'What—?' Elsqare began saying, but his words were drowned out.

The rumbling had grown in volume.

Bingo realised that the sound was not issuing from the Gobblin horde. It was coming from the ground beneath him.

Kluk, still clutching the Barkingstone, looked to the mountain, and for the first time his expression of triumph was replaced by one of fear. Bingo turned and looked up.

From where they stood they could just see the little plateau where the dwarfs and Gandef and Bingo had camped days before. Gouts of smoke were pouring from that side of the mountain.

'The chimney,' he cried with sudden understanding.

Then fire burst from the mountain. A huge, blinding spout of light and heat thrust from the mountainside into the sky. Lava, boiling and spitting, poured in great waves from the mountain's western flank, rolling down the side of the peak, bunching on itself like bales of rolling cloth, burning the mountain grasses and bushes in a hundred flare-ups as it proceeded.

A second mass of fire burst from the mountainside, and again molten magma poured from above, but this time it flew into the air, hurling in a wide arc, spraying north and west and – Bingo could see – spraying south as well, gobs of lava that curled and gripped at themselves in the air and descended upon them.

'It is the end of all things!' shrieked Elsqare.

And so it seemed, for the airborne wave of liquid rock was coming down with a terrible inevitability. The shouts of triumph in the Gobblin army had been replaced with gibbers and wails of terror. The archers had dropped their weapons, and were struggling to press backwards, prevented from escape by their fellows behind them. Kluk himself opened his mouth to say something, but he never spoke again, for a house-size gob of lava caught him and his bodyguard square on the front, and swept up his instantly burning remains and carried them downhill tangled inside the flowing rock. Bingo and Thorri cowered, and the elves and men hid their faces, as the scorching heat of lava engulfed a hundred of the Gobblin soldiers closest to Kluk and hurled them backwards. Spatters of hot rock sprayed all around, and yet none of these boiling fragments struck any of the remnants of the four armies. But more lava, and more, hurled through the air, and landed again and again amongst the Gobblins.

Bingo looked back at the mountain, and saw the searing stream of molten rock rushing down towards them. The air above it was so hot it seemed to tremble with fear, and smoke and dust turned the sky above dark. 'This must surely be it,' he said. 'This great stream of fire will devour us all.'

And yet it did not. The mighty river of molten rock struck a boulder a little way up the mountainside above the ledge where the remnants of the four armies stood – and divided. To Bingo's left and to his right the scorching fiery river flowed, and it ploughed into the Gobblins and licked them up with its fiery breath.

For many long minutes the burning river flooded on, pouring down and eating into the mass of Gobblins. They shrieked, they thrashed, they tried to run, but they were caught in the crush of their own bodies, and stream after stream of magma ploughed them down and burnt them up and buried them under.

Those few elves, men and dwarfs, and the one soddit, left alive on the little ledge clung together and hid their faces from the terrible heat of the lava streams that rushed past them. For an age and an age, or so it seemed, the heat lay on their backs like a huge weight. Sweat poured from Bingo's skin like rain. His throat was parched and aching. He could taste nothing but hot ashes and death, and his eyeballs felt as if they were boiling in his head. His very hair smouldered, as if it would catch fire – and, truly, only his prodigious sweating prevented that chance.

But, after a long time, the heat began to diminish. When Bingo dared look, the rivers of fire had solidified into two vast trunks of blackened rock. Smoke rushed off them, and they were palpably hot through the air. Sometimes veins of fire would glow upon them, and the rock would shrug and change shape, and the fire would die away again.

There was little to be seen through the smoke and steam, and yet Bingo noticed the occasional grisly relic of the Gobblin horde: an arm encased in rock. Burnt arrows like bristles in the skin of the black rock.

'It's unbelievable,' said Bingo. 'I don't believe it.'

'Is it over?' gasped Mori, from the ground. 'Did we win? Or is it moot?'

'We won,' said Elsqare, his face grimed and slick with sweat. 'It is not moot.'

'Grand,' said Mori. 'Look you.' And he passed into unconsciousness.

It was hours before the new rocks were cool enough for the party to leave their ledge. Seven men, eleven elves, three dwarfs and a soddit were all that were left alive of the four armies. And of the three dwarfs, only Thorri and Gofur were awake. Mori had passed into a kind of swoon; he was sorely wounded.

'It's unbelievable,' said Bingo, for the nineteenth time. He was slumped on the ground, more tired than he had ever been before, and yet unable to sleep. 'How did the lava *miss* us? It destroyed the whole of the Gobblin army, and yet it just *happened* to miss us altogether? That's an incredible chance. That's un-believable.'

'Is it?' asked Elsqare. 'What was it that you spoke through the Thing® Was it the magic of that device that summoned up this volcanic destruction?'

'I . . .' said Bingo. 'I didn't know what to say. I said one word only.'

'What word?'

'I said, "war".'

Elsqare nodded, and sat down on the hot ground next to the exhausted soddit. 'I think I see,' he said.

'You do?' said Bingo.

'It wathn't the Thing® that called up the molten rock,' said Thorri. 'That wath Gandef.'

'Gandef?' said Bingo, leaping up. 'How?'

'We were afraid of it,' said Thorri. 'The tranthforma-tion from wizard to dragon ith a mighty tranthforma-tion. A being changed from a being of earth and water, thuch ath you and me, to a being of fire and air, which ith what a dragon ith. A great amount of magic power

~ 311 ~

ith produthed in the tranthformation. It'th an inherently unthtable time.'

'From earth and water to fire and air,' said Bingo. 'Is that what caused the mountain to explode? Is Gandef all right?'

'Thith,' said Thorri, 'ith why we wanted an experienthed dragon looking after him as he tranthformed. Ith he all right? I don't know if he'th all right. I don't know.'

'I think he's all right,' said Gofur. 'He is not what he was before. Fire would have burnt up the old Gandef – but he's a new creature now. Fire can't hurt him now.'

'He has become a dragon?' said Elsqare. 'How interesting. His transformation happened at exactly the right time as far as we were concerned. Most fortuitous.'

'It wath – fortuitouth,' agreed Thorri. 'Five minuteth more and Kluk would have thlain uth all, killed uth – and all would have been lotht.'

'I do not believe it was fortuitous,' said Bingo.

'Nor I,' said Gofur. 'Bingo said the word "war" into the Thing®, and it has brought about peace.'

But Elsqare shook his head. 'Yet the Thing® is evil in its making and its mode, and will bring misery wherever it can. I do not believe it has brought peace. For what is war but struggle? And the opposite of struggle is not peace but death.'

'It has certainly brought death,' said Gofur, looking around.

'Elsqare is right,' said Bingo. 'The Thing® was not happy with me – it was positively twitching and struggling in my hand, yearning to be free. Had the Gobblins seized it then it would have been able to do much more damage to the world, and that's what it wants. It *yearned* towards the Gobblins. I could feel its yearning, as an almost palpable force. But, luckily, it was in my hands, not theirs. When I spoke the word "war" through it, it brought about the opposite. Lord Elsqare is correct – for all those at war it brought death. We were saved because we surrendered. We were not at war when the word was spoken, or the lava would have devoured us also.'

Gofur barked a shout of laughter. 'And had the Gobblin King accepted our surrender, then the war would have been over – and the Thing® would have been powerless to destroy him! Do you remember what he said? "You may not be at war with *us* – but *we* are at war with *you* – always!" Those words brought his doom. They meant that the Thing®'s magic applied to him and his army. But not to us.'

'Verily,' said Bingo. 'Blimey,' he added.

'You speak truly, Sir Dwarf,' said Elsqare. 'The Gobblin King's pride destroyed him. He could have accepted our surrender and then he would not have been at war, and Bingo's word would not have harmed him.'

'The Thing® thertainly found the motht dethtructive manner of inverting Bingo'th word,' said Thorri.

They carried Mori, sorely wounded and still unconscious, over the warm black rocks, bearing him towards the main doorway of the mountain. The lava had not flowed here, because the Gobblins had been swarming around their King and had not been concerned with access to the mountain – that would have come later, when they would have burst the stone doors asunder and looted the halls within. Now the stream trickled thinly in its bank, and the only Gobblins were corpses, and there were other corpses there too – elves and men.

As the sun rose in the east, Elsqare found a trampled silk pavilion, paw marks and footprints all over the white cloth. With his surviving elves he pulled it out of the dirt and bound up the splintered poles that supported it, and made a tent again in that place. Mori was taken inside, his armour removed and his wounds tended. But he was badly hurt.

Elves scavenged amongst the fields to the west and brought back rabbits, which they cooked in the morning. The survivors drank from the stream, and then slept. Bingo himself was roused by Thorri after a few hours.

'Come,' said the dwarfish King. 'Inthide.'

In the tent Mori had regained consciousness, but his eyes were wild and wandering. 'Soddit?' he said. 'Are you there?'

'I'm here.'

'We won, then?'

'We won. It was a great victory. The mountain exploded, and carried the Gobblin horde away with it, leaving the survivors untouched.'

'Really!' said Mori. 'Really! Extraordinary, look you. A few clods fly through the air, and the Gobblins are blown away.'

'It was more than a few clods, actually,' said Bingo.

'And the survivors! Were many killed on our side?'

'Oh,' said Bingo, embarrassed. 'We got off lightly. Compared to the Gobblins certainly. Indeed, at least one of the armies suffered no casualties at all.'

'I'm going to choose to believe,' said Mori, in a fading voice, 'that that's the dwarf army you're talking about. But never mind,' he added, his eyes clouding. 'Glad to have known you, boyo,' he said, his voice very faint. 'All the best. Where to now?'

'Where indeed?' whispered the soddit.

Mori grunted. 'Moot,' he said. And so he died.

That's not all folks!

Chapter Twelve

THE RETURN JOURNEY

၆nu၅

The survivors of the battle of the Famous Five Armies numbered no more than twenty one. Thorri and Gofur alone remained from the troop of dwarfs that had departed from Soddlesex. The men of Lakeside had lost their mayor. It was a grim day.

The eruption of Strebor had laid swathes of jagged black rock over the western and southern flanks of the mountain, a desolate and wasted prospect. Yet the meads by the river were clear of lava, and the water still flowed. Bingo, Thorri and Gofur dug a deep grave for Mori and buried him. Gofur sang an ancient dwarf lament at the graveside.

> *So, farewell*
> *then*
> *Mori the dwarf.*
> *You fought*
> *bravely,*
> *but now you're dead.*

Trevor's mum says that
if Trevor were
half the man
you were, he'd be
a fifth of the man he is.

Then she laughs, which
I don't think is very
appropriate.

Bingo didn't understand it, but it brought tears to his eyes.

The survivors rested, but on the second day after the battle it became clear that disposal would have to be made of the many corpses that still littered the open ground. 'The mountain did much of our work for us,' said Elsqare. 'Most of the Gobblins tens of thousands are encased in the new rock – very hygienic, that. But there are many hundreds of bodies that the lava did not touch, and amongst them are some of our own comrades.'

They spent that day and the next searching amongst the dead. It was terrible work, or at least Bingo thought so at the beginning. But after a few hours he became used to it, immune to the shock of hauling dead Gobblins. There was a place where the lava had settled into a basin, forty yards across and twenty deep, and the Gobblin dead were placed there. The occasional elfen or human body was carried respectfully to the river's edge. On the evening of the third day elven runners brought back wood and also pigeons from the nearest copse. The victorious four armies ate the pigeons and drank water from the clear stream. As the sun set, the bodies of elvish and mannish warriors were burnt on a funeral pyre.

'I am sorry,' said Elsqare, 'that we have not discovered any of the dwarfish fallen.'

'We are content,' said Thorri. 'As dwarfth, we require burial in rock – and the mountain hath provided that for uth in iths eruption.'

'It is a bitter and a sweet victory,' said Elsqare.

'Quite,' said Thorri.

On the morning of the fourth day, seven days after he entered his great sleep, Gandef the Dragon stirred in his mountain home. He padded down his corridor on his new legs, and drew back the brass lock of the main entrance. Then he pushed the mighty stone doors apart and put his enormous dragonish head out into the sunshine.

'Hello,' he said. 'What's new?'

Bingo, Thorri and Gofur were overjoyed to see him again, for all that he had changed and grown out of almost all recognition. A grey-skinned, bright-eyed young dragon greeted them, its wings black, its claws obsidian. And yet there was something familiar in its gaze, and its voice – though deeper and huger than the wizard's had been – was nonetheless familiar.

He perched on a spur of black rock that lay, newly created by the eruption, parallel with the meads, and listened politely to Gofur and Bingo's account of the battle. 'Dear me,' he rumbled. 'And I missed it all?'

'You played a crucial part,' insisted Bingo. 'Your fire brought us victory.'

'Excellent,' he said. 'Excellent.'

Then Gandef reared into the air and flew around the mountain's peak, trying his new wings. He flew over the pile of Gobblin dead and blasted down with a spout of blue-grey fire, burning up the bodies in a purifying conflagration. After that he flew far to the north, and returned clutching two heifers, one in each hind claw. One of these beasts he gave to the survivors of the battle, and the other he ate himself, roasting it with puffs from his nostrils.

'Peckish,' he announced. 'Haven't eaten in seven days.'

The men roasted the cow on a spit, and the veterans of the battle ate heartily.

The following morning the Lakeside men departed, beginning their march downstream to their town. They carried with them a portion of the wealth from inside the Only Mountain – 'Take it, take it,' Gandef insisted.

'Fat lot of good it'll do me. When am I ever going to go shopping? I couldn't so much as fit inside a shop any more. Take it – take it.'

The elves were similarly rewarded, and they struck out over the new black rocks and beyond them to the fields westward, making for the forest. 'My cousin the woodelf, Ele the Elcoholic, has a place there,' Elsqare explained. 'It's all feasting and drinking, and it gets tiresome after a while, but it'll do for now. Then it's back over the Minty Mountains. Things should be quieter in our lands now that the Gobblins have been overthrown. Farewell!'

'Farewell!' said Bingo.

And so it was that only Thorri, Gofur, Bingo and Gandef remained. 'What will you do?' asked the soddit.

'We'll thtay here,' said Thorri. 'That'd be betht. There's plenty of room inthide – room for a whole population of dwarfth, in fact. And you?'

'I'd like to go home,' said Bingo. 'But I do not know the way.'

'I'll carry you,' said Gandef, rumbling and smoking. 'I need an excuse to stretch my wings, and I quite fancy a really long fly.'

'Thank you, Sir Dragon,' said Bingo, bowing.

The soddit spent his last night inside the mountain, sleeping on a huge bed that had once, Gofur said, been the bed of a King. The walls of his rock-carved chamber were hung with antique armour, rusty pikes, gold and silver chain mail, works of fine carving and art. It was a spooky place, but Bingo slept deeply and slept long.

In the morning he said his farewells. 'We'll thee you again thoon, I hope,' said Thorri. 'Pop by, any time. You know – if you're paththing, on your way, thome-where, you know.'

'Likewise,' said Bingo. 'I'm sure. Do you know a strange thing?'

'What?'

'My feet haven't hurt in weeks. Or I haven't noticed it if they have.'

'Bit of exerthithe,' said the dwarf King sagely. 'Doth the world of good.'

Finally Bingo clambered up Gandef's leg, and settled himself between the dragon's great shoulder blades. 'Righto,' rumbled Gandef. 'Off we go.'

He sprung upwards, and soared into the air. The ground shrunk beneath them like a craven thing, and the wind boomed in Bingo's ears. Clutching the swaying stalk at the base of Gandef's left wing, the soddit leaned a little out to stare in frank amazement.[1] In moments the

---

[1] Frank Gerard Amazement II was a fabled prince of the realm of RororoHyorboat, far to the south. His amazement and ingenuous open-mindedness had become a byword amongst his own people, and this byword had, evidently, spread far to the north as well.

river had become a silver strand, the fields were no bigger than leaves, Lake Escargot shone like a puddle of mercury in the sunlight. Mighty Strebor itself had dwindled below them to a conical stump, splotched about its western and southern skies with black marks, like pitch spilt on a grey wizard's hat. And peering forward, over the undulating shoulders of the dragon, Bingo saw the whole expanse of Mykyurwood laid below them like a rough-woven quilt of green and black.

'You all right?' Gandef asked.

'It's marvellous,' called Bingo, his voice swamped by the white rushing of the wind through which they flew. 'Marvellous!' They had left the earth far behind, and moved now amongst air and space and sunlight. The sun, rising behind them, was sharper, clearer, its light purer and more enormous. Bingo scrunched up his eyes and gazed at the sun for long minutes, its outpouring fountain of light. When he looked down again, clouds swept past below them like pipesmoke, and hurried away. It was blue all around them, dazzling blue above, blue-hued greens below.

'Marvellous!' he called again.

They flew on and on.

'I meant to say,' thundered Gandef, twisting his neck and bringing his head a little way round so that he could observe the soddit from one eye. 'Thorri told me about the Thing® you know.'

'Don't you remember it,' Bingo said, 'from before your transformation?'

'No,' rumbled the dragon. 'I was far gone before you told the dwarfs that it was in your possession, I think.'

'Oh,' shouted Bingo.

'May I see it?' the dragon asked. Bingo looked into the beast's eye, and hesitated. But he took the Thing® out of his pocket and held it up.

The dragon's snaky neck curled again, and his head – large as a horse's and considerably more intelligent – swung in towards Bingo. The great wings continued beating, the wind continued rushing past them, although the pilot was not, now, looking where he was going. The dragon's nostrils were wide as inkwells, and as black, and they approached the Thing® with a sniffing eagerness. Bingo controlled the urge to snatch the Thing® away, and held it out.

Eventually Gandef withdrew his head, faced forward again and flew on for a long while in silence.

'Well?' Bingo prompted.

'It is as I feared,' said the dragon. 'A terrible device, filled with evil potential. My own magic is much greater now than it was when I was a wizard, and I can sense much wickedness in it – I can smell it, if you like. But,' and here he turned his head and met Bingo's gaze a second time, 'I can tell you something else. It has been long separated from its evil creator, the dreaded Sharon, and accordingly its magic is greatly weakened. In fact, it is nearly exhausted – it has been used recently, and used several times, and each usage has drained more of its magic potential. It would take only a very little spell now to drain it completely.'

Bingo's clothes were fluttering and wrestling in the wind. 'And then would it be safe?'

'Safer. Not wholly safe, for Sharon could recharge its power. But safer – much less likely to do mischief in the wrong hands.'

'A little spell,' said Bingo thoughtfully. 'What must I say?'

'You are the Thing®-carrier,' said Gandef. 'It is for you to decide. Say, "my clothes are green", or "fish have two eyes", or "gherkins are unpleasant food", and the Thing® will try and make the reverse true, but it will be unable to – it will become denuded of all power, exhausted, worn out in the process.'

'A spell as small as that?' cried Bingo.

'I think so,' said the dragon, turning his head again to face the direction of flight. 'It has only the merest trickle of magic left inside it. Or so it smells to me.'

'And a larger spell. What if I say "the oceans are blue", or "two and two are four"? How would a larger spell effect it?'

'A larger spell would be more sure to exhaust the

Thing®. It is very weary, its magic very small, a mere shadow of what it once was.'

Bingo pondered this for a while. He did not have the sureness in his mind that the dragon seemed to possess, and he knew from his own experience how sly the device was. Could it have hidden its true power from Gandef? Was it even now scheming, hoping to trap the soddit into saying something that it could twist to evil? He thought of many possible phrases, trying them out.

Below them the forest had come to an end, and the sharp clean lines, white and blue, of the Minty Mountains were visible. Bingo could see the expanse of the mountain chain now, a tremendous ridge in the landscape running to the horizon left and right. Then he looked up again at the blue of the sky and the pouring, clean, bright light of the sun.

On an impulse he lifted the Thing® to his mouth and spoke.

He said, 'The sun shines.' And so it did, it shone with a glorious and an undiminished brightness.

Have you enjoyed *The Soddit*?

Why not read the three volumes of A. R. R. R. Roberts's
magical sequel *The Lord of the Dancings*[1]

The Lord of the Dancings Volume I: *The Yellow Ship of the Thing*®

Wrenched again from his ordinary, peaceful life as a soddit,
Bingo the Thing®-Mule becomes embroiled in the rise to
power of the Evil Sharon. A group, well, more a party, a –
what would you call it – band, no group – yes, *band* – of
individuals from all the races of Upper Middle Earth as-
semble to help Bingo on his quest: to sail *over the sea* to the
Whirlpool of Dshwshrs (a feature of the oceans of Upper
Middle Earth that was named, clearly, onomatopoeically)
and there to cast the Thing® into the swirling waters and rid
the world of its deadly threat for ever, and for ever!! (Or just
'for ever' now that I come to think of it, that second 'for ever'
is redundant, really, isn't it, like saying 'infinity plus infinity'
that's just infinity, not double-infinity or anything like that.
Anyway. There you go.)

'But how shall we travel across the waves?' asked Bingo in a

[1] **Attention:** This is *a rhetorical question.* Do not attempt to answer
this question. NonWin Books accepts no liability for anybody who
attempts to answer this question and injures themselves in the
process.

querulous voice. 'Are they not wet? Is there not the risk of wetting? Not to mention drowning?'

'Fear not, young soddit,' said Strudel. 'In the land where I was born there lived a man who *sailed* the sea.'

'Will you tell me of his life in the land of such marine,' Bingo pressed, 'adventures?'

'Tell you of his life?' repeated Strudel, a pastry halfway to his mouth and a startled look in his eye. 'You what? I don't know anything about his life. Why do you want to know about that? What's to know? Only that he proved that it *is possible* to sail the sea. He did it in a big yellow boat of some kind. You and I and the rest of our band will do so too – we shall charter a Yellow Ship and sail the sea of green. Y,' he added, thinking more carefully about it. 'Green-*y* bluey sort of colour.'

'Hurrah,' said Bingo weakly.

The Lord of the Dancings Volume II: *The Twins' Tower*

After the abject failure of the question to destroy the Thing®
in the Whirlpool of Dshwshrs (*warning, the previous sentence may contain spoilers: do not read the previous sentence if you wish to preserve narrative suspense during* The Yellow Ship of the Thing®), the quest passes to Bingo's cousin, three-times removed (by court order), Frodeo. Frodeo and his faithful companion Scram – his, shall we say, um, servant? Or just friend? Yes – friend, his friend. But nothing funny, no funny business about their friendship, they just happen to be extremely close friends that's all. Where was I? Oh yes, Frodeo and Scram cross a landscape of razor-sharp rocks

and stagnant pools, attended by Sollum – a foul, skinny philosopher who, thanks to a piece of malign magic exists not as a real person, but as an animated Manuscript Illumination-cum-Illustration. Although he's terribly realistic. Terribly. Some of those monks who did that sort of artwork were *terribly* talented you know, geniuses some of them, although of course we don't know their names in the way that we know Raphael and Picasso and so on. Anyway, this threesome must make their way to the great tower in which the Twins live, Tomson and Tombson (the 'b' is silent, as in 'basilica'), and recruit their twinnish excellence in the process of destroying the Thing®. Meanwhile Strudel can no longer fit into his lederhosen, and reveals himself to be the Secret King of Sh!-Tellnoone! The survivors of the original sea quest to destroy the Thing® reassemble.

'We can only pray,' said Gandef, 'that the Tomson twins will be able to help Frodeo and Scram.'

'Help them,' said Strudel, chuckling to himself, 't'win. Do you get it? To win. Twin. Yeah?'

Gandef addressed the whole company. 'To horse!' he cried. 'We must ride to the Land of Helpmi Rhondor, and there gather an army to confront Sharon's hordes of Gobblin warriors!

The nine of them cheered, and leapt on to their horses. Gandef himself leapt on to his horse, Shadowemail, the fleetest, most intelligent horse in all of Upper Middle Earth, inadvertently crushing it to death. 'Oops,' he said. 'I forgot myself there for a moment. Damn it; it's easily done, though, isn't it? Damn.' He stood, and tried to scrape the remnants of the beast from his hindquarters.

The Lord of the Dancings Volume III: *The Rerun of the Sequel of* Thing® *Part 2: Son of* Thing® *Rides Again*

Just when you thought the story couldn't possibly have anywhere else to go, a whole new chapter opens up in the saga of the Thing®. *The Rerun of the Sequel* is the most spectacular *Lord of the Dancings* episode yet. Scaryman the Evil reveals himself – astonishingly, and to the complete and utter surprise of everybody who knew him, and who thought he was one of the good guys – to be evil, and allies himself with Sharon, renaming himself Scaryman the Evil the Evil. You could have knocked me down with a *feather* when I heard. Blimey. Then there's lots and lots of fighting, and more fighting. Gobblins get killed in *such* large numbers. Finally Frodeo and Scram must don the Tap Shoes of Fate and confront the Lord of the Dancings in person – uncovering a mystery that will rock Upper Middle Earth to its very core. To its very core! I know . . . I know . . . exciting, isn't it?

> He looked up in terror to see a Gobblin flying the air sitting astride his hideous winged mount. It was the Lord of the Seagul – the Seaguls of Sharon that struck such horror into the Armies of Good by their persistence in trying to grab bits of food from about your person, their screeching, their pooping, and the way they appear in the sky above your head even though you're dozens of leagues from the sea . . .

Have you enjoyed *The Soddit*? Then be sure and purchase some of Professor Roberts's other delightful works.

> *The Garble-de-Hwaet (the 1375 recension)*
An Anglo Saxon poem of great length, subject-matter and tedium, edited by Professor Roberts in his academic years before he achieved fame as a story-teller, now reissued by his publisher with a misleading sword-and-sorcery style cover painting and 'by the author of *The Soddit* and *Lord of the Dancings*' under his name. Disappointment guaranteed! Buy it, flick through it, and put it on your shelf never to look at it again!

> *Lame-o! Lame-o!*
Charming and magical lyrics written by Professor Roberts, and put to music by a Fey Friend from Oxford for an evening of musical delight and a tombola in 1951. Includes such masterpieces as 'I'll Twist the Sense to Fit the Rhyme-O!', 'They Used To Write Verse This Way in the Old Days-O (It's as if Eliot, Pound and Wallace Stevens Never Happened)' and 'Hark, the Tweetings!':

> *Hark, the Tweetings!*
> *Fair the sweetings!*
> *Spring is bursting!*
>   *Sing fal-dol-yellow-yellow-up-wahey!*
> *The flutter-by fleetings*
> *Sing all the greetings*

~ 333 ~

Poetic sheetings
Sound your zitherlings
Sense-the-less blitherings
Sing fal-dol-yellow-yellow-up-wahey!

Now re-issued by his publisher with a misleading painting on the front of a dragon screaming through the night sky pouring fire and destruction on an army of foul-looking monsters beneath, but you won't find anything one-tenth as exciting as that inside the covers, I'm sorry to say, and 'by the author of *The Soddit* and *Lord of the Dancings*' under his name.

> A. R. R. Roberts's *The Soddit Companion*

Issued in exactly the same livery as all of Roberts's other books, and with only Roberts's name on the cover, you'll have picked this off the bookshop shelf, paid for it and got it home before you realise that it wasn't written by him at all, but instead by a jobbing hack called Daniel Gibbons as a cynical exercise in hasty cashing-in. Includes encyclopedia-style entries on all the main characters, monsters, place-names, but nothing quoted from the original book for copyright reasons.

PlayGameBoxCube 2 presents

The Soddit: Wrath of Morbore

Combining all the challenges of a role-playing game with the excitement of a hack-and-slash fight-'em platformer, *The Soddit: Wrath of Morbore* is the first ever fully licensed video game based on the works of A. R. R. Roberts (excluding the games *Lord of the Dancings 1, 2, 3, Return of Lord of the Dancings, Dance!; The Wrath of Morbore, SimSoddit, Metal Gear Soddit, Quake, Night of the Mutant Soddits, Soddit 1944: Assault on Normandy, Formula 1: Soddit Pony-Carts at Silverstone*).

Choose from one of any two lead characters, with different strengths and weaknesses; and choose from a list of intimidating weapons (axe, sword, spear, longer sword, sword with sort of hook at the end, nunchuk, nunchuk with a sort of hook at the end, bigger axe, a different sort of sword, uzi nine mil and sten gun). Then fight your way through an intimidating array of opponents:

- Slash! Your way out of the Putting Dragon Inn in Hobbld-Ahoy!
- Hack! The elves in the last homely house west of the mountains.
- Kill! Random passers-by on the road to the east.
- Try! To deviate from the path to explore the woods on the right, just to see what's there, only to find that your control-pad doesn't allow you to go past an unrealistic little wooden fence.

- Desperately! Bash away at the fence with your sword to vent your frustration.
- Notice! The way, however far you walk, the mountains on the horizon never seem to get any closer. Your mate Dave once left the control-pad on the floor with a heavy book leaning on 'forward' so that the character walked forward *all night long* from midnight to about ten a.m. the next day and when he came down again the mountains were *still on the bloody horizon*, can you believe it? They weren't any closer at all. I mean how hard would it be to program mountains that came a little bit closer as you walked towards them? It's not asking for the moon on a stick, is it? And then when you fight the troll at the river ford thing *suddenly* you're in the mountains with the goblins underground and everything. How is that supposed to happen? It simply lacks verisimilitude, that's what it lacks.
- Give up! On level two, and play a racing game instead.

'This is the . . . good . . . a . . . game . . . under any circumstances' – *PlayGameBoxCube 2 Magazine.*

'Another hack 'em-wander-about game. 97%' – *PlayGameBoxCube 2 Monthly*, *'We Never Give Any Game Less Than a 90% Rating No Matter How Poor It Is' Magazine.*

'A hundred uses. As a coaster, for instance, or part of an interesting mobile' – *Recycle Your Old CDs and DVDs Magazine.*

With original vocal stylings by Sir Ian McEllen and Lady Ellen McIan

Play *The Soddit: Wrath of Morbore* with a friend, or play with yourself.

Other Children's Classics from NonWin Books

WIND IN THE PILLOWS
by Graham Wosdafree Quincy Kennethe

'. . . teaches your children to love vermin . . .' *The Times*.

'. . . as yet unsurpassed, and indeed unprosecuted' – *The Times of Delhi*

In this classic children's tale, a Rat, a Toad, a Cockroach, a Dead Sparrow Left Floating in a Waterbutt for Two Weeks, a Smallpox Bacillus and a Tory MP enjoy a sequence of magical, flatulent adventures in and out of the Wild Wood and through the Gaye Fields of Merrie Englande, Cornwalle, Walese and Eiree. In the character of Lord 'call me Mr' Toad, Kennethe created one of the most enduring characters in all of children's fiction.

In the words of Professor Roberts himself, 'My favourite scene was the one in which the amphibian is locked away in prison and dresses as a transvestite in order to make good his escape. So true to life. I mean, if *you* saw a six-foot transsexual man-toad with green blistered skin and a peerage trying to wriggle out of a barred window, would *you* stand in his way? I know I wouldn't. Not after that unfortunate affair of the failed citizen's arrest and the Marquis of Turkley's younger son, at any rate.'

HAIRY POTSDAM
By J. K. 'not from Jamiroquai' Rollinint

Imagine a small child, abused and neglected in his earliest years, who suddenly discovers that he has incredibly potent magical powers of life-giving and death-dealing at the emotionally unstable age of thirteen, and who decides to wreak a terrible vengeance upon all the people who mocked and cuffed him, all those who humiliated him before, who told him that he'd never amount to anything, making him sleep under the stairs, *him?* Treat *him* like dirt, would they? Well they picked the *wrong boy* to ***k with, the *wrong boy*. Let's see how *they* like it when my magical force breaks every bone in their body and rips off their limbs, picking them off one by one in the shopping mall as they run, cowering and pleading – *pleading!* – for mercy hahahahaha! Who's the brat *now*? Eh? Eh? Ha-ha-ha-ha-ha-ha, I saw this on a video round at Pete's hee-hee where they hee-hee *squash this guy's head* like a grape with their telepathic powers, hee-hee. Let's see how that goes in real life my so-called-parents, ha! Ha! Splat! I am vengeance! I AM VENGEANCE! The whole town will PAY – PAY! Oh I bet they're sorry now, I'll *make* them sorry – HAHAHAHAHA! Die! Die! Die, all of you!

This book isn't anything like that.

'A Dorothy Parkeresque rollercoaster of wit, rudeness and girly hilarity; forget all pretenders to the chick-lit crown, the tiara belongs to . . .' *Daily Mirror*. (This press endorsement

may have appeared in earlier editions of a completely different book.)

£3.99. Also available: exactly the same book with a moody
photographic cover in black and white, £12.99.

JAMIE OLIVER TWIST
by Delia Dickings

Annoying cockney scamp falls in with gipsies, tramps and
thieves. Includes a forty-page supplement of Victorian Slum
Recipes, amongst them 'Lard on Bread', 'Stale Crust *cuisine
ironique*', 'Lard on Bread topped with unrefined sugar', 'Grit'
and 'Mississippi Mud Pie with Mud rather than Chocolate'.

Includes the songs, 'You've Got To Pick Enough Rocket
for Two', 'Consider Your Shellfish at Home', 'Whe-eh-eh-eh-
ere is Lard?' and the barn-storming 'Food Recipes, Glori-
ously Marketable Food Recipes' (Hot Sausage and Custard,
for that soursweet tang).

'*Most Likely to Say*: "Dad, do I have to read this? Can't I read the new Hellboy
instead?" *Least Likely to Say*: "Please, sir, can I have some more?"' – *Guardian*

MARY POPPINS
By P. L. Travesty

Mary comes to the Winsbury family in Old London Town as
an au pair, and transforms their lives by weeping noisily in
her room, talking on the phone to Czechoslovakia for hours,
eating all the ice cream in the freezer, bringing her malodor-

ous and piercings-riddled boyfriend home to stay with her 'just for ze two daias, pliz? Pliz?' and him still being in the house a month later, coming up with three separate and frankly incompatible excuses to weasel out of looking after Algernon and Jasmine for *one evening*, for crying out loud, and Van Morrison is only playing the one night in London, it's not as if we'll get the chance to see him again, and – in a rousing conclusion – threatening to tell your wife that you've made a pass at her, look, really, it's a misunderstanding, a culture-clash thing, it's actually quite funny if you think about it, no really, no *really*.

'Not so much a novel, more a (cont. p. 17)' – *Hair and Makeup Monthly*

Join the Soddit Society

Are you *ma-aa-aad!* for Soddits?

Do you live, breathe and dream of A. R. R. R. Roberts's works, morning, noon, night and in-between times? Have worried relatives expressed gentle-voiced sentiments of concern about your neglecting homework, friends, food and play to devote all your time to what they call 'this odd little book'? Are you prepared to sacrifice the quivering body of the one you love most on the bloodstained altar of your fascination for A. R. R. R. Roberts's work?

Would you like to meet people as *cra-ay-zee!* for soddits as you?

Join the Roberts-robot, the fantasy-fan, the Upper-Middle-Earth-Madman and the soddit-schizophrenic in the SODDIT SOCIETY.

For a mere £95 annual membership fee plus VAT and trauma insurance, you can join the obese, the inverted, the talk-to-themselves-in-the-toilet and the threadworm-infested to discuss the greatness of *The Soddit*, and mutter darkly how *'they'* don't understand.

Meet your fellow SODDIT SOCIETY MEMBERS once every six months and

- Dress up in costumes based on the world of A. R. R. R. Roberts's World of Soddit.
- Repeat phrases such as 'it's my absolute favourite book ever', 'my favourite part is *(insert favourite part here)*', and

'that other book, about the, like, mercenaries in fairyland, I didn't like that nearly so much'.

• Sigh, and look at the floor.

As Professor Roberts himself said, '*Fan* as we know is derived etymologically from *fanatic* – and to this day the "fan" is an alarming figure, starbursts of madness twinkling in his eye, obsessed, possessed with madness, fundamentalist, divorced from reality, a suitable case for treatment, or incarceration in my opinion, dear me yes.' He forgot to add 'And having the best fun in the world!'

Abandon the real world for this musty obsessive fantasy TODAY!

NEW FROM NONWIN BOOKS

The Spuddit

Read this hilarious, light-hearted, thoroughly respectful, not-cashing-in-at-all **Parody of A. R. R. R. Roberts's classic *The Soddit***. There's a laugh in every sentence, or your money back! (*Offer not valid in UK, Commonwealth, North America, South America, territories above the tropic of Capricorn, or signatories of the Book Charter.*) The Perfect Gift for the person who already has a copy of *The Soddit*, and you want to buy him a present that's geared as it were to his personal tastes, not socks or gloves or something generic, but something that he'd actually like. The only problem is that you can't think of anything else about him than that he likes *The Soddit* and he's already got that.

In this irreverent, brilliant parody – *all the parts of the original are taken by potatoes!!*

> Bingo . . . a marin piper
> Gandef . . . a King Edward
> Mori the Dwarf . . . a roasting potato
> Elsqare . . . Jersey royal
>
> Will Smug the Dragon *get his chips??!!*

A *Tatty* (i.e. 'tasty') Treat!

From all *good booksellers* – good meaning '*wickedd*' (youth slang for 'good')!!

'I'm prepared to say that I did laugh' – *Sir George Graham, former manager of 'The Spurs' (Tottenham Football Club).*